Java™
Structures

Data Structures in Java™ for
the Principled Programmer

Java™
Structures

Data Structures in Java™ for the Principled Programmer

Duane A. Bailey
Williams College

Boston   Burr Ridge, IL   Dubuque, IA   Madison, WI
New York   San Francisco   St. Louis
Bangkok   Bogotá   Caracas   Lisbon   London   Madrid
Mexico City   Milan   New Delhi   Seoul   Singapore   Sydney
Taipei   Toronto

WCB/McGraw-Hill

A Division of The **McGraw·Hill** *Companies*

JAVA™ STRUCTURES: DATA STRUCTURES IN JAVA™ FOR THE PRINCIPLED PROGRAMMER

This book is printed on acid-free paper.

1 2 3 4 5 7 8 9 0 QPF/QPF 9 3 2 1 0 9 8

ISBN 0-07-289179-3

Vice president and editorial director: *Kevin T. Kane*
Publisher: *Tom Casson*
Executive editor: *Elizabeth A. Jones*
Senior developmental editor: *Kelley Butcher*
Editorial assistant: *Emily J. Gray*
Marketing manager: *John T. Wannemacher*
Project manager: *Christine Parker*
Senior production supervisor: *Heather D. Burbridge*
Cover designer: *Z Graphics*
Printer: *Quebecor Printing Book Group/Fairfield*

Library of Congress Cataloging-in Publication Data

Bailey, Duane A.
    Java™ structures: data structures in Java™ for the principled
  programmer / Duane A. Bailey
       p. cm.
    Includes index.
    ISBN 0-07-289179-3
    1. Java (Computer program language) 2. Data structures (Computer
  science).   I. Title
  QA76.73.J38B34 1999
  005.13'3--dc21   98-18625

http://www.mhhe.com

Contents

for Mary,
my wife and best friend

without
the model of my mentors,
the comments of my colleagues,
the support of my students,
the friendship of my family
this book would never be

thank you!

Preface

Envoi

God, thou great symmetry,
Who put a biting lust in me
From whence my sorrows spring,
For all the frittered days
That I have spent in shapeless ways,
Give me one perfect thing.

—Anna Wickham

"IT'S A WONDERFUL TIME TO BE ALIVE." At least that's what I've found myself saying over the past couple of decades. When I first started working with computers, they were resources used by a privileged (or in my case, persistent) few. They were physically large, and logically small. They were cast from iron. The challenge was to make these behemoths solve complex problems quickly.

Today, computers are everywhere. They are in the office and at home. They speak to us on telephones; they zap our food in the microwave. They make starting cars in New England a possibility. Everyone's using them. What has aided their introduction into society is their diminished size and cost, and increased capability. The challenge is to make these behemoths solve complex problems quickly.

Thus, while the computer and its applications have changed over time, the challenge remains the same: *How can we get the best performance out of the current technology?* The design and analysis of data structures lay the fundamental groundwork for a scientific understanding of what computers can do efficiently. The motivations for data structure design work accomplished three decades ago in assembly language at the keypunch are just as familiar to us today as we practice our craft in modern languages on computers on our laps. The focus of this material is the identification and development of relatively *abstract* principles for structuring data in ways that make programs efficient in terms of their consumption of resources, *as well as efficient in terms of "programmability."*

In the past, my students have encountered this material in Pascal, Modula-2, and, most recently, C++. None of these languages has been ideal, but each has been met with increasing expectation. This text uses The Java Programming Language[1]—"Java"—to structure data. Java is a new and exciting language that has received considerable public attention. At the time of this writing, for example, Java is one of the few tools that can effectively use the Internet as a computing resource. That particular aspect of Java is not touched on greatly in

---

[1] Java is a trademark of Sun Microsystems Corporation.

this text. Still, Internet-driven applications in Java will need supporting data structures. This book attempts to provide a fresh and focused approach to the design and implementation of classic structures in a manner that meshes well with existing Java packages. It is hoped that learning this material in Java will improve the way working programmers craft programs, and the way future designers craft languages.

Pedagogical Implications. This text was developed specifically for use with CS2 in a standard Computer Science curriculum. It is succinct in its approach, and requires, perhaps, a little more effort to read. I hope, though, that this text becomes not a brief encounter with object-oriented data structure design, but a touchstone for one's programming future.

The material presented in this text follows the syllabus I have used for several years at Williams. As students come to this course with experience using Java, the outline of the text may be followed directly. Where students are new to Java, a couple of weeks early in the semester will be necessary with a good companion text to introduce the student to new concepts, and an introductory Java language text or reference manual is recommended. For students that need a quick introduction to Java we provide a tutorial in Appendix A. While the text was designed as a whole, some may wish to eliminate less important topics and expand upon others. Students may wish to drop (or consider!) the section on induction (Section 4.2.2). The more nontraditional topics—including, for example, iteration and the notions of symmetry and friction—have been included because I believe they arm programmers with important mechanisms for implementing and analyzing problems. In many departments the subtleties of more advanced structures—dictionaries (Chapter 13) and graphs (Chapter 14)—may be considered in an algorithms course. Chapter 5, a discussion of sorting, provides very important motivating examples and also begins an early investigation of algorithms. The chapter may be dropped when better examples are at hand, but students may find the refinements on implementing sorting interesting.

List

Associated with this text is a Java package of data structures that is freely available over the Internet for noncommercial purposes. I encourage students, educators, and budding software engineers to download it, tear it down, build it up, and generally enjoy it. In particular, students of this material are encouraged to follow along with the code online as they read. Also included is extensive documentation gleaned from the code by `javadoc`. All documentation—within the book and on the Web—includes pre- and postconditions. The motivation for this style of commenting is provided in Chapter 2. While it's hard to be militant about commenting, this style of documentation provides an obvious, structured approach to minimally documenting one's methods that students can appreciate and users will welcome. These resources, as well as many others, are available from McGraw-Hill at `http://www.mhhe.com/javastructures`.

nim

Three icons appear throughout the text, as they do in the margin. The top "compass" icon highlights the statement of a *principle*—a statement that encourages abstract discussion. The middle icon marks the first appearance of a particular class from the `structure` package. Students will find these files at

McGraw-Hill, or locally, if they've been downloaded. The bottom icon similarly marks the appearance of example code.

Finally, I'd like to note an unfortunate movement away from studying the implementation of data structures, in favor of studying applications. In the extreme this is a disappointing and, perhaps, dangerous precedent. The design of a data structure is like the solution to a riddle: the process of developing the answer is as important as the answer itself. The text may, however, be used as a reference for using the `structure` package in other applications by selectively avoiding the discussions of implementation.

Acknowledgments. The trajectory of this manuscript is the product of many forces. First, all of the eating establishments mentioned within this text are real and, after extensive testing, I recommend them to Berkshire programmers, authors, and tourists. My gratitude goes to colleagues Kim Bruce and Bill Lenhart, whose use of various versions of this text in their courses has generated productive feedback. Long discussions with Kim and Bill have also had the greatest impact on design of the `structure` package. Changes to many parts of this text come from students, including Udai Haraguchi, James Rowe, Qiang Sun, and Robin Yan (all of Williams), as well as Sarah Peterson (Grinnell). The reviewers—Zoran Duric (George Mason University), William Hankley (Kansas State University), Van Howbert (Colorado State), Brian Malloy (Clemson University), Daniel D. McCracken (City College of New York), David A. Poplawski (Michigan Technical University), John E. Rager (Amherst College), Stuart Reges (University of Arizona), Susan Rodger (Duke University), Dale Skrien (Colby College), Louis Steinberg (Rutgers University), Deborah A. Trytten (University of Oklahoma), and Allen Tucker (Bowdoin College)—all worked hard to meet fast and strict deadlines. Their efforts directly shape this work. I am particularly indebted to Dale, who used this text in its rawest form at Colby, and to the institutions using this text in preprint and beta editions. Kimberly Tabtiang (University of Wisconsin) and Claude Anderson (Rose-Hulman Institute of Technology) scoured the text and code and found more errors than seemed possible. Kim is also responsible for much of the careful design and implementation of the `Graph` classes. Adams Technologies is responsible for our Web-site design. My editors at McGraw-Hill—Betsy Jones, Kelley Butcher, and Christine Parker—have kindly kept this multithreaded project on an understanding schedule. Finally, despite this work, life with Ryan, Kate, and Megan (tolerant children) and Mary (reviewer, therapist, and loving wife) remains, for me, that perfect thing.

Enjoy!

Duane A. Bailey
Williamstown, May 1998

Chapter 0

Introduction

"This is an important notice.
Please have it translated."
—The Phone Company

YOUR MOTHER probably provided you with constructive toys, like blocks or Tinker Toys[1] or Legos. These toys are educational: they teach us to think spatially and to build increasingly complex structures. You develop modules that can be stuck together and rules that guide the building process.

If you are reading this book, you probably enjoyed playing with constructive toys. You consider writing programs an artistic process. You have grown from playing with blocks to writing programs. The same guidelines for building structures apply to writing programs, save one thing: there is, seemingly, no limit to the complexity of the programs you can write.   *I lie.*

Well, almost. When writing large programs, the *data structures* that maintain the data in your program govern the space and time consumed by your running program. In addition, large programs take time to write. Using different structures can actually have an impact on how long it takes to *write* your program. Choosing the wrong structures can cause your program to run poorly, or be difficult or impossible to implement effectively.

Thus, part of the program-writing process is choosing between different structures. Ideally you arrive at solutions by analyzing and comparing their various merits. This book focuses on the creation and analysis of traditional data structures in a modern programming environment, The Java Programming Language, or Java for short.

0.1 Read Me

As might be expected, each chapter is dedicated to a specific topic. Many of the topics are concerned with specific data structures. The structures we will investigate are abstracted from working implementations in Java that are available to you if you have access to the Internet.[2] Other topics concern the "tools of the trade." Some are mathematical and others are philosophical, but all consider the process of programming well.

---

[1] All trademarks are recognized.
[2] For more information, see http://www.mhhe.com/javastructures.

The topics we cover are not all-inclusive. Some useful structures have been left out. Instead, we will opt to learn the *principles of programming data structures*, so that, down the road, you can design newer (and probably better) structures yourself.

Perhaps the most important aspect of this book is the set of problems at the end of each section. *All are important for you to consider*. For some problems I have attempted to place a reasonable hint or answer in the back of the book. Why should you do problems? Practice makes perfect. I could show you how to ride a unicycle, but if you never practiced, you would never learn. If you study and understand these problems, you will find your design and analytical skills are improved. And your mother will be proud.

Unicycles: the ultimate riding structure.

This text is brief and to the point. Most of us are interested in experimenting. We will save as much time as possible for solving problems, perusing code, and practicing writing programs. As you read through each of the chapters, you might find it useful to read through the source code online. As we first consider the text of files online, I'll refer to the file name in the margin, as you see here. The top icon refers to files in the `structure` package, while the bottom icon refers to files supporting examples.

structure

example

One more point—this book, like most projects, is an ongoing effort, and the latest thoughts are unlikely to have made it to the printed page. If you are in doubt, turn to the Web for the latest comments. You will also find online documentation for each of the structures, generated from the code using `javadoc`. It is best to read the online version of the documentation for the most up-to-date details, as well as documentation of several structures not formally presented within this text.

0.2   He Can't Say That, Can He?

Sure! Throughout this book are little political comments. These remarks, on first blush, may not be interesting. Skip them! If, however, you are interested in ways to improve your skills as a programmer and a computer scientist, I invite you to read on. Sometimes these comments are so important that they appear as *principles*:

Principle 1   *The principled programmer understands a principle well enough to form an opinion about it.*

Now, let's get to work!

Problems

0.1⋆   All starred problems have answers. Where do you find answers to problems? (Hint: See page 355)

0.2⋆   You are an experienced programmer. What five serious pieces of advice would you give a new programmer?

0.3   Surf to the Web site associated with this text and review the resources available to you.

0.4⋆   Which of the following structures are described in this text (see Appendix D, "Structure Package Hierarchy"): `BinarySearchTree`, `BinaryTree`, `BitSet`, `Dictionary`, `Hashtable`, `List`.

0.5   Surf to `http://www.javasoft.com` and review the Java resources available from Sun, the developers of Java.

0.6⋆   Review documentation for Sun's `java.util` package. (See the Core API Documentation at `http://www.javasoft.com`.) Which of the following data structures are available in this package: `BinarySearchTree`, `BinaryTree`, `BitSet`, `Dictionary`, `Hashtable`, `List`?

0.7   Check your local library or bookstore for Java reference texts.

0.8   If you haven't done so already, learn how to use your local Java programming environment by writing a Java application to write a line of text. (Hint: Read Appendix A.)

0.9   Find the local documentation for the `structure` package. If none is to be found, remember that the same documentation is available over the Internet, from `http://www.mhhe.com/javastructures`.

0.10   Find the examples distributed with the `structure` package. Many of the examples are discussed later in this text.

Chapter 1

The Object-Oriented Method

> *" 'I will pick up the hook.*
> *You will see something new.*
> *Two things. And I call them*
> *Thing One and Thing Two.*
> *These Things will not bite you.*
> *They want to have fun.' "*
> —Theodor Seuss Geisel

COMPUTER SCIENCE DOES NOT SUFFER the great history of many other disciplines. While other subjects have well-founded paradigms and methods, computer science still struggles with one important question: *What is the best method to write programs?* To date, we have no best answer. The focus of language designers is to develop programming languages that are simple to use but provide the power to accurately and efficiently describe the details of large programs and applications. The development of Java is one such effort.

Throughout this text we focus on developing data structures using *object-oriented programming*. Using this paradigm the programmer spends time developing templates for structures called *classes*. The templates are then used to construct *instances* or *objects*. A majority of the statements in object-oriented programs involve *sending messages* to objects to have them change their state. Programs involve, then, the construction and coordination of objects. In this way languages like Java are *object-oriented*.

OOP: Object-oriented programming.

In all but the smallest programming projects, *abstraction* is a useful tool for writing working programs. In programming languages such as Pascal and C, the details of a program's implementation are hidden away in its procedures or functions. This approach involves *procedural abstraction*. In object-oriented programming the details of the implementation of data structures are hidden away within its objects. This approach involves *data abstraction*. Many modern programming languages use object orientation to support basic abstractions of data. We review the details of this support in this chapter.

1.1 Data Abstraction and Encapsulation

If you purchase a muffin from the Clarksburg Bread Company you can identify it as a muffin without knowing its ingredients. Muffins are dome-shaped, bread-like, and sometimes sweet. Whether or not there's baking powder in a muffin is of little concern to you. Of course, the baker is free to switch from baking powder to other leavening without much impact. The muffin's ingredients list and its construction are details that probably do not interest you.

Likewise, it is often unimportant to know how data structures are *implemented* in order to appreciate their *use*. For example, most of us are familiar with the workings or *semantics* of strings or arrays, but, if pressed, we might find it difficult to describe their *mechanics*: *Do all consecutive locations in the array appear close together in memory in your computer, or are they far apart?* The answer is: *it is unimportant*. As long as the array "behaves like an array" or the string "behaves like a string" we are happy. The less one knows about how arrays or strings are implemented, the less one becomes dependent on a particular implementation. Another way to think about this abstractly is that the data structure lives up to an implicit "contract": *a string is an ordered list of characters*, or *elements of an array may be accessed in any order*. The implementor of the data structure is free to construct it in any reasonable way, as long as all the terms of the contract are met. Since different implementors are in the habit of making very different implementation decisions, anything that helps to hide the implementation details—any means of using *abstraction*—serves to make the world a better place to program.

Macintosh and Unix store strings differently.

When used correctly, object-oriented programming allows the programmer to separate the details that are important to the user from the details that are only important to the implementation. Those details that are important to the user of the structure make up its *contract* or *interface*. The interface describes the look and feel of the structure, from a programmer's point of view. Most of us would agree that while strings and arrays are very similar structures, they behave differently: you can shrink or expand a string, while you cannot directly do the same with an array; you can print a string directly, while printing an array involves explicitly printing each of its elements. These distinctions suggest they have different interfaces.

The unimportant details hidden from the user are part of what makes up the *implementation*. We might decide (see Figure 1.1) that a string is to be constructed from a large array of characters with an attendant character count. Alternatively, we might specify the length implicitly by terminating the string with a special *end-of-string mark* that is not used for any other purpose. Both of these approaches are perfectly satisfactory, but there are tradeoffs. The first implementation (called a *counted string*) has its length stored explicitly, while the length of the second implementation (called a *terminated string*) is implied. It takes longer to determine the length of a terminated string because we have to search for the end-of-string mark. On the other hand, the size of a terminated string is limited only by the amount of available memory, while the longest counted string is determined by the range of integers that can be stored in its length field (often this is only several hundred characters). If implementors can hide these details, users do not have to be distracted from their own important design work.

Data abstraction in languages like Java allows a structure to take responsibility for its own state. The structure knows how to maintain its own state without bothering the programmer. If two strings have to be concatenated into

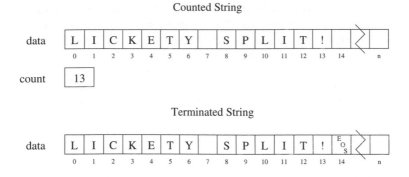

Figure 1.1 Two methods of implementing a string. A counted string explicitly records its length. The terminated string's length is determined by an end-of-string mark.

a single string structure, the string might have to request new memory. Thankfully, because strings know how to perform operations on themselves, the user doesn't have to worry about managing memory.

1.2 The Object Model

To facilitate the construction of well-designed objects, it is useful to have a design method in mind. As alluded to earlier, we will often visualize the data for our program as being managed by its objects. Each object manages its own data that determine its state. A point on a screen, for example, has two coordinates. A medical record maintains a name, a list of dependents, a medical history, and a reference to an insurance company. To maintain a consistent state we imagine the program manipulates the data within its objects only through messages or *method calls* to the objects. A string might receive a message "tell me your length," while a medical record might receive a "change insurance" message. The string message simply accesses information, while the medical record method may involve changing several pieces of information in this and other objects in a consistent manner. If we directly modify the reference to the insurance company, we may forget to modify similar references in each of the dependents. For large applications with complex data structures, it can be extremely difficult to remember to coordinate all the operations that are necessary to move a single complex object from one consistent state to another. We opt, instead, to have the designer of the data structure provide us a method for carefully moving between states; this method is activated in response to a high level message sent to the object.

This text, then, focuses on two important topics: (1) how we implement and evaluate objects with methods that are logically complex and (2) how we might use the objects we create. Traditionally, these objects represent *data structures*, but occasionally we will develop *control structures*—structures whose purpose is to control other data structures. This latter form of structure is described in some detail in Chapter 8.

1.3   Object-Oriented Terminology

In Java, data abstraction is accomplished through *encapsulation* of data in an *object*—an instance of a *class*. Like a *record* in other languages, an object has *fields*. Unlike records, objects also contain *methods*. Fields and methods of an object may be declared `public`, which means that they are visible to entities outside the class, or `protected`, in which case they may only be accessed by code within methods of the class.[1] A typical class declaration is demonstrated by the following (almost trivial) class that keeps track of the ratio of two integer values:

Ratio

```
public class Ratio
{ // an object for storing a fraction
    protected int numerator;   // numerator of ratio
    protected int denominator; // denominator of ratio

    public Ratio(int top, int bottom)
    // pre: bottom != 0
    // post: constructs a ratio equivalent to top/bottom
    {
        numerator = top;
        denominator = bottom;
    }

    public int getNumerator()
    // post: return the numerator of the fraction
    {
        return numerator;
    }

    public int getDenominator()
    // post: return the denominator of the fraction
    {
        return denominator;
    }

    public double value()
    // post: returns the real value equivalent to ratio
    {
        return (double)numerator/(double)denominator;
    }
```

---

[1] This is not quite the truth. For a discussion of the facts, see Appendix B.

```
        public Ratio add(Ratio other)
        // pre: other is non-null
        // post: return new fraction --- the sum of this and other
        {
            return new Ratio(this.numerator*other.denominator+
                             this.denominator*other.numerator,
                             this.denominator*other.denominator);
        }
}
```

First, a `Ratio` object maintains the numerator and denominator as protected `ints` that are not directly modifiable by the user. The first method is the `Ratio` *constructor*: a method whose name is the same as that of the class. (The formal comments at the top of methods are pre- and postconditions; we discuss these in detail in the next chapter.) This special method is called whenever a new `Ratio` object is constructed. Constructors initialize all the fields of the associated object, placing the object into a predictable and consistent initial state. We declare the constructors for a class `public`. To construct a new `Ratio` object, users will have to call these methods. The `value` method returns a `double` that represents the ratio, while the `getNumerator` and `getDenominator` methods fetch the current values of the numerator and denominator of the fraction. Finally, we have provided a method for adding one `Ratio` to another; the result is a newly constructed `Ratio` object.

As with the `Ratio` class, data fields are often declared `protected`. To manipulate protected fields the user must invoke `public` methods. The following trivial example demonstrates the use of the `Ratio` class:

```
public static void main(String[] args)
{
    Ratio r = new Ratio(1,1);      // r == 1.0
    r = new Ratio(1,2);            // r == 0.5
    r.add(new Ratio(1,3));         // r still 0.5
    r = r.add(new Ratio(1,4));     // r == 0.75
    System.out.println(r.value()); // 0.75 printed
}
```

To understand the merit of this technique of class design, we might draw an analogy between a well-designed object and an alternator for a car. The protected fields and methods of an object are analogous to the internal design of the alternator. The observable features, including the alternating current appearing on wires, are provided without giving any details about the implementation of the object. If automobile designers made use of particular implementations of alternators, it might ultimately restrict the suppliers of alternators in the future. Likewise, manufacturers of alternators should be able to have a certain freedom of implementation. As long as they provide a current in an agreed-upon way, they should be free to use whatever design they want.

In the same way that fields are encapsulated by a class, classes may be encapsulated by a *package*. A package is a collection of related classes that implement some set of structures with a common theme. The classes of this text, for example, are members of the `structure` package. In the same way that there are users of classes, there are users of packages, and much of the analogy holds. In particular, classes may be declared `public`, in which case they may be used by anyone who *imports* the package into their program. If a class is not `public`, it is automatically considered `protected`. These `protected` classes may only be constructed and used by other classes within the same package.

1.4   Sketching an Example: A Word List

Suppose we're interested in building a game of Hangman. The computer selects random words and we try to guess them. Over several games, the computer should pick a variety of words and, as each word is used, it should be removed from the word list. Using an object-oriented approach, we'll determine the essential features of a `WordList`, the Java object that maintains our list of words.

The operations necessary to support a list of words can be sketched out easily, even if we don't know the intimate details of constructing the Hangman game itself. Once we see how the data structure is used, we have a handle on the design of the interface. "Squinting our eyes" as we consider the Hangman program design, we can identify the following general use of the `WordList` object:

WordList

```
WordList list;                          // declaration
String targetWord;

list = new WordList(10);                // construction
list.add("Ephraim");                    // building
list.add("Jeffrey");
list.add("John");
while (!list.isEmpty())                 // game loop
{
    targetWord = list.selectAny();      // selection
    // ...play the game using target word...
    list.remove(targetWord);            // update
}
```

Let's consider these lines. One of the first lines (labeled `declaration`) declares a *reference* to a `WordList`. For a reference to refer to an object, the object must be constructed. We require, therefore, a constructor for a `WordList`. The `construction` line allocates an initially empty list of words ultimately containing as many as 10 words. We provide an upper limit on the number of words that are potentially stored in the list. (We'll see later that providing such information can be useful in designing efficient data structures.) On the three lines marked `building`, three words are added to the list.

The `while` loop accomplishes the task of playing Hangman with the user. This is possible as long as the list of words is not empty. We use the `isEmpty` method to test this fact. At the beginning of each round of Hangman, a random word is selected (`selectAny`), setting the `targetWord` reference. To make things interesting, we presume that `selectAny` selects a random word each time. Once the round is finished, we `remove` the word from the word list, eliminating it as a choice in future rounds.

There are insights here. First, we have said very little about the Hangman game other than its interaction with our rather abstract list of words. The details of the screen's appearance, for example, do not play much of a role in understanding how the `WordList` structure works. We knew that a list was necessary for our program and we considered the program *from the point of view of the object*. Second, we don't really know how the `WordList` is implemented. The words may be stored in an array, or in a file on disk, or they may use some technology that we don't currently understand. All that is important is that we have *faith* that the structure can be implemented. We have sketched out the `WordList` *interface*, and we have faith that an *implementation* supporting the interface can be built. Finally we note that what we have written is not a complete program. Still, from the viewpoint of the `WordList` structure, there are few details of the interface that are in question. A reasoned individual should be able to look at this design and say "this will work—provided it is implemented correctly." If a reviewer of the code were to ask a question about how the structure works, it would lead to a refinement of our understanding of the interface.

We have, then, the following required interface for the `WordList` class:

```java
public class WordList
{
    public WordList(int size)
    // pre: size >= 0
    // post: construct a word list capable of holding "size" words

    public boolean isEmpty()
    // post: return true iff the word list contains no words

    public void add(String s)
    // post: add a word to the word list, if it is not already there

    public String selectAny()
    // pre: the word list is not empty
    // post: return a random word from the list

    public void remove(String word)
    // pre: word is not null
    // post: remove the word from the word list
}
```

We will leave the implementation details of this example until later. You might consider various ways that the `WordList` might be implemented. As long as the methods of the interface can be supported by your data structure, your implementation is valid.

1.5   A Special Purpose Class: A Bank Account

We now take a serious look at the detailed construction of a simplistic class: a `BankAccount`. Many times, it is necessary to provide a tag associated with an instance of a data structure. You might imagine that your bank balance is kept in a database at your bank. When you get money for a trip through the Berkshires, you swipe your card through an automated teller bringing up your account. Your account number, presumably, is unique to your account. Nothing about you or your banking history is actually stored in your account number. Instead, that number is used to find the record linked to your account: the bank searches for a structure associated with the number you provide. Thus a `BankAccount` is a simple, but important, data structure. It has a *key* (an account number that never changes) and a *value* (a bank balance that potentially *does* change). The public methods of such a structure are as follows:

Automated teller: a robotic palm reader.

BankAccount

```
public class BankAccount
{
    public BankAccount(String account, double balance)
    // pre: account is a string identifying the bank account
    //      balance is the starting balance
    // post: constructs a bank account with desired balance

    public boolean equals(BankAccount other)
    // pre: other is a valid bank account
    // post: returns true if this bank account is the same as other

    public String account()
    // post: returns the bank account number of this account

    public double balance()
    // post: returns the balance of this bank account

    public void setBalance(double balance)
    // post: set the value of the bank account to balance
}
```

The substance of these methods has purposefully been removed because, again, it is unimportant for a us to know exactly how a `BankAccount` is implemented. We have ways to construct and compare `BankAccount`s, as well as ways to read the account number or balance, or update the balance.

Let's look at the implementation of these methods, individually. To build a new bank account, you must use the **new** operator to call the constructor with two parameters. The account number provided never changes over the life of the BankAccount—if it were necessary to change the value of the account number, a new BankAccount would have to be made, and the balance would have to be transferred from one to the other. The constructor plays the important role of initializing the account number field, and ensuring that a suitable key is always part of the BankAccount. Here is the code for a BankAccount constructor:

```
protected String key;
protected double value;

public BankAccount(String account, double balance)
// pre: account is a string identifying the bank account
//      balance is the starting balance
// post: constructs a bank account with desired balance
{
    key = account;
    value = balance;
}
```

Two fields—key and value—of the BankAccount object are responsible for maintaining the object's state. The key keeps track of the account number, while the value field maintains the balance.

Since account numbers are unique to BankAccounts, to check to see if they are the same, we need only compare the key fields. Here's the code:

```
public boolean equals(BankAccount other)
// pre: other is a valid bank account
// post: returns true if this bank account is the same as other
{
    // two accounts are the same if account numbers are the same
    return this.key.equals(other.key);
}
```

Notice that the BankAccount equals method calls the equals method of the key, a String. Both BankAccount and String are nonprimitive types, or examples of Objects. Every object in Java has an equals method. If you don't explicitly provide one, the system will write one for you. In the case of the BankAccount object, the default equals method would have compared each of the respective fields, an unnecessary level of complexity.

One can ask the BankAccount about various aspects of its state by calling its account or balance methods:

```
public String account()
// post: returns the bank account number of this account
{
    return key;
}
```

```
public double balance()
// post: returns the balance of this bank account
{
    return value;
}
```

These methods do little more than pass along the information found in the `key` and `value` fields respectively. In a different implementation of the `BankAccount`, the balance would not have to be explicitly stored—the value might be, for example, the difference between two fields, `deposits` and `drafts`. Given the interface, it is not much of a concern to the user which implementation is used.

We provide one more method, `setBalance`, that explicitly sets the balance to a new value:

```
public void setBalance(double balance)
// post: set the value of the bank account to balance
{
    value = balance;
}
```

Because we would like to change the balance of the account, it is important to have a method that allows us to modify it. On the other hand, we purposefully don't have a `setAccount` method because we do not want the account number to be changed without a considerable amount of work (work that, by the way, models reality).

Here is a simple application that determines whether it is better to deposit $100 in an account that bears 5 percent interest for 10 years, or to deposit $100 in an account that bears $2\frac{1}{2}$ percent interest for 20 years. It makes use of the `BankAccount` object outlined above:

```
public static void main(String[] args)
{
    // Question: is it better to invest $100 over 10 years at 5%
    //           or to invest $100 over 20 years at 2.5% interest?
    BankAccount jd = new BankAccount("Jain Dough",100.00);
    BankAccount js = new BankAccount("Jon Smythe",100.00);

    for (int years = 0; years < 10; years++)
    {
        jd.setBalance(jd.balance() * 1.05);
    }
    for (int years = 0; years < 20; years++)
    {
        js.setBalance(js.balance() * 1.025);
    }
    System.out.println("Jain invests $100 over 10 years at 5%.");
    System.out.println("After 10 years " + jd.account() +
                       " has $" + jd.balance());
    System.out.println("Jon invests $100 over 20 years at 2.5%.");
```

```
        System.out.println("After 20 years " + js.account() +
                             " has $" + js.balance());
    }
```

It is left to the reader to answer this financial question.

1.6   A General Purpose Class: An Association

The following small application implements a Pig Latin translator based on a dictionary of nine words. The code makes use of an array of **Associations**, each of which establishes a relation between an English word and its Pig Latin translation. For each string passed as the argument to the **main** method, the dictionary is searched to determine the appropriate translation.

At least Dr. Seuss started with 50 words!

atinlay

```
public class atinlay {
    // a pig latin translator for 9 words
    public static void main(String args[])
    {
        // build and fill out an array of 9 translations
        Association dict[] = new Association[9];
        dict[0] = new Association("a","aay");
        dict[1] = new Association("bad","adbay");
        dict[2] = new Association("had","adhay");
        dict[3] = new Association("dad","adday");
        dict[4] = new Association("day","ayday");
        dict[5] = new Association("hop","ophay");
        dict[6] = new Association("on","onay");
        dict[7] = new Association("pop","oppay");
        dict[8] = new Association("sad","adsay");

        for (int argn = 0; argn < args.length; argn++)
        {   // for each argument
            for (int dictn = 0; dictn < dict.length; dictn++)
            {   // check each dictionary entry
                if (dict[dictn].key().equals(args[argn]))
                    System.out.println(dict[dictn].value());
            }
        }
    }
}
```

When this application is run with the arguments **hop on pop**, the results are:

```
ophay
onay
oppay
```

While this application may seem rather trivial, it is easy to imagine a large scale application with similar needs.

We now consider the design of the `Association`. Notice that while the *type* of data maintained is different, the *purpose* of the `Association` is very similar to that of the `BankAccount` class we discussed in the previous section. An `Association` is a key-value pair such that the `key` cannot be modified. Here is the interface for the `Association` class:

Association

```
public class Association
{
    public Association(Object key, Object value)
    // pre: key is non-null
    // post: constructs a key-value pair

    public Association(Object key)
    // pre: key is non-null
    // post: constructs a key-value pair; value is null

    public boolean equals(Object other)
    // pre: other is non-null Association
    // post: returns true iff the keys are equal

    public Object value()
    // post: returns value from association

    public Object key()
    // post: returns key from association

    public void setValue(Object value)
    // post: sets association's value to value
}
```

What distinguishes an `Association` from a `BankAccount` is that the fields of an `Association` are of type `Object`. The use of the word `Object` in the definition of an `Association` makes the definition very general: any data value that is of type `Object`—any nonprimitive data type in Java–can be used for the `key` and `value` fields.

Unlike the `BankAccount` class, this class has two different constructors:

```
protected Object theKey; // the key of the key-value pair
protected Object theValue; // the value of the key-value pair

public Association(Object key, Object value)
// pre: key is non-null
// post: constructs a key-value pair
{
    Assert.pre(key != null, "Key must not be null.");
    theKey = key;
    theValue = value;
}
```

```
public Association(Object key)
// pre: key is non-null
// post: constructs a key-value pair; value is null
{
    this(key,null);
}
```

The first constructor—the constructor distinguished by having two parameters—allows the user to construct a new `Association` by initializing both fields. On occasion, however, we may wish to have an `Association` whose key field is set, but whose `value` field is left referencing nothing. (An example might be a medical record: initially the medical history is incomplete, perhaps waiting to be forwarded from a previous physician.) For this purpose, we provide a single parameter constructor that sets the `value` field to null. Note that we use `this(key,null)` as the body. The one-parameter constructor calls this object's two-parameter constructor with `null` as the second parameter. We write the constructors in this dependent manner so that if the underlying implementation of the association had to be changed, only the two-parameter method would have to be updated. It also reduces the complexity of the code, and saves your fingerprints!

Now, given a particular `Association`, it is useful to be able to retrieve the key or value. Since the implementation is hidden, no one outside the class is able to see it, and must depend on the accessors to observe the data.

```
public Object value()
// post: returns value from association
{
    return theValue;
}

public Object key()
// post: returns key from association
{
    return theKey;
}
```

When necessary, the method `setValue` can be used to change the value associated with the key. Thus, the `setValue` method simply takes its parameter and assigns it to the `value` field:

```
public void setValue(Object value)
// post: sets association's value to value
{
    theValue = value;
}
```

There are other methods that are made available to users of the `Association` class, but we will not discuss the details of that code until later. Some of the methods are required, some are useful, and some are just nice to have around. While the code may look complicated, we take the time to implement it correctly, so that *we will not have to implement it again, in the future.*

Principle 2 *Free the future: reuse code.*

The temptation to design data structures "from scratch" is difficult to fight. We shall see, however, that many of the more complex structures would be very difficult to construct if we could not base our implementations on the results of previous work.

1.7   Interfaces

Sometimes it is useful to describe the interface for a number of different classes, without committing to an implementation. For example, in later sections of this text we will implement a number of data structures that are able to report on their "size." We can, for all of these classes, specify a portion of their interface by using the Java **interface** declaration:

Store

```java
public interface Store
{
    public int size();
    // post: returns the number of elements contained in the store

    public boolean isEmpty();
    // post: returns true iff store is empty

    public void clear();
    // post: clears the store
}
```

Notice that the body of each method has been replaced by a semicolon. It is, in fact, illegal to specify any code in a Java interface. Specifying an interface is like writing "boilerplate" for a contract without committing to any implementation. When we decide that we are interested in constructing a new class, we can choose to have it *implement* the `Store` interface. For example, our `WordList` structure of Section 1.4 might have made use of our `Store` interface by beginning its declaration as follows:

WordList

```java
public class WordList implements Store
```

When the `WordList` class is compiled by the Java compiler, it checks to see that each of the methods mentioned in the `Store` interface—`size`, `isEmpty`, and `clear`—is actually implemented. In this case, only `isEmpty` is part of the `WordList` specification, so we must either (1) not have `WordList` implement the `Store` interface or (2) add the methods demanded by `Store`.

Interfaces may be extended. Here, we have a definition of what it means to be a `Collection`, in the `structure` package:

```
public interface Collection extends Store
{
    public boolean contains(Object value);
    // pre: value is non-null
    // post: returns true iff the collection contains the value

    public void add(Object value);
    // pre: value is non-null
    // post: the value is added to the collection
    //       the replacement policy is not specified.

    public Object remove(Object value);
    // pre: value is non-null
    // post: removes an object "equal" to value within collection.

    public Iterator elements();
    // post: returns an iterator for traversing collection
}
```

Collection

A `Collection` requires four methods—`contains`, `add`, `remove`, and `elements`—as well as the methods demanded by being a `Store`. Thus, in order to be considered a `Collection`, you must implement at least seven different methods. If we implement those seven methods for the `WordList` class and indicate that `WordList implements Collection`, the `WordList` class could be used wherever a `Collection` or `Store` is required. Currently, our `WordList` is close to, but not quite, a `Collection`. Applications that demand the functionality of a `Collection` will not be satisfied with a `WordList`. Having the class implement an interface increases the flexibility of its use. Still, it may require considerable work for us to upgrade the `WordList` class to the level of a `Collection`. It may even work against the design of the `WordList` to provide the missing methods. The choices we make are part of an ongoing design process that attempts to provide the best implementations of structures to meet the demands of the user.

1.8 Who Is the User?

When implementing data structures using classes and interfaces, it is sometimes hard to understand *why* we might be interested in hiding the implementation. After all, perhaps we know that ultimately we will be the only programmers making use of these structures. That might be a good point, except that if you are really a successful programmer, you will implement the data structure flawlessly this week, use it next week, and not return to look at the code for a long time. When you *do* return, your view is effectively that of a user of the code, with little or no memory of the implementation.

One side effect of this relationship is that we have all been reminded of the need to write comments. If you do not write comments, you will not be able to read the code. If, however, you design, document, and implement your interface carefully, you might not ever have to look at the implementation! That's good news because, for most of us, in a couple of months our code is as foreign to us as if someone else had implemented it. The end result: consider yourself a user and design and abide by your interface wherever possible. If you know of some public field that gives a hint of the implementation, do not make use of it. Instead, access the data through appropriate methods. You will be happy you did later, when you optimize your implementation.

Principle 3 *Design and abide by interfaces as though you were the user.*

A quick corollary to this statement is the following:

Principle 4 *Declare data fields* `protected`*.*

If the data are protected, you cannot access them from outside the class, and you are forced to abide by the restricted access of the interface.

1.9   Conclusions

The construction of substantial applications involves the development of complex and interacting structures. In object-oriented languages, we think of these structures as objects that communicate through the passing of messages or, more formally, the invocation of methods.

We use object orientation in Java to write the structures found in this book. It is possible, of course, to design data structures without object orientation, but any effective data structuring model ultimately depends on the use of some form of abstraction that allows the programmer to avoid considering the complexities of particular implementations.

In many languages, including Java, data abstraction is supported by separating the interface from the implementation of the data structure. To ensure that users cannot get past the interface to manipulate the structure in an uncontrolled fashion, the system controls access to fields, methods, and classes. The implementor plays an important role in making sure that the structure is usable, given the interface. This role is so important that we think of implementation as supporting the interface—sometimes usefully considered a *contract* between the implementor and the user. This analogy is useful because, as in the real world, if contracts are violated, someone gets upset!

Initial design of the interfaces for data structures arises from considering how they are used in simple applications. Those method calls that are required by the application determine the interface for the new structure and constrain, in various ways, the choices we make in implementing the object.

In our implementation of an `Association`, we can use the `Object` class—that class inherited by all other Java classes—to write very general data structures.

The actual type of value that is stored in the **Association** is determined by the values passed to the constructors and mutators of the class. This ability to pass a subtype to any object that requires a super type is a strength of object-oriented languages—and helps to reduce the complexity of code.

Problems

1.1⋆   Which of the following are primitive Java types: `int`, `Integer`, `double`, `Double`, `String`, `char`, `Association`, `BankAccount`, `boolean`, `Boolean`?

1.2⋆   Which of the following variables are associated with valid constructor calls?

```
BankAccount a,b,c,d,e,f;
Association g,h;
a = new BankAccount("Bob",300.0);
b = new BankAccount(300.0,"Bob");
c = new BankAccount(033414,300.0);
d = new BankAccount("Bob",300);
e = new BankAccount("Bob",new Double(300));
f = new BankAccount("Bob",(double)300);
g = new Association("Alice",300.0);
h = new Association("Alice",new Double(300));
```

1.3   For each pair of classes, indicate which class extends the other:

a. `java.lang.Number`, `java.lang.Double`

b. `java.lang.Number`, `java.lang.Integer`

c. `java.lang.Number`, `java.lang.Object`

d. `java.util.Stack`, `java.util.Vector`

e. `java.util.Hashtable`, `java.util.Dictionary`

1.4   Rewrite the compound interest program (discussed when considering `BankAccount`s) so that it uses `Association`s.

1.5   Write a program that attempts to modify one of the private fields of an `Association`. When does your environment detect the violation? What happens?

1.6   Finish the design of a `Ratio` class that implements a ratio between two integers. The class should support standard math operations: addition, subtraction, multiplication, and division. You should also be able to construct `Ratio`s from either a numerator-denominator pair, or a single integer, or with no parameter at all (what is a reasonable default value?).

1.7   In order to maintain a `Ratio` (see above) in reduced terms, you would find it useful to be able to determine the greatest common divisor of two values. Assuming this method is a part of the `Ratio` class, should it be declared public or private? Explain.

1.8   Design a class to represent a U.S. telephone number. It should support three types of constructors—one that accepts three numbers, representing area code, exchange, and extension; another that accepts two integers, representing a number within your local area code; and a third constructor that accepts a string of letters and numbers that represent the number (e.g., `"900-410-TIME"`). Provide a method that determines if the number is provided "toll free" (such numbers have "area codes" of 800, 877, or 888).

1.9   Sometimes it is useful to measure the length of time it takes for a piece of code to run. (For example, it may help determine where optimizations of your code would be most effective.) Design a `Stopwatch` class to support timing of events. (You should consider use of the millisecond clock in the Java environment, `System.currentTimeMillis()`.) Like many stopwatches, it should support starting, temporary stopping, and a reset. The design of the private section of the stopwatch should hide the implementation details.

1.10   Design a data structure in Java that represents a musical pitch. A `pitch` can be completely specified as a number of cycles per second (or hertz, abbreviated "Hz"), or the number of half steps above a commonly agreed-upon pitch, such as A (in modern times, in the United States, considered to be 440 Hz). Higher pitches have higher frequencies. Two pitches are an octave (12 semitones) apart if one has a frequency twice the other. A half-step or semitone increase in pitch is $\sqrt[12]{2} \approx 1.06$ times higher. Your `pitch` constructors should accept a frequency (a `double`) or a number of half-steps (an `int`) above A. Imperfect frequencies should be tuned to the nearest half pitch. Once constructed, a pitch should be able to provide its frequency in either cycles per second or half-steps above A.

1.11   Extend the previous problem to allow a second parameter to each constructor to specify the definition of A upon which the `pitch`'s definition is based. What modern pitch most closely resembles that of modern middle C (9 semitones below A) if A is defined to be 415 Hz?

1.12   Design a data structure to represent a combination lock. When the lock is constructed, it is provided with an arbitrary length array of integers between 0 and 25 specifying a combination (if no combination is provided, $9 - 0 - 21 - 0$ is the default). Initially, it is locked. Two methods—`press` and `reset`—provide a means of entering a combination: `press` enters the next integer to be used toward matching the combination, while `reset` re-readies the lock for accepting the first integer of the combination. Only when `press` is used to match the last integer of the combination does the lock silently unlock. Mismatched integers require `reset` before the combination can again be entered. The `isLocked` method returns true if and only if the lock is locked. The `lock` method locks and resets the lock. In the unlocked state only the `isLocked` and `lock` methods have effect.

1.13   Design a data structure to simulate the workings of a car radio. The state of the radio is on or off, and it may be tuned to an AM or FM frequency. A dozen modifiable push buttons allow the listener to store and recall AM or FM frequencies. AM frequencies can be represented by multiples of 10 in the range 530 to 1610. FM frequencies are found at multiples of 0.2 in the range 87.9 to 107.9.

1.14⋆   Design a data structure to maintain the position of m coins of radius 1 through m on a board with $n \geq m$ squares numbered 0 through $n-1$. You may provide whatever interface you find useful to allow your structure to represent any placement of coins, including stacks of coins in a single cell. A configuration is *valid* only if large coins are not stacked on small coins. Your structure should have an `isValid` method that returns true if the coins are in a valid position. (A problem related to this is discussed in Section 7.2.1.)

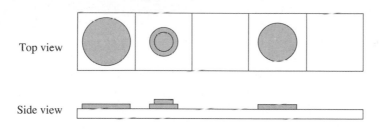

Top view

Side view

Chapter 2

Comments, Conditions, and Assertions

"/* This is bogus code.
Wizards are invited to improve it.   */"
—Anonymous

CONSIDER THIS: WE CALL OUR PROGRAMS "CODE"! The languages we learn, including Java, have features that are driven by the need to express algorithms and manipulations of data in a manner that a machine can understand. A step toward making a program run more efficiently often makes it less understandable. If language design was driven by the need to make the program readable, it would be hard to argue against programming in English.

Okay, perhaps French!

The *comment* is a carefully crafted piece of text that describes the state of the machine, the use of a variable, or the purpose of a control construct. Many of us, though, write comments for the same reason that we exercise: we feel guilty. You feel that, if you do not write comments in your code, you "just *know*" something bad is going to happen. Well, you are right. A comment you write today will help you out of a hole you dig tomorrow.

Ruth Krauss: "A hole is to dig."

All too often comments are hastily written after the fact, to help understand what is really going on in the code. The time you spent thinking about the code has long since passed, and the comment might not be right. If you write comments beforehand, while you are designing your code, it is more likely your comments will describe what you want to do as you carefully think it out. Then, when something goes wrong, the comment is there to help you figure out the code. In fairness, the code and the comment have a symbiotic relationship. Writing one or the other does not really feel complete, but writing both provides you with the redundancy of concept: one lucid and one as clear as Java.

The one disadvantage of comments is that, unlike code, they cannot be checked. Occasionally, programmers come across comments such as *If you think you understand this, you don't!* or *Are you reading this?* One could, of course, annotate programs with mathematical formulæ. As the program is compiled the mathematical comments are distilled into very concise descriptions of what should be going on. When the output from the program's code does not match the result of the formula, something is clearly wrong with your logic. But *which* logic? The writing of mathematical comments is a level of detail most programmers would prefer to avoid.

Semiformal convention: a meeting of tie haters.

A compromise is a semiformal convention for comments that provide a reasonable documentation of *when* and *what* a program does. In the code associated with this book, we see one or two comments for each method or function that describe its purpose. They are the *precondition* and *postcondition*.

2.1   Pre- and Postconditions

The *precondition* describes, as succinctly as possible in your native tongue, the conditions under which a method may be called and expected to produce correct results. Ideally the precondition is expressed in terms of the *state* of the program. This state is usually cast in terms of the parameters passed to the routine. For example, the precondition on a square root function might be

sqrt

```
// pre: x is nonnegative
```

The authors of this square root function expect that the parameter is not a negative number. It is perfectly fine to call a function or method if the precondition is not met, but it might not produce the desired result. When there is no precondition on a procedure, it may be called without failure.

The *postcondition* describes the state of the program once the routine has been completed, *provided the precondition was met*. Every routine should have some postcondition. If it does not, then the routine does not change the state of the program, and the routine has no effect.

Pre- and postconditions do not force you to write code correctly. Nor do they help you find the problems that *do* occur. They can, however, provide you with a uniform method for documenting the programs you write, and they require more thought than the average comment. More thought put into programs lowers your average blood pressure and ultimately saves you time you might spend more usefully playing outside, visiting museums, or otherwise bettering your mind.

2.2   Assertions

In days gone by, homeowners would sew firecrackers in their curtains. If the house were to catch fire, the curtains would burn, setting off the firecrackers. It was an elementary but effective fire alarm.

And the batteries never needed replacing.

An *assertion* is an assumption you make about the state of your program. In Java, we will encode the assertion as a call to a function that verifies the state of the program. That function does nothing if the assertion is true, but it halts your program with an error message if it is false. It is a firecracker to sew in your program. If you sew enough assertions into your code, you will get an early warning if you are about to be burned by your logic.

Principle 5 *Test assertions in your code.*

The **Assert** class provides four functions to help you test the state of your program as it runs:

```
public class Assert
{
    static public void pre(boolean test, String message)
    // pre: result of precondition test
    // post: does nothing if test true, otherwise abort w/message

    static public void post(boolean test, String message)
    // pre: result of postcondition test
    // post: does nothing if test true, otherwise abort w/message

    static public void condition(boolean test, String message)
    // pre: result of general condition test
    // post: does nothing if test true, otherwise abort w/message

    static public void fail(String message)
    // post: throws error with message
}
```

Assert

Each of **pre**, **post**, and **condition** tests to see if its first argument—the assertion—is true. The **message** is used to indicate the condition tested by the assertion. Here's an example of a check to make sure that the precondition for the **sqrt** function was met:

```
public static double sqrt(double x)
// pre: x is nonnegative
// post: returns the square root of x
{
    Assert.pre(x >= 0,"the value is nonnegative.");
    double guess = 1.0;
    double guessSquared = guess * guess;

    while (Math.abs(x-guessSquared) >= 0.00000001) {
        // guess is off a bit, adjust
        guess += (x-guessSquared)/2.0/guess;
        guessSquared = guess*guess;
    }
    return guess;
}
```

Should we call **sqrt** with a negative value, the assertion fails, the message is printed out, and the program comes to a halt. Here's what appears at the display:

```
structure.FailedPrecondition:
Assertion that failed: A precondition: the value is nonnegative.
        at Assert.pre(Assert.java:17)
        at sqrt(examples.java:24)
        at main(examples.java:15)
```

The first two lines of this message indicate that a precondition (that x was non-negative) failed. This message was printed within `Assert.pre` on line 17 of the source, found in `Assert.java`. The next line of this *stack trace* indicates that the call to `Assert.pre` was made on line 24 of `examples.java` at the start of the `sqrt` function. This is the call shown above. The problem is (probably) on line 15 of the main procedure of `examples.java`. Debugging our code should probably start in the `main` routine.

The code within this book makes use of assertion testing. Including assertion testing in the code you write can help to find errors in logic early.

2.3   Craftsmanship

If you *really* desire to program well, a first step is to take pride in your work—pride enough to sign your name on everything you do. Through the centuries, fine furniture makers signed their work, painters finished their efforts by dabbing on their name, and authors inscribed their books. Programmers should stand behind their creations.

Computer software has the luxury of immediate copyright protection—it is a protection against piracy, and a modern statement that you stand behind the belief that what you do is worth fighting for. If you have crafted something as best you can, add a comment at the top of your code:

```
// Image compression barrel for downlink to robotic cow tipper.
// (c) 2001, 2002 duane r. bailey
```

If, of course, you *have* stolen work from another, avoid the comment and consider, heavily, the appropriate attribution.

2.4   Conclusions

The effective programmer approaches his work like a craftsman. His constructions are well considered and documented. Comments are not necessary, but documentation makes working with the program much easier. One of the most important comments you can provide is your name—it suggests you are taking credit *and* responsibility for things you create. It makes our programming world less anonymous and more humane.

Special comments, including conditions and assertions, help the user and implementor of a method determine whether the method is used correctly. While it is difficult for compilers to determine the "spirit of the routine," the implementor is usually able to provide succinct checks of the sanity of the function. *I've done my time!* Five minutes of appropriate condition description and checking provided by the implementor can prevent hours of debugging by the user.

Problems

2.1⋆   Why is it necessary to provide pre- and postconditions?

2.2   What can be assumed if a method has no precondition?

2.3   Why is it not possible to have a method with no postcondition?

2.4⋆   Object orientation allows us to hide unimportant details from the user. Why, then, must we put pre- and postconditions on hidden code?

2.5⋆   What are the pre- and postconditions for the `length` method of the `java.lang.String` class?

2.6⋆   What are the pre- and postconditions for `String`'s `charAt` method?

2.7⋆   What are the pre- and postconditions for `String`'s `concat` method?

2.8   What are the pre- and postconditions for the `IEEEremainder` function in the `java.lang.Math` class?

2.9   Improve the comments on an old program.

2.10   Each of the methods of `Assert` (`pre`, `post`, and `condition`) takes the same parameters. In what way do the methods function differently? (Write a test program to find out!)

2.11   What are the pre- and postconditions for `java.lang.Math.asin` class?

Chapter 3

Vectors

"Climb high, climb far,
your goal the sky, your aim the star."
—Inscription on a college staircase

THE BEHAVIOR OF A PROGRAM usually depends on its input. Suppose, for example, that we wish to write a program that reads in n String values. One approach would keep track of the n values with n String variables:

```
public static void main(String args[])
{
    // read in n = 4 strings
    ReadStream r = new ReadStream();
    String v1, v2, v3, v4;
    v1 = r.readString();  // read a space-delimited word
    v2 = r.readString();
    v3 = r.readString();
    v4 = r.readString();
}
```

StringReader

This approach is problematic for the programmer of a *scalable* application—an application that works with large sets of data as well as small. As soon as n changes from its current value of 4, it has to be rewritten. Scalable applications are not uncommon, and so we contemplate how they might be supported.

One approach is to use *arrays*. An array of n values acts, essentially, as a collection of similarly typed variables whose names can be computed at run time. A program reading n values is shown below:

```
public static void main(String args[])
{
    // read in n = 4 strings
    ReadStream r = new ReadStream();
    String data[];
    int n = 4;
    // allocate array of n String references:
    data = new String[n];
    for (int i = 0; i < n; i++)
    {
        data[i] = r.readString();
    }
}
```

Here, n is a constant whose value is determined at compile time. As the program starts up, a new array of n integers is constructed and referenced through the variable named `data`.

All is fine, unless you want to read a different number of values. Then n has to be changed, and the program must be recompiled and rerun. Another solution is to pick an *upper bound* on the length of the array and only use the portion of the array that is necessary. Here's a modified procedure that uses up to one million array elements:

```java
public static void main(String args[])
{
    // read in up to 1000000 Strings
    ReadStream r = new ReadStream();
    String data[];
    int n = 0;
    data = new String[1000000];
    // read in strings until we hit end of file
    for (r.skipWhite(); !r.eof(); r.skipWhite())
    {
        data[n] = r.readString();
        n++;
    }
}
```

Unfortunately, if you are running on a small machine, and have small amounts of data, you are in trouble (see Problem 3.8). Because the array is so large, it will not fit on your machine—even if you want to read small amounts of data. You have to recompile the program with a smaller upper bound and try again. All this seems rather silly, considering how simple the problem appears to be.

We might, of course, require the user to specify the maximum size of the array before the data are read, at *run time*. Once the size is specified, an appropriately sized array can be allocated. While this may appear easier to program, the burden has shifted to the *user* of the program: the user has to commit to a specific upper bound—beforehand:

```java
public static void main(String args[])
{
    // read in as many Strings as demanded by input
    ReadStream r = new ReadStream();
    String data[];
    int n;
    // read in the number of strings to be read
    n = r.readInt();
    // allocate references for n strings
    data = new String[n];
    // read in the n strings
    for (int i = 0; i < n; i++)
```

```
        {
            data[i] = r.readString();
        }
    }
```

A nice solution is to build a *vector*—an array whose size may easily be changed. Here is our `String` reading program retooled one last time, using `Vectors`:

```
public static void main(String args[])
{
    // read in an arbitrary number of strings
    ReadStream r = new ReadStream();
    Vector data;
    int n;
    // allocate vector for storage
    data = new Vector();
    // read strings, adding them to end of vector, until eof
    for (r.skipWhite(); !r.eof(); r.skipWhite())
    {
        String s = r.readString();
        data.addElement(s);
    }
}
```

The `Vector` starts empty and expands (using `addElement`) with every `String` read from the input. Notice that the program doesn't explicitly keep track of the value of `n`.

3.1   Application: The Word List Revisited

We now reconsider an implementation of the word list part of our Hangman program of Section 1.4 implemented directly using Vectors:

WordList

```
Vector list;
String targetWord;
java.util.Random generator = new java.util.Random();

list = new Vector(10);
list.addElement("Ephraim");
list.addElement("Jeffrey");
list.addElement("John");
while (list.size() != 0)
{
    {   // select a word from the list
        int index = Math.abs(generator.nextInt())%list.size();
        targetWord = (String)list.elementAt(index);
    }
```

```
        // ... play the game using target word ...
        list.removeElement(targetWord);
}
```

Here, the operations of the `Vector` are seen to be very similar to the operations of the `WordList` program fragment shown on page 10. The `Vector` class, however, does not have a `selectAny` method. Instead, the bracketed code accomplishes that task. Since only `String`s are placed within the `Vector`, the assignment of `targetWord` involves a cast from `Object` (the type of value returned from the `elementAt` method of `Vector`) to `String`. This cast is necessary for Java to be reassured that you're expecting an element of type `String` to be returned. If the cast were not provided, Java would complain that the types involved in the assignment were incompatible.

Now that we have an implementation of the Hangman code in terms of both the `WordList` and `Vector` structures, we can deduce an implementation of the `WordList` structure in terms of the `Vector` class. In this implementation, the `WordList` contains a `Vector` that is used to hold the various words, as well as the random number generator (`generator`, above). To demonstrate the implementation, we look at the implementation of the `WordList`'s constructor and `selectAny` method:

```
        protected Vector theList;
        protected java.util.Random generator;

        public WordList(int n)
         */
        public WordList2(int n)
        {
            theList = new Vector(n);
            generator = new java.util.Random();
        }

        public String selectAny()
        {
            int i = Math.abs(generator.nextInt())%theList.size();
            return (String)theList.elementAt(i);
        }
}
```

Clearly, the use of a `Vector` within the `WordList` is an improvement over the direct use of an array, just as the use of `WordList` is an improvement over the complications of directly using a `Vector` in the Hangman program.

3.2   Application: Word Frequency

Suppose one day you read a book, and within the first page you read "behemoth" twice. A mighty unusual writing style! Word frequencies within documents can yield interesting information. Here is a little application for computing the frequency of words appearing on the input:

WordFreq

```java
public static void main(String args[])
{
    Vector vocab = new Vector(1000);
    ReadStream r = new ReadStream();
    int i;

    // for each word on input
    for (r.skipWhite(); !r.eof(); r.skipWhite())
    {
        Association wordInfo; // word-frequency association
        String vocabWord;     // word in the list

        // read in and tally instance of a word
        String word = r.readString();
        for (i = 0; i < vocab.size(); i++)
        {
            // get the association
            wordInfo = (Association)vocab.elementAt(i);
            // get the word from the association
            vocabWord = (String)wordInfo.key();
            if (vocabWord.equals(word))
            {   // match: increment integer in association
                Integer f = (Integer)wordInfo.value();
                wordInfo.setValue(new Integer(f.intValue() + 1));
                break;
            }
        }
        // mismatch: add new word, frequency 1.
        if (i == vocab.size())
        {
            vocab.addElement(
                new Association(word,new Integer(1)));
        }
    }
    // print out the accumulated word frequencies
    for (i = 0; i < vocab.size(); i++)
    {
        Association wordInfo = (Association)vocab.elementAt(i);
        System.out.println(
            wordInfo.key()+" occurs "+
            wordInfo.value()+" times.");
    }
}
```

First, for each word found on the input, we maintain an `Association` between the word (a `String`) and its frequency (an `Integer`). Each element of the `Vector` is such an `Association`. Now, the outer loop at the top reads in each word. The inner loop scans through the `Vector` searching for matching words that might have been read in. Matching words have their values updated. New words cause the construction of a new `Association`. The second loop scans through the `Vector`, printing out each of the `Associations`.

Each of these applications demonstrates the most common use of `Vectors`—keeping track of data when the number of entries is not known far in advance. In later chapters, we will consider the efficiency of these algorithms and, if necessary, seek improvements.

3.3   The Interface

As we have seen, the semantics of a `Vector` are similar to the semantics of an array. Both can store multiple values that may be accessed in any order. We call this property *random access*. Unlike the array, however, the `Vector` starts empty and is extended to hold object references. In addition, values may be removed from the `Vector` causing it to shrink. To accomplish these same size-changing operations in an array, the array would have to be reallocated.

With these characteristics in mind, let us consider a portion of the interface for this structure:

Vector

```
public class Vector implements Cloneable
{
    public Vector()
    // post: constructs an empty vector

    public Vector(int initialCapacity)
    // pre: initialCapacity >= 0
    // post: constructs an empty vector with initialCapacity capacity

    public void addElement(Object obj)
    // post: adds new element to end of possibly extended vector

    public Object elementAt(int index)
    // pre: 0 <= index && index < size()
    // post: returns the element stored in location index

    public void insertElementAt(Object obj, int index)
    // pre: 0 <= index <= size()
    // post: inserts new value in vector with desired index,
    //    moving elements from index to size()-1 to right

    public boolean isEmpty()
    // post: returns true iff there are no elements in the vector

    public boolean removeElement(Object element)
    // post: element equal to parameter is removed

    public void removeElementAt(int where)
```

```
        // pre: 0 <= where && where < size()
        // post: indicated element is removed, size decreases by 1

        public void setElementAt(Object obj, int index)
        // pre: 0 <= index && index < size()
        // post: element value is changed to obj

        public int size()
        // post: returns the size of the vector
    }
```

First, the constructors allow construction of a `Vector` with an optional initial *capacity*. The capacity is the initial number of `Vector` locations that are reserved for expansion. The `Vector` starts empty and may be freely expanded to its capacity. At that point the `Vector`'s memory is reallocated to handle further expansion. While the particulars of memory allocation and reallocation are hidden from the user, there is obvious benefit to specifying an appropriate initial capacity.

The `addElement` method adds a value to the end of the `Vector`, expanding it. To insert a new value in the middle of the `Vector`, we use `insertElementAt`. To access an existing element, one calls `elementAt`. The `removeElement` removes at most one element, selected by value. The `removeElementAt` method shrinks the logical size of the `Vector` by removing an element at a particular location. The `setElementAt` method is used to change a value in the `Vector`. Finally, two methods provide feedback about the current logical size of the `Vector`: `size` and `isEmpty`. The `size` method returns the number of values stored within the `Vector`. As elements are added to the `Vector`, the size increases from zero up to the capacity of the `Vector`. When the size is zero, then `isEmpty` returns `true`. The result is a data structure that provides constant-time access to data within the structure, without concern for determining explicit bounds on the structure's size.

There are several ways that a `Vector` is different than its array counterpart. First, while both the array and `Vector` maintain a number of references to objects, the `Vector` typically grows with use and stores a non-`null` reference in each entry. An array is a static structure whose entries may be initialized and used in any order, and are often `null`. Second, the `Vector` has an *end* where elements can be appended, while the array does not directly support the concept of appending values. There are times, of course, when the append operation might not be a feature desired in the structure; either the `Vector` or array would be a suitable choice.

The interface for `Vector`s in the `structure` package was driven, almost exclusively, by the interface for Java's proprietary `java.util.Vector` class. Thus, while we do not have access to the code for that class, any program written to use Java's `Vector` class can be made to use the `Vector` class described here, because their interfaces are consistent.

At this point, it may be useful to review the string-reading program of page 33. That code is frequently used as the basis for more complex programs.

3.4   The Implementation

Clearly, the `Vector` must be able to store a large number of similar items. We choose, then, to have the implementation of the `Vector` maintain an array of `Objects`, along with an integer that describes its current *size* or *extent*. When the size is about to exceed the *capacity* (the length of the underlying array), the `Vector`'s capacity is increased to hold the growing number of elements.

The constructor is responsible for allocation of the space and initializing the local variables. The number of elements initially allocated for expansion can be specified by the user:

```
protected Object elementData[];    // the data
protected int elementCount;        // # of elements in vector

public Vector()
// post: constructs an empty vector
{
    this(10); // call one-parameter constructor
}

public Vector(int initialCapacity)
// pre: initialCapacity >= 0
// post: constructs an empty vector with initialCapacity capacity
{
    Assert.pre(initialCapacity >= 0,"Nonnegative capacity.");
    elementData = new Object[initialCapacity];
    elementCount = 0;
}
```

Unlike other languages, all arrays within Java must be explicitly allocated. At the time the array is allocated, the number of elements is specified. Thus, in the constructor, the `new` operator allocates the number of elements desired by the user. Since the size of an array can be gleaned from the array itself (by asking for `elementData.length`), the value does not need to be explicitly stored within the `Vector` object.[1]

To access and modify elements within a `Vector`, we use the following operations:

```
public Object elementAt(int index)
// pre: 0 <= index && index < size()
// post: returns the element stored in location index
{
    return elementData[index];
}
```

---

[1] It could, of course, but explicitly storing it within the structure would mean that the implementor would have to ensure that the stored value was always consistent with the value accessible through the array's `length` variable.

```
public void setElementAt(Object obj, int index)
// pre: 0 <= index && index < size()
// post: element value is changed to obj
{
    elementData[index] = obj;
}
```

The arguments to both methods identify the location of the desired element. Because the index should be within the range of available values, the precondition states this fact.

For the accessor (`elementAt`), the desired element is returned as the result. The `setElementAt` method allows the `Object` reference to be changed to a new value, or `null` if no reference is desired. These operations, effectively, translate operations on `Vector`s into operations on arrays.

Now consider the addition of an element to the `Vector`. One way this can be accomplished is through the use of `addElement`. The task requires extending the size of the `Vector`, and then storing the element at the location indexed by the current number of elements (this is the first free location within the `Vector`). Here is the Java method:

```
public void addElement(Object obj)
// post: adds new element to end of possibly extended vector
{
    ensureCapacity(elementCount+1);
    elementData[elementCount] = obj;
    elementCount++;
}
```

(We will discuss the method `ensureCapacity` later. Its purpose is simply to ensure that the data array actually has enough room to hold the indicated number of values.) Notice that, as with many modern languages, arrays are indexed starting at zero. There are many good reasons for doing this. There are probably just as many good reasons for not doing this, but the best defense is that this is what programmers are currently used to.

Principle 6 *Maintaining a consistent interface makes a structure useful.*

If one is interested in inserting an element in the middle of the `Vector`, `insertElementAt` is the necessary method. The operation first creates an unused location at the desired point by shifting elements out of the way. Once the opening is created, the new element is inserted.

```
public void insertElementAt(Object obj, int index)
// pre: 0 <= index <= size()
// post: inserts new value in vector with desired index,
//    moving elements from index to size()-1 to right
{
    int i;
    ensureCapacity(elementCount+1);
    // N.B. must copy from right to left to avoid destroying data
```

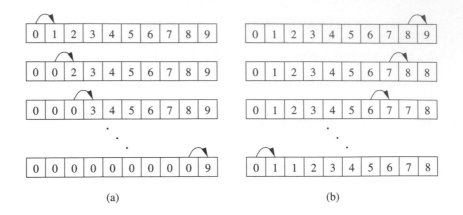

Figure 3.1 The incorrect (a) and correct (b) way of moving values in an array to make room for an inserted value.

```
    for (i = elementCount; i > index; i--) {
        elementData[i] = elementData[i-1];
    }
    // assertion: i == index and element[index] is available
    elementData[index] = obj;
    elementCount++;
}
```

Note that the loop that moves the elements higher in the array runs *backward*. To see why, it is only necessary to see what happens if the loop runs forward (see Figure 3.1a): the lowest element gets copied into higher and higher elements, ultimately copying over the entire **Vector** to the right of the insertion point. Figure 3.1b demonstrates the correct technique.

Removing an element from a specific location in the **Vector** is very similar, reversing the effect of **insertElementAt**. Here, using an argument similar to the one above, the loop moves in the forward direction:

```
    public void removeElementAt(int where)
    // pre: 0 <= where && where < size()
    // post: indicated element is removed, size decreases by 1
    {
        elementCount--;
        while (where < elementCount) {
            elementData[where] = elementData[where+1];
            where++;
        }
        elementData[elementCount] = null; // free reference
    }
```

We also allow the removal of a specific value from the **Vector**, using **removeElement** (not shown). Within this code, the **equals** method of the value passed to the routine is used to compare it to values within the **Vector**. When (and if) a match is found, it is removed using the technique described above.

The methods having to do with size are relatively straightforward:

```
public boolean isEmpty()
// post: returns true iff there are no elements in the vector
{
    return size() == 0;
}

public int size()
// post: returns the size of the vector
{
    return elementCount;
}
```

The logical size of the **Vector** is the number of elements stored within the **Vector**, and it is empty when this size is zero.

3.5   Extensibility: A Feature

Sometimes, our initial estimate of the maximum number of values is too small. In this case, it is necessary to extend the capacity of the **Vector**, carefully maintaining the values already stored within the **Vector**. Fortunately, because we have packaged the implementation within an interface, it is only necessary to extend the functionality of the existing operations, and provide some additional methods to describe the features.

A first approach might be to extend the **Vector** to include just as many elements as needed. Every time an element is added to the **Vector**, the number of elements is compared to the capacity of the array. If the capacity is used up, an array that is one element longer is allocated. This reallocation also requires copying of the existing data from one array to the other. Of course, for really long arrays, these copying operations would take a proportionally long time. Over time, as the array grows to n elements, the array data get copied many times. Problem 3.7 of this section demonstrates that this process causes approximately n^2 data items to be copied. This is expensive since, if in the beginning we had just allocated the **Vector** with a capacity of n elements, none of the data items would have to be copied during extension!

It turns out there is a happy medium: every time you extend the array, just double its capacity. Now, if we reconsider the number of times that an item gets copied during the extension process, the result is dramatically different. Suppose, for neatness only, that n is a power of two, and that the **Vector** started with a capacity of 1. What do we know? When the **Vector** was extended from capacity 1 to capacity 2, one element was copied. When the array was extended from capacity 2 to capacity 4, two elements were copied. When the array was extended from capacity 4 to 8, four elements were copied. This continues until the last extension, when the **Vector** had its capacity extended from $\frac{n}{2}$ to n: then $\frac{n}{2}$ elements had to be preserved. The total number of times elements were copied is

$$1 + 2 + 4 + \ldots + \frac{n}{2} = n - 1$$

Thus, extension by doubling allows unlimited growth of the **Vector** with an overhead that is proportional to the ultimate length of the array. Another way to think about it is that there is a constant overhead in supporting each element of a **Vector** extended in this way.

The Java language specifies a **Vector** interface that allows the user to specify how the **Vector** is to be extended if its capacity is not sufficient for the current operation. When the **Vector** is constructed, a **capacityIncrement** is specified. This is simply the number of elements to be added to the underlying array when extension is required. A nonzero value for this increment leads to the n^2 behavior we saw above, but it may be useful if, for example, one does not have the luxury of being able to double the size of a large array. If the increment is zero, the doubling strategy is used.

Our design, then, demands another protected value to hold the increment; we call this **capacityIncrement**. This value is specified in a special constructor and is not changed during the life of the **Vector**:

```
protected int capacityIncrement;     // the rate of growth for vector

public Vector(int initialCapacity, int capacityIncr)
// pre: initialCapacity >= 0, capacityIncr >= 0
// post: constructs an empty vector with initialCapacity capacity
//     that extends capacity by capacityIncr, or doubles if 0
{
    Assert.pre(initialCapacity >= 0, "Nonnegative capacity.");
    elementData = new Object[initialCapacity];
    elementCount = 0;
    capacityIncrement = capacityIncr;
}
```

We are now prepared to investigate **ensureCapacity**, a method that, if necessary, resizes **Vector** to have a capacity of at least **minCapacity**:

```
public void ensureCapacity(int minCapacity)
// post: the capacity of this vector is at least minCapacity.
{
    if (elementData.length < minCapacity) {
        int newLength = elementData.length; // initial guess
        if (capacityIncrement == 0) {
            // increment of 0 suggests doubling (default)
            if (newLength == 0) newLength = 1;
            while (newLength < minCapacity) {
                newLength *= 2;
            }
```

```
        } else {
            // increment != 0 suggests incremental increase
            while (newLength < minCapacity)
            {
                newLength += capacityIncrement;
            }
        }
        // assertion: newLength > elementData.length.
        Object newElementData[] = new Object[newLength];
        int i;
        // copy old data to array
        for (i = 0; i < elementCount; i++) {
            newElementData[i] = elementData[i];
        }
        elementData = newElementData;
        // N.B. Garbage collector will pick up old elementData
    }
    // assertion: capacity is at least minCapacity
}
```

This code deserves a careful investigation. If the current length of the underlying array is already sufficient to provide `minCapacity` elements, then the method does nothing. On the other hand, if the `Vector` is too short, it must be extended. We use a loop here that determines the new capacity by doubling (if `capacityIncrement` is zero) or by directly incrementing if `capacityIncrement` is nonzero. In either case, by the time the loop is finished, the desired capacity is determined. At that point, an array of the appropriate size is allocated, the old values are copied over, and the old array is dereferenced in favor of the new.

3.6 Application: The Matrix Class

One application of the `Vector` class is to support a two-dimensional `Vector`-like object: the *matrix*. Matrices are used in applications where two dimensions of data are needed. Our `Matrix` class has the following methods:

Matrix

```
public class Matrix
{
    public Matrix(int h, int w)
    // pre: h >= 0, w >= 0;
    // post: constructs an h row by w column matrix

    public Object elementAt(int row, int col)
    // pre: 0 <= row < height(), 0 <= col < width()
    // post: returns object at (row, col)

    public void setElementAt(Object value, int row, int col)
    // pre: 0 <= row < height(), 0 <= col < width()
    // post: changes location (row,col) to value
```

```
public void insertRowAt(int r)
// pre: 0 <= r <= height()
// post: inserts row of null values to be row r

public void insertColAt(int c)
// pre: 0 <= c <= width()
// post: inserts column of null values to be column c

public Vector removeRowAt(int r)
// pre: 0 <= r < height()
// post: removes row r and returns it as a Vector.

public Vector removeColAt(int c)
// pre: 0 <= c < width
// post: removes column c and returns it as a vector

public int width()
// post: returns number of columns in matrix

public int height()
// post: returns number of rows in matrix
}
```

The two-parameter constructor specifies the width and height of the `Matrix`. Elements of the `Matrix` are initially `null`, but may be reset with the `setElementAt` method. This method, along with the `elementAt` method, accepts two parameters that identify the row and the column of the value. To expand and shrink the `Matrix`, it is possible to insert and remove both rows and columns at any location. When a row or column is removed, a `Vector` of removed values is returned. The methods `height` and `width` return the number of rows and columns found within the `Matrix`, respectively.

To support this interface, we imagine that a `Matrix` is a `Vector` of rows, which are, themselves, `Vectors` of values (see Figure 3.2). While it is not strictly necessary, we explicitly keep track of the height and width of the `Matrix` (if we determine at some later date that keeping this information is unnecessary, the interface would hide the removal of these fields). Here, then, is the constructor for the `Matrix` class:

```
protected int height, width; // size of matrix
protected Vector rows;       // vector of row vectors

public Matrix(int h, int w)
// pre: h >= 0, w >= 0;
// post: constructs an h row by w column matrix
{
    height = h;  // initialize height and width
    width = w;
    // allocate a vector of rows
```

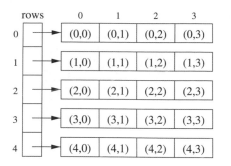

Figure 3.2   The `Matrix` class is represented as a `Vector` of rows, each of which is a `Vector` of references to `Objects`. Above, elements are labeled with their indices.

```
rows = new Vector(height);
for (int r = 0; r < height; r++)
{   // each row is allocated and filled with nulls
    Vector theRow = new Vector(width);
    rows.addElement(theRow);
    for (int c = 0; c < width; c++)
    {
        theRow.addElement(null);
    }
}
}
```

We allocate a `Vector` for holding the desired number of rows, and then, for each row, we construct a new `Vector` of the appropriate width. All the elements are initialized to `null`. It's not strictly necessary to do this initialization, but it's a good habit to get into.

The process of manipulating individual elements of the matrix is demonstrated by the `elementAt` and `setElementAt` methods:

```
public Object elementAt(int row, int col)
// pre: 0 <= row < height(), 0 <= col < width()
// post: returns object at (row, col)
{
    Assert.pre(0 <= row && row <= height, "Row in bounds.");
    Assert.pre(0 <= col && col <= width, "Col in bounds.");
    Vector theRow = (Vector)rows.elementAt(row);
    return theRow.elementAt(col);
}

public void setElementAt(Object value, int row, int col)
// pre: 0 <= row < height(), 0 <= col < width()
// post: changes location (row,col) to value
```

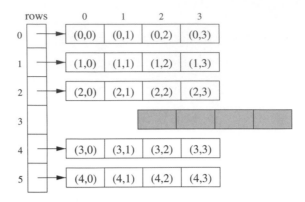

Figure 3.3 The insertion of a new row (gray) into an existing matrix. Indices are those associated with matrix *before* `InsertRowAt`. Compare with Figure 3.2.

```
{
    Assert.pre(0 <= row && row <= height, "Row in bounds.");
    Assert.pre(0 <= col && col <= width, "Col in bounds.");
    Vector theRow = (Vector)rows.elementAt(row);
    theRow.setElementAt(value,col);
}
```

The process of manipulating an element requires looking up a row within the rows table and finding the element within the row. It is also important to notice that in `setElementAt`, the row is found using `elementAt`, while the element within the row is changed using `setElementAt`. Although the element within the row changes, the row itself is represented by the same vector.

Many of the same memory management issues discussed in reference to `Vectors` hold as well for the `Matrix` class. When a row or column needs to be expanded to make room for new elements (see Figure 3.3), it is vital that the management of the arrays within the `Vector` class be hidden. Still, with the addition of a row into the `Matrix`, it is necessary to allocate the new row object, and to initialize each of the elements of the row to `null`:

```
public void insertRowAt(int r)
// pre: 0 <= r <= height()
// post: inserts row of null values to be row r
{
    Assert.pre(0 <= r && r <= width, "Row in bounds.");
    height++;
    Vector theRow = new Vector(width);
    for (int c = 0; c < width; c++)
    {
        theRow.addElement(null);
```

Chapter 4

Design Fundamentals

> *"We shape clay into a pot,*
> *but it is the emptiness inside*
> *that holds whatever we want."*
> —Lao-Tzu

PROGRAMMERS ARE CRAFTSMEN. Their medium—their programming language—often favors no particular design, and pushes for an individual and artistic decision. Given the task of implementing a simple program, any two individuals are likely to make different decisions about their work. Because programmers are allowed a large degree of personal expression, implementations of structures reflect considerable personal choice.

Some aspects of writing programs are, of course, taught and learned. The need to comment code is well understood. The desirability of writing small, easily grasped procedures is easily seen. Other aspects of the design of structures, algorithms, and programs are not easily identified, and are only appreciated after considerable experience. As a result, we have only recently developed even the most basic tools for understanding what it means to say that an algorithm is implemented nicely, or that a data structure works efficiently. Since the performance features of many data structures are quite subtle, it is important to develop a rich set of tools for developing and analyzing these structures.

In this chapter, we consider several important conceptual tools. *Big-O* complexity analysis provides a means of classifying the growth of functions and, therefore, the performance of the structures they describe. The concepts of *recursion* and *self-reference* make it possible to concisely code solutions to complex problems, and *mathematical induction* helps us demonstrate the important properties—including trends in performance—of traditional data structures. Finally, notions of symmetry and friction help us understand how to design data structures so that they have a reasonable look and feel.

4.1 Asymptotic Analysis Tools

We might be satisfied with evaluating the performance or *complexity* of data structures by precisely counting the number of statements executed or objects referenced. The main argument against any analysis that involves this counting is that the analysis is prone to significant misinterpretation. If, for example, we count integer-based operations, our evaluation is accurate to the extent that we know the length of time that it takes to perform these operations. Yet, modern architectures may have speeds that vary as much as a factor of 10 or more. The accurate counting of any specific kind of operation alone does not give us much information about the time of a specific implementation. Thus, while this technique is sometimes useful for understanding the fine distinctions between similar implementations, it is not generally necessary to make such detailed analyses of behavior. Distinctions between structures and algorithms can often be identified with coarser techniques. We consider those here.

4.1.1   Time and Space Complexity

In reality, what concerns us most are trends suggested by the *growth* of various metrics as the size of the problem becomes large. Clearly, an algorithm that takes linear time grows more slowly than one that is quadratic, and a quadratic algorithm grows more slowly than an exponential. Each of these rough characterizations—linear, quadratic, and so on—identifies a class of functions with similar growth behavior. To give us a better grasp on these classifications, we use *asymptotic* or *big-O* analysis to help us to describe and evaluate a function's growth.

Definition 4.1 *A function $f(n)$ is $O(g(n))$ (read "order g" or "big-O of g"), if and only if there exist two positive constants, c and n_0, such that*

$$|f(n)| \leq c \cdot g(n)$$

for all $n \geq n_0$.

In this text, f will usually be a function that describes the utilization of some precious resource (e.g., time or space) as the size of the structure or problem increases. This is a subtle definition (and one that is often stated incorrectly), so let's carefully consider why each of the parts of the definition is necessary.

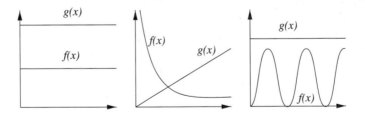

Figure 4.1   Examples of functions, $f(n)$, that are $O(g(n))$.

First, a "scaled-up" instance of $g(n)$ forms an upper bound for the function $f(n)$ (see Figure 4.1). In the loosest of terms, we would like to think that after some point (when $n \geq n_0$), the magnitude of $f(n)$ does not exceed a scaled-up version of $g(n)$. You will note that if $f(n)$ is $O(g(n))$ it is also $O(10 \cdot g(n))$ and

$O(5 + g(n))$. The selection of an appropriate c allows us to scale up $g(n)$ to the extent necessary to make it an upper bound. So, while $g(n)$ may not directly exceed $f(n)$, it might if it is multiplied by 10. If so, we would be happy to say that $f(n)$ has a shape that does not grow any faster than $g(n)$. Note, also, that c is positive. It does not help us understand the shape of $f(n)$ if we consider functions scaled by a negative or zero factor.

Second, we are looking for long-term behavior. Since the most dramatic growth in functions is most evident for large values, we are happy to ignore "glitches" and anomalous behavior up to a certain point—that point is n_0. We do not really care how big n_0 gets, as long as it can be nailed down to some fixed value when relating specific functions f and g.

Nails = proofs.

Third, we are not usually interested in whether the function $f(n)$ is negative or positive; we are just interested in the magnitude of its growth. In reality, most of the resources we consider (e.g., time and space) are measured as positive values and larger quantities of the resource are consumed as the problem grows in size, so the rates of growth are usually positive.

Most functions we encounter fall into one of a few categories. A function that is bounded above by a constant is classified as $O(1)$.[1] The constant factor can be completely accounted for in the value of c in the above definition. These functions measure size-independent characteristics of data structures. For example, the time it takes to assign a value to an arbitrary element of an array of size n is constant.

What's your best guess for the time to assign a value? $\frac{1}{1000}$ second? $\frac{1}{1000000}$ sec.? $\frac{1}{1000000000}$ s.?

When a function grows at most *linearly*, we say it is $O(n)$. Depending on what's being measured, this can be classified as "nice behavior." Summing the values in an n-element array, for example, can be accomplished in linear time. If we double the size of the array, we expect the time of the summation process to grow proportionately. Similarly, the Vector takes linear space. Most methods associated with the Vector class, if not constant, are linear in time and space. If we develop methods that manipulate the n elements of a Vector of numbers in *superlinear* time—time that grows faster than linear—we should not be pleased, as we know it can be accomplished more efficiently.

Other functions grow *polynomially* and are $O(n^c)$ where c is some constant greater than 1. The function $n^2 + n$ is $O(n^2)$ (let $c = 2$ and $n_0 = 1$) and therefore grows as a quadratic. Many simple methods for sorting n elements of an array are quadratic. The space required to store a square matrix of size n takes quadratic space. Usually, we consider functions with polynomial growth to be fairly efficient, though we would like to see c remain small in practice. Because a function n^{c-1} is $O(n \cdot n^{c-1})$ (i.e., $O(n^c)$), we only need consider the growth of the most significant term of a polynomial function. (It is, after all, most significant!) The less significant terms are ultimately outstripped by the leading term.

Grass could be greener.

Some functions experience *exponential* growth (see Figures 4.2 and 4.3). The functions are $O(c^n)$, where c is a constant greater than 1. Enumerating

---

[1] It is also $O(13)$, but we try to avoid such distractions.

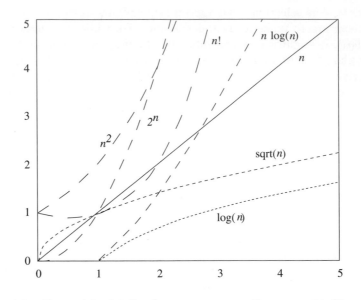

Figure 4.2   Near-origin details of common curves. Compare with Figure 4.3.

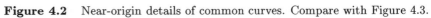

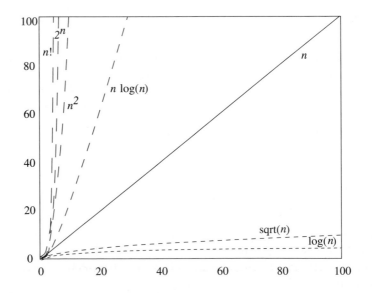

Figure 4.3   Long-range trends of common curves. Compare with Figure 4.2.

all strings of length n or checking topological equivalence of circuits with n devices are classic examples of exponential algorithms. Constructing a list of the n-digit palindromes requires exponential time and space. The demands of an exponential process grow too quickly to make effective use of resources. As a result, we often think of functions with exponential behavior as being *intractable*. In the next section we will see that some recursive solutions to problems are exponential. While these solutions are not directly useful, simple insights can sometimes make these algorithms efficient.

"2002" is a palindrome.

4.1.2 Examples

We now consider the analysis of the running times of several simple methods.

A "Modulo Table"

Suppose we're interested in printing a 10 by 10 table of modular (`row%col`) values. Each value in the table corresponds to the remainder when the row number is divided by the column number:

```
0 1 1 1 1 1 1 1 1 1
0 0 2 2 2 2 2 2 2 2
0 1 0 3 3 3 3 3 3 3
0 0 1 0 4 4 4 4 4 4
0 1 2 1 0 5 5 5 5 5
0 0 0 2 1 0 6 6 6 6
0 1 1 3 2 1 0 7 7 7
0 0 2 0 3 2 1 0 8 8
0 1 0 1 4 3 2 1 0 9
0 0 1 2 0 4 3 2 1 0
```

Analysis

As with most two-dimensional forms of output, we consider the use of a nested pair of loops:

```java
public static void modTable(int n)
// pre: n >= 0
// post: print modulo table of width n
{
    for (int row = 1; row <= n; row++)        // 1
    {
        for (int col = 1; col <= n; col++)    // 2
        {
            System.out.print(row%col+" ");    // 3
        }
        System.out.println();                 // 4
    }
}
```

Each of the loops executes n times. Since printing a value (line 3) takes constant time c_1, the inner loop at line 2 takes $c_1 n$ time. If line 4 takes constant time c_2, then the outer loop at line 1 takes $n(c_1 n + c_2) = c_1 n^2 + c_2 n$ time. This polynomial is clearly $O(n^2)$ (take $c = c_1 + c_2$ and $n_0 = 1$). Doubling the problem size approximately quadruples the running time.

As a rule of thumb, each loop that performs n iterations multiplies the complexity of each iteration by a factor of n. Nested loops multiply the complexity of the most deeply nested code by a power of n. As we have seen above, loops doubly nested around a simple statement often consume quadratic time.

Since there are only three variables in our modulo method, it takes constant space—an amount of space that is independent of problem size.

A Multiplication Table

Unlike the modulo operator, the multiplication operator is commutative. Therefore, when printing a multiplication table of size n, only the "lower triangular" region is needed. Here is the Java implementation:

```java
public static void multTable(int n)
// pre: n >= 0
// post: print multiplication table
{
    for (int row = 1; row <= n; row++)        // 1
    {
        for (int col = 1; col <= row; col++)  // 2
        {
            System.out.print(row*col+" ");    // 3
        }
        System.out.println();                 // 4
    }
}
```

Clearly, this table can be printed at least as fast as our modulo table—it has about half the entries—so it must be $O(n^2)$. Can this limit be improved? If lines 3 and 4 take constant times c_1 and c_2, respectively, then the overall time is approximately

$$(1c_1 + c_2) + (2c_1 + c_2) + \ldots + (nc_1 + c_2) = \frac{c_1 n(n+1)}{2} + nc_2$$

Clearly, no scaled linear function will bound this function above, so the bound of $O(n^2)$ is tight.

Notice that both of the above programs print an "area" of values, each of which can be computed in constant time. Thus, the growth rate of the function is the growth rate of the area of the output—which is $O(n^2)$.

Building a `Vector` of Values

Often, it is useful to build a `Vector` containing specific values. For the purposes of this problem, we will assume the values are integers between 0 and $n-1$, inclusive. Our first (and best) attempt expands the `Vector` in the natural manner:

```
public static Vector buildVector1(int n)
// pre: n >= 0
// post: construct a vector of size n of 1..n
{
    Vector v = new Vector(n);                   // 1
    for (int i = 0; i < n; i++)                 // 2
    {
        v.addElement(new Integer(i));           // 3
    }
    return v;                                    // 4
}
```

We will assume (correctly) that lines 1 and 4 take constant time. The loop at line 2, however, takes n times the length of time it takes to add a single element. Review of that code will demonstrate that the addition of a new element to a **Vector** takes constant time, provided expansion is not necessary. Thus, the total running time is linear, $O(n)$. Notice that the process of building this **Vector** requires space that is linear as well. Clearly, if the method's purpose is to spend time initializing the elements of a **Vector**, it would be difficult for it to consume space at a faster rate than time.

A slightly different approach is demonstrated by the following code:

```
public static Vector buildVector2(int n)
// pre: n >= 0
// post: construct a vector of size n of 1..n
{
    Vector v = new Vector(n);                   // 1
    for (int i = 0; i < n; i++)                 // 2
    {
        v.insertElementAt(new Integer(i),0);// 3
    }
    return v;                                    // 4
}
```

All of the assumptions of **buildVector1** hold here, except that the cost of inserting a value at the *beginning* of a **Vector** is proportional to the **Vector**'s current length. On the first insertion, it takes about 1 unit of time, on the second, 2 units, and so on. The analysis of this method, then, is similar to that of the triangular multiplication table, above. Its running time is $O(n^2)$. Its space utilization, however, remains linear.

Finding a Space in a String

Some problems appear to have behavior that is more variable than the examples we have seen so far. Consider, for example, the code to locate the first space in a string:

```
static int findSpace(String s)
// pre: s is a string, possibly containing a space
// post: returns index of first space, or -1 if none found
```

```
{
    int i;
    for (i = 0; i < s.length(); i++)
    {
        if (' ' == s.charAt(i)) return i;
    }
    return -1;
}
```

This simple method checks each of the characters within a string. When one is found to be a space, the loop is terminated and the index is returned. If, of course, there is no space within the string, this must be verified by checking each character. Clearly, the time associated with this method is determined by the number of loops executed by the method. As a result, the time taken is linear in the length of the string.

We can, however, be more precise about its behavior using *best-*, *worst-*, and *average-case analyses*:

Worst case. The worst-case behavior is the longest time that any problem of size n might take. In our string-based procedure, our method will take the longest when there is no space in the string. In that case, the method consumes at most linear time. Unless we specify otherwise, the worst-case consumption of resources is used to determine the complexity.

Best case. The best-case behavior is the shortest time that any problem might take. Usually, best cases are associated with particularly nice problems— here, perhaps, a string with a space in the first position. In this case, our method takes at most constant time!

Average case. The average-case behavior is the complexity of solving an "average" problem of size n. Analysis involves computing a weighted sum of the cost (in time or space) of problems of size n. The weight of each problem is the probability that the problem would occur. If, in our example, we knew (somehow) that there was exactly one space in the string, and that it appears in any of the n positions with equal probability, we would deduce that, on average,

$$\frac{1}{n} + \frac{1}{n}2 + \ldots + \frac{1}{n}n = \frac{1}{n}\frac{n(n+1)}{2} = \frac{n+1}{2}$$

iterations would be necessary to locate the space. Our method has linear average-time complexity. If, however, we knew that the string was English prose of length n, the average complexity would be related to the average length of the first word, a value easily bounded above by a constant (say, 10). The weights of the first few terms would be large, while the weights associated with a large number of iterations or more would be zero. The average complexity would be constant. (In this case, the worst case would be constant as well.) Obviously determining the average-case complexity

German prose may require larger constants.

requires some understanding of the particular distributions of data to be used.

Best-, worst-, and average-case analyses will be imporant in helping us evaluate the theoretical complexities of the structures we develop. Some care, however, must be used when determining the growth rates of real Java. It is tempting, for example, to measure the space or time used by a data structure and fit a curve to it in hopes of getting a handle on its long-term growth. This approach should be avoided, if possible, as such statements can rarely be made with much security. Still, such techniques can be fruitfully used to verify that there is no *unexpected* behavior.

4.1.3   The Trading of Time and Space

The two resources most coveted by programmers are time and space. When programs are run, the algorithms they incorporate and the data structures they utilize work together to consume time. This time is the direct result of executing machine instructions. The fewer instructions executed, the faster the program is likely to go.

Most of us have had an opportunity to return to old code and realize that useless instructions can be removed. Arguably, most programs are susceptible to some form of this weeding, or *optimization*. On the other hand, it is clear that there must be a limit to the extent that an individual program can be improved. At some stage, the removal of any statement causes the program to run incorrectly. This limit, in some sense, is an *information theoretic limit*: given the approach of the algorithm and the design of a data structure, no improvements can be made to the program to make it run faster. To be convinced that there is a firm limit, we would require a formal proof that each statement was necessary. Such proofs can be difficult, especially without intimate knowledge of the language, its compiler, and the architecture that supports the running code. Nonetheless, the optimization of code is an important feature of making programs run quickly. Considerable effort has been put into designing compilers to make automated optimization decisions. Most compilers, for example, will not generate instructions for *dead code*—statements that will never be executed. In the following Java code, for example, it is clear the "then" portion of this code may be removed without fear:

```
if (false)
{
    System.out.println("Man in the moon.");
} else {
    System.out.println("Pie in the sky.");
}
```

After compiler optimizations have been employed, though, there is a limit that can be placed on how fast the code can be made to run. We will assume — whenever we consider a time–space tradeoff—that all reasonable efforts have been made to optimize the time and space utilization of a particular approach. Notice, however, that most optimizations performed by a compiler do not significantly impact the asymptotic running time of an algorithm. At most, they tend to speed up an algorithm by a constant factor, which is easily absorbed in any theoretical analysis using big-O methods.

The selection of appropriate implementations of data structures can have an impact. Such decisions about data structure design involve weighing—often using results of big-O analysis—the time and space utilization of the algorithms that manipulate them. For example, in the `Vector` class, we opted to maintain a field, `elementCount`, that kept track of how many elements within the underlying array are actually being used. This variable became necessary when we realized that as the `Vector` expanded, the constant reallocation of the underlying memory could lead to quadratic time complexity over the life of the `Vector`. By storing a little more information (here, `elementCount`) we reduce the total complexity of expanding the `Vector`—our implementation, recall, requires a linear number of element copies as the `Vector` expands. Since `Vector`s are likely to be used in this way, we find it worthwhile to use this extra space. In other situations we will see that the tradeoffs are less obvious and sometimes lead to the development of several data structures for use by an informed user.

The choice between implementations is sometimes difficult, and may require analysis of the problems that are to be solved using the structure: if the `addElement` method is to be called relatively infrequently, then the time spent "resizing" the value is relatively insignificant. On the other hand, if elements are to be added frequently, maintaining `elementCount` saves time. In any case, the careful analysis of time–space tradeoffs is an important facet of good data structure design.

4.2   Self-Reference

One of the most elegant techniques for construction of algorithms, data structures, and proofs is to utilize self-reference. In this section we discuss applications of self-reference in programming—called *recursion*—and in proofs—called *proof-by-induction*. In both cases the difficulties of solving the problem outright are circumvented by developing a language that is rich enough to support the self-reference. The result is a compact technique for solving complex problems.

4.2.1   Recursion

When faced with a difficult problem of computation or structure, often the best solution can be specified in a *self-referential* or *recursive* manner. Usually, the difficulty of the problem is one of management of the resources that are to be used by the program. Recursion helps us tackle the problem by focusing on reducing the problem to one that is more manageable in size and then building up the answer. Through multiple, nested, progressive applications of the algorithm, a solution is constructed from the solutions of smaller problems.

Summing Integers

We first consider a simple, but classic, problem: suppose we are interested in computing the sum of the numbers from 0 through n.

$$\sum_{i=0}^{n} i = 0 + 1 + 2 + 3 + \ldots + n$$

One approach to the problem is to write a simple loop that, over n iterations accumulates the result:

Recursion

```
public static int sum1(int n)
// post: compute the sum of 0..n
{
    int result = 0;
    for (int i = 1; i <= n; i++)
    {
        result = result + i;
    }
    return result;
}
```

The method starts by setting a partial sum to zero. If n is a value that is less than 1, then the loop will never execute. This is the result we expect if $n = 0$. As the loop executes, the initial portion of the partial sum is computed. After $n - 1$ loops, the sum of the first $n - 1$ terms is computed; the nth iteration simply adds in n. This method works as advertised in the postcondition.

Suppose, now, that a second programmer is to solve the same problem. If the programmer is particularly lazy and has access to sum1, the following code also solves the problem:

```
public static int sum2(int n)
// post: compute the sum of 0..n
{
    if (n < 1) return 0;
    else return sum1(n-1) + n;
}
```

For the most trivial problem (any number less than 1), we return 0. For all other values of n, the programmer turns to sum1 to solve the next simplest problem (the sum of integers 0 thru $n - 1$), and then adds n. Of course, this algorithm works as advertised in the postcondition, because it depends on sum1 for all but the last step, and it then adds in the correct final addend, n.

Actually, if sum2 calls *any* method that is able to compute the sum of numbers 0 through $n - 1$, sum2 works correctly. But, wait! The sum of integers is precisely what sum2 is supposed to be computing! We use this observation to derive, then, the following self-referential method:

```
public static int sum3(int n)
// post: compute the sum of 0..n
{
    if (n < 1) return 0;           // base case
    else return sum3(n-1) + n;     // reduction, progress, sol'n
}
```

This code requires careful inspection (Figure 4.4). First, in the simplest or *base* cases (for $n < 1$), sum3 returns 0. The second line is executed in every other computation. It reduces the problem to a simpler problem—the sum of integers between 0 and $n - 1$. As with all recursive programs, this requires a little "work" (a subtraction) to reduce the problem to one that is closer to the base case. Considering the problem $n + 1$ would have been fatal because it doesn't make suitable *progress* toward the solution. The subproblem is passed off to *another invocation* of sum3. Once that procedure computes its result (either immediately or, if necessary, through further recursion), a little more work is necessary to convert the solution of the problem of size $n - 1$ into a solution for a problem of size n. Here, we have simply added in n. Notice the operation involved in building the answer (addition) opposes the operation used to reduce the problem (subtraction). This is common in recursive procedures.

Principle 7 *Recursive structures must make "progress" toward a "base case."*

We cast this principle in terms of "structures" because much of what we say about self-referential execution of code can be applied to self-referential structuring of data. Most difficulties with recursive structures (including recursive methods) stem from either incorrectly stating the base case or making improper progress toward the base case.

Returning to sum3, we note it is an example of a *tail recursive* method. Any recursion happens just before exiting from the method. Tail recursive methods are particularly nice because good compilers can translate them into loops of the form found in sum1. Each iteration of the loop simulates the computation and return of another of the nested recursive procedure calls, traveling up the arrows of Figure 4.4 from bottom-right to top-left. Since there is one call for each value between 1 and n, and the procedure performs a constant amount of math, the entire process takes $O(n)$ time.

Inserting a Value into a Vector

Recursion is a natural method for accomplishing many complicated tasks. For example, the insertElementAt method of the Vector class discussed on page 39 can be written as a recursive procedure. The essential concept is to insert the value into the Vector only after having moved the previous value out of the way. That value is inserted at the next larger location. This leads us to the following alternative to the standard Vector method:

Vector

```
public void insertElementAt(Object value, int index)
// pre: 0 <= index <= size()
// post: inserts new value in vector with desired index
```

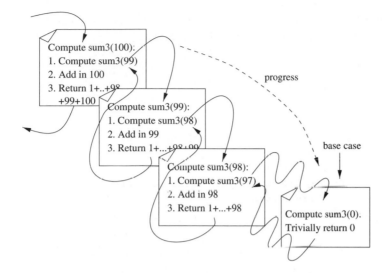

Figure 4.4 The "unrolling" of a procedure to recursively sum integers. Rightward arrows break the problem down; leftward arrows build up the solution.

```
//   moving elements from index to size()-1 to right
{
    if (index >= size()) addElement(value); // base case
    else {
        Object previous = elementAt(index); // work
        insertElementAt(previous,index+1);  // progress
        setElementAt(value,index);   // work
    }
}
```

Note that the base case is identified through the need to apply a *trivial operation* rather than, say, the size of the index. Indeed, progress is determined by how close the index gets to the size of the **Vector**. Again, this is a linear or $O(n)$ process.

Printing a **Vector** *of Values*

In the previous example, the recursive routine was suitable for direct use by the user. Often, though, recursion demands additional parameters that encode, in some way, progress made toward the solution. These parameters can be confusing to users who, after all, are probably unaware of the details of the recursion. To avoid this confusion, we "wrap" the call to a protected recursive method in a public method. This hides the details of the initial recursive method call. Here, we investigate a printing extension to the **Vector** class:

```
public void print()
// post: print the elements of the vector
{
    printFrom(0);
}

protected void printFrom(int index)
// pre: index <= size()
// post: print elements indexed between index and size()
{
    if (index < size()) {
        System.out.println(elementAt(index));
        printFrom(index+1);
    }
}
```

The `print` method wraps or hides the call to the recursive `printFrom` method. The recursive method accepts a single parameter that indicates the index of the first element that should be printed out. As progress is made, the initial index increases, leading to linear performance. To print the entire `Vector`, the recursive method is called with a value of zero.

Notice that the base case appears to be missing. In fact, it is indicated by the failure of the `if` statement. Even though the base case is to "do nothing," the `if` statement is absolutely necessary. Every terminating recursive method should have some conditional statement.

Computing Change in Postage Stamps

Suppose, when receiving change at the post office, you wished to be paid your change in various (useful) stamps. For example, at current rates, you might be interested in receiving either 32 cent stamps, 20 cent postcards, or penny stamps (just in case of a postage increase). For a particular amount of change, what is *the smallest number of stamps required* to meet your demands?

This problem is fairly complex because, after all, the minimum number of stamps needed to make 42 cents involves 4 stamps—two postcard stamps and two penny stamps—and *not* 11—a 32 cent stamp and 10 penny stamps. (The latter solution might be suggested by postal clerks used to dealing with U.S. coinage, which is fairly easily minimized.) We will initially approach this problem using recursion. Our solution will only report the minimum number of stamps returned. We leave it as an exercise to report the number of each type of stamp (consider Problem 4.20); that solution does not greatly impact the approach of the problem.

If no change is required, the solution is simple: hand the customer zero stamps. If the change is anything more, we'll have to do some work. Consider the "42 cent problem." We know that some stamps will have to be given to the customer, but not the variety. We *do* know that the "last stamp" handed to the customer will either be a penny, a 20 cent, or a 32 cent stamp. If we could only solve three smaller minimization problems—the "41 cent problem," the "22 cent problem," and the "10 cent problem"—then our answer would be one stamp more than the minimum of the answers to those three problems. (The answers to the three problems are 3, 3, and 10, respectively, so our answer should be 4.) Of course, we should ignore meaningless reduced problems: the "−3 cent problem" results from considering handing a 20 cent stamp over to solve the "17 cent problem."

Here is the `stampCount` method that computes the solution:

```
public static int stampCount(int amount)
// pre: amount >= 0
// post: return *number* of stamps needed to make change
//       (only use 1 cent, 20 cent, and 32 cent stamps)
{
    int minStamps;
    Assert.pre(amount >= 0,"Reasonable amount of change.");
    if (amount == 0) return 0;
    // consider use of a penny stamp
    minStamps = 1+stampCount(amount-1);
    // consider use of a 20 cent stamp
    if (amount >= 20) {
        int possible = 1+stampCount(amount-20);
        if (minStamps > possible) minStamps = possible;
    }
    // consider use of a 32 cent stamp
    if (amount >= 32) {
        int possible = 1+stampCount(amount-32);
        if (minStamps > possible) minStamps = possible;
    }
    return minStamps;
}
```

Recursive-Postage

For the nontrivial cases, the variable `minStamps` keeps track of the minimum number of stamps returned by any of these three subproblems. Since each method call potentially results in several recursive calls, the method is not tail recursive. While it is possible to solve this problem using iteration, recursion presents a very natural solution.

An Efficient Solution to the Postage Stamp Problem

If the above procedure were used to compute the minimum number of stamps to make 42 cents change, the `stampCount` procedure would be called 395 times. This number increases exponentially as the size of the problem increases. Because 395 is greater than 42, some subproblems are recomputed many times. For example, the "2 cent problem" must be re-solved by every larger problem.

Making currency is illegal. Making change is not!

To reduce the number of calls, we can incorporate an array into the method. Each location n of the array stores either 0 or the answer to the problem of size n. If, when looking for an answer, the entry is 0, we invest time in computing the answer and *cache* it in the array for future use. This technique is called *dynamic programming* and yields an efficient linear algorithm. Here is our modified solution:

FullPostage

```
public static int stampCount(int amount)
// pre: amount >= 0
// post: return *number* of stamps needed to make change
//       (only use 1 cent, 20 cent, and 32 cent stamps)
{
    return stampCount(amount, new int[amount+1]);
}


protected static int stampCount(int amount, int answer[])
// pre: amount >= 0; answer array has length >= amount
// post: return *number* of stamps needed to make change
//       (only use 1 cent, 20 cent, and 32 cent stamps)
{
    int minStamps;
    Assert.pre(amount >= 0,"Reasonable amount of change.");
    if (amount == 0) return 0;
    if (answer[amount] != 0) return answer[amount];
    // consider use of a penny stamp
    minStamps = 1+stampCount(amount-1,answer);
    // consider use of a 20 cent stamp
    if (amount >= 20) {
        int possible = 1+stampCount(amount-20,answer);
        if (minStamps > possible) minStamps = possible;
    }
    // consider use of a 32 cent stamp
    if (amount >= 32) {
        int possible = 1+stampCount(amount-32,answer);
        if (minStamps > possible) minStamps = possible;
    }
    answer[amount] = minStamps;
    return minStamps;
}
```

When we call the method for the first time, we allocate an array of sufficient size (amount+1 because of zero origin arrays) and pass it as answer in the protected two-parameter version of the method. If the answer is not found in the array, it is computed using up to three recursive calls that pass the array of previously computed answers. Just before returning, the newly computed answer is placed in the appropriate slot. In this way, when solutions are sought for this problem again, they are cached away where they can be retrieved without the overhead of redundant computation.

42: the ultimate answer. When we seek the solution to the "42 cent problem," 77 calls are made to the procedure. Only 42 of these get past the first few statements to potentially make recursive calls. The combination of the power recursion and the efficiency of dynamic programming yields elegant solutions to many seemingly difficult problems.

In the next section, we consider *induction*, a recursive proof technique. Induction is as elegant a means of proving theorems as recursion is for writing programs.

4.2.2 Mathematical Induction

The accurate analysis of data structures often requires mathematical proof. An effective proof technique that may be applied to many computer science problems is *mathematical induction*. The technique is, essentially, the construction of a recursive proof. Just as some problems can be elegantly solved recursively, some properties may be elegantly investigated using induction.

A common template for proving statements by mathematical induction is as follows:

1. Begin your proof with "We will prove this using induction on the size of the problem." This informs the reader of your approach.

2. Directly prove whatever base cases are necessary. Strive, whenever possible to keep the number of cases small and the proofs as simple as possible.

3. State the assumption that the observation holds for all values from the base case, up to but not including the nth case. Sometimes this assumption can be relaxed in simple inductive proofs.

4. Prove, from simpler cases, that the nth also holds.

5. Claim that, by mathematical induction on n, the observation is true for all cases more complex than the base case.

Individual proofs, of course, often require special modifications to the inductive argument, but most fit the outline, above.

As an initial example, we construct a formula for computing the sum of integers between 0 and $n \geq 0$ inclusively. Recall this result was used in Section 3.5 when we considered the cost of extending vectors, and earlier in this chapter when analyzing `buildVector2`. Proof of this statement also yields a constant time method for implementing `sum3`.

Observation 4.1 $\sum_{i=0}^{n} i = \frac{n(n+1)}{2}$.

Proof: We prove this by induction. First, consider the simplest case or *base case*. If $n = 0$, then the sum is 0. The formula gives us $\frac{0(0+1)}{2} = 0$. The observation appears to hold.

Now, suppose we know—for some reason—that our closed-form formula holds for all values between 0 (our base case) and $n - 1$. This knowledge may help us solve a more complex problem, namely the sum of integers between 0 and n. The sum

$$0 + 1 + 2 + \ldots + (n - 1) + n$$

conveniently contains the sum of the first $n - 1$ integers, so we rewrite it as

$$[0 + 1 + 2 + \ldots + (n - 1)] + n$$

Because we have assumed the sum of the natural numbers to $n - 1$ can be computed by the formula, we may rewrite the sum as

$$\left[\frac{(n - 1)n}{2}\right] + n$$

The terms of this expression may be simplified and reorganized:

$$\frac{(n - 1)n + 2n}{2} = \frac{n(n + 1)}{2}$$

Thus given only the knowledge that the formula worked for $n - 1$, we have been able to extend it to n. It is not hard to convince yourself, then, that the observation holds for any nonnegative value of n. Our base case was for $n = 0$, so it must hold as well for $n = 1$. Since it holds for $n = 1$, it must hold for $n = 2$. In fact, it holds for any value of $n \geq 0$ by simply proving it holds for values $0, 1, 2, \ldots, n - 1$ and then observing it can be extended to n.◇

99 cases left to prove! Take one down, pass it around, 98 cases left to prove!...

The induction can be viewed as a recursively constructed proof (consider Figure 4.5). Suppose we wish to see if our observation holds for $n = 100$. Our method requires us to show it holds for $n = 99$. Given that, it is a simple matter to extend the result to 100. Proving the result for $n = 99$, however, is *almost*[2] as difficult as it is for $n = 100$. We need to prove it for $n = 98$, and extend *that* result. This process of developing the proof for 100 eventually unravels into a recursive construction of a (very long) proof that demonstrates the observation holds for values 0 through 99, and then 100.

The whole process, like recursion, depends critically on the proof of appropriate base cases. In our proof of the above observation, for example, we proved the observation held for $n = 0$. If we do not prove this simple case, then our recursive construction of the proof for any value of $n \geq 0$ does not terminate: when we try to prove it holds for $n = 0$, we have no base case, and therefore must prove it holds for $n = -1$, and in proving that we prove it holds for $-2, -3, \ldots$, *ad infinitum*. The proof construction never terminates!

Our next example of proof by induction is a *correctness proof*. Our intent is to show that a piece of code runs as advertised. In this case, we reinvestigate `sum3` from earlier in the chapter:

Recursion

```
public static int sum3(int n)
// post: compute the sum of 0..n
{
    if (n < 1) return 0;          // 1
    else return                   // 2
                sum3(             // 3
                    n-1           // 4
                ) + n;            // 5
}
```

_____

[2] It is important, of course, to base your inductive step on simpler problems—problems that take you closer to your base case. If you avoid basing it on simpler cases, then the recursive proof will never be completely constructed, and the induction will fail.

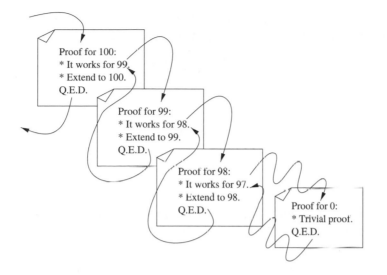

Figure 4.5 The process of proof by induction simulates the recursive construction of a proof. Compare with Figure 4.4.

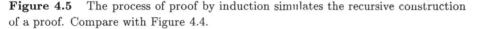

(The code has been reformatted to allow discussion of portions of the computation.) As with our mathematical proofs, we state our result formally:

Observation 4.2 *The method* sum3 *computes the sum of the integers 0 through n, inclusive.*

Proof: Our proof is by induction, based on the parameter n. First, consider the action of sum3 when passed the parameter 0. The if statement of line 1 is true, and the program returns 0, the desired result.

We now consider n>0, and assume that the method computes the correct result for all values less that n. We extend our proof of correctness to the parameter value of n. Since n is greater than zero, the if of line 2 fails, and the else is considered. On line 4, the parameter is decremented, and on line 3, the recursion takes place. By our assumption, this recursive call returns the correct result—the sum of values between 0 and n-1, inclusive. Line 5 adds in the final value, and the entire result is returned. The program works correctly for a parameter n greater than zero. By induction on n, the method computes the correct result for all n>=0.◇

Proofs of correctness are important steps in the process of verifying that code works as desired. Clearly, since induction and recursion have similar forms, the application of inductive proof techniques to recursive methods often leads to straightforward proofs. Even when iteration is used, however, induction can be used to demonstrate assumptions made about loops, no matter the number of iterations.

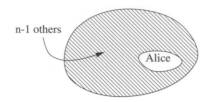

Figure 4.6   A group of n computer scientists composed of Alice and $n-1$ others.

We state here an important result that gives us a closed form expression for computing the sum of powers of 2.

Observation 4.3 $\sum_{i=0}^{n} 2^i = 2^{n+1} - 1$.

Proof: Left to the reader.⋄

There are, of course, ways that the inductive proof can go awry. Not proving the appropriate base cases is the most common mistake, and can lead to some interesting results. Here we prove what few have suspected all along:

Observation 4.4 *All computer scientists are good programmers.*

Warning: bad proof!

Proof: We prove the observation is true, using mathematical induction. First, we use traditional techniques (examinations, etc.) to demonstrate that Alice is a good programmer.

Now, assume our observation is true of any group of fewer than n computer scientists. Let's extend our result: select n computer scientists, including Alice (see Figure 4.6). Clearly, the subgroup consisting of all computer scientists that are "not Alice" is a group of $n-1$ computer scientists. Our assumption states that this group of $n-1$ computer scientists is made up of good programmers. So Alice and all the other computer scientists are good programmers. By induction on n, we have demonstrated that all computer scientists are good programmers.⋄

This is a very interesting result, especially since it is not true. (Among other things, some computer scientists do not program computers!) How, then, were we successful in proving it? If you look carefully, our base case is Alice. The assumption, on the other hand, is based on *any* group of $n-1$ programmers. Unfortunately, since our only solid proof of quality programming is Alice, and non-Alice programmers cannot be reduced to cases involving Alice, our proof is fatally flawed.

Still, a slight reworking of the logic might make the proof of this observation possible. Since Alice is a computer scientist, we can attempt to prove the observation by induction on groups of computer scientists *that include Alice:*

Warning: bad proof, take 2!

Proof: We prove the observation by induction. First, as our base case, consider Alice. Alice is well known for being a good programmer. Now, assume that for

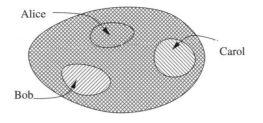

Figure 4.7   A group of n computer scientists, including Alice, Bob, and Carol.

any group of fewer than n computer scientists that includes Alice, the members are excellent programmers. Take n computer scientists, including Alice (see Figure 4.7). Select a non-Alice programmer. Call him Bob. If we consider all non-Bob computer scientists we have a group of $n - 1$ computer scientists— including Alice. By our assumption, they must all be good. What about Bob? Select another non-Alice, non-Bob computer scientist from the group of n. Call her Carol. Carol must be a good programmer, because she was a member of the $n - 1$ non-Bob programmers. If we consider the $n - 1$ non-Carol programmers, the group includes both Alice and Bob. Because it includes Alice, the non-Carol programmers must all be good. Since Carol is a good programmer, then all n must program well. By induction on n, all groups of computer scientists that include Alice must be good programmers. Since the group of all computer scientists is finite, and it includes Alice, the entire population must program well. The observation holds!◇

This proof looks pretty solid—until you consider that in order for it to work, you must be able to distinguish between Alice, Bob, and Carol. There are three people. The proof of the three-person case depends directly on the observation holding for just two people. But we have not considered the two-person case! In fact, *that* is the hole in the argument. If we know of a bad programmer, Ted, we can say nothing about the group consisting of Alice and Ted (see Figure 4.8). As a result, we have a worrisome hole in the proof of the group consisting of Alice, Bob, and Ted. In the end, the attempt at a complete proof unravels.

What have we learned from this discussion? For an inductive proof, the base cases must be carefully enumerated and proved. When proving the inductive step, the step must be made upon a proved foundation. If not, the entire statement collapses. The subtlety of this difficulty should put us on alert: even the most thoughtful proofs can go awry if the base case is not well considered.

Lesson: it's hard to find good programmers.

We can now reverse our analogy with recursion, and make a similar statement there: it is important to identify and correctly code the base cases you need. If you don't you run the risk that your method will fail to stop, or will compute the wrong answer. One of the most difficult debugging situations occurs when multiple base cases are to be considered and only a few are actually programmed.

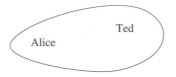

Figure 4.8   The proof does not hold for the simplest nontrivial case: Alice and any bad programmer.

4.3   Properties of Design

This section is dedicated to two informal properties of design that are referenced elsewhere within this text. The property of *symmetry* describes the predictability of a design, while *friction* describes the difficulty of moving a data structure from one state to another. Both terms extend the vocabulary of implementors when discussing design decisions.

4.3.1   Symmetry

For the most part, our instruction of computers occurs through programs. As a result, programs can be nonintuitive and hard to understand if they are not designed with human-readability in mind. On the other hand, a well-designed program can be used by a novice without a significant learning curve. Systems that are easy to use tend to survive longer.

The programmer, as a designer of a data structure, is responsible for delivering a usable implementation of an abstract data structure. For an implementation to be usable, it should provide access to the structure with methods that are predictable and easy to use. The notion of predictability is particularly difficult for designers of data structures to understand, and it is something often overlooked by novice programmers.

When designing a system (here, a program or data structure) a useful principle is to make its interface *symmetric*. What is symmetry? Symmetry allows one to view a system from different points of view, and see similarities. Mathematicians would say that a system exhibits a symmetry if "it looks like itself under a nontrivial transformation." Given this, programmers consider asymmetries in transformed programs to be early warning signs of errors in logic.

Consider the following method (you will see this as part of the `swap` procedure of page 78). It exchanges two object references—`data[i]` and `data[j]`.

```
int temp;
temp = data[i];
data[i] = data[j];
data[j] = temp;
```

Close inspection of this code demonstrates that it does what it claims to do. Even if we stand back, not thinking so much about the actual workings of the code, we can see that the code is pretty symmetric. For example, if we squint our eyes and look at the code from the standpoint of variable `data[i]`, we see it as:

```
int ...;
... = data[i];
data[i] = ...;
... = ...;
```

Here, `data[i]` is assigned to a variable, and a value is assigned to `data[i]`. We see a similar pattern with `data[j]`:

```
int ...;
... = ...;
... = data[j];
data[j] = ...;
```

While this is not direct proof that the code works, it is an indication that the code is, in some way, "symmetric," and that helps make the argument that it is well designed.

Not everything we do is symmetric. If we consider the `Association` class, for example, the `key` and `value` components of the `Association` are different. The `value`, of course, has two associated methods, `value` and `setValue`. The first of the methods reads and returns a value, while the second method consumes and sets a value. Everything is in "balance," and so we are hopeful that the design of the structure is correct. On the other hand, the `key` associated with this structure can only be read: while there is a `key` method, there is no `setKey`. We have suggested good reasons for doing this. As long as you can make a good argument for asymmetry in design, the breaking of symmetry can be useful. Unreasoned asymmetry, however, is a sign of poor and unpredictable design.

Here are various ways that one can look at a system to evaluate it for symmetry:

1. Compare methods that extend the structure with methods that trim the structure. Do they have similar approaches? Are they similar in number?

2. Consider methods that read and write values. Can the input methods read what is written by the output methods? Can the writing methods write all values that can be read?

3. Are procedures that consume parameters matched by functions that deliver values?

4. Can points of potential garbage collection be equally balanced by `new` invocations?

5. In linked structures, does unlinking a value from the structure appear to be the reverse of linking a new value into the structure?

When asymmetries are found, it is important to consider why they occur. Arguments such as *I can't imagine that anyone would need an opposite method!* are usually unconvincing. Many methods are added to the structures, not because they are obviously necessary, but because there is no good argument against them. Sometimes, of course, the language or underlying system forces an asymmetry. In Java, for example, every `Object` has a `toString` method that converts an internal representation of an object to a human readable form, but there's no `fromString` required method that reads the value of an `Object` from a `String`.

Should ≠ will. There *should be*, but there isn't.

4.3.2   Friction

One of the obvious benefits of a data structure is to provide a means of storing information. The ease with which the structure accepts and provides information about its contents can often be determined by its interface. Likewise, the difficulty of moving a data structure from one state to another determines, in some way, its "stiffness" or the amount of *friction* the structure provides when the state of the structure is to be modified.

One way that we might measure friction is to determine a sequence of logical states for the structure, and determine the number of operations that are necessary to move the structure from each state to the next. If the number of operations is high, we imagine a certain degree of friction; if the operation count is low, the structure moves forward with relative ease.

Often we see that the less space provided to the structure, the more friction appears to be inherent in its structure. This friction can be good—it may make it less possible to get our structure into states that are inconsistent with the definition of the structure, or it may be bad—it may make it difficult to get something done that is necessary.

4.4   Conclusions

Several formal concepts play an important role in modern data structure design—the use of big-O analysis to support claims of efficiency, the use of recursion to develop concise but powerful structures, and the use of induction to prove statements made about both data structures and algorithms. Mastery of these concepts improves one's approach to solving problems of data structure design.

The purpose of big-O analysis is to demonstrate upper bounds on the growth of functions that describe behavior of the structures we use. Since these are upper bounds, the tightest bounds provide the most information. Still, it is often not very difficult to identify the fastest-growing component of a function—analysis of that component is likely to lead to fairly tight bounds and useful results.

Self-reference is a powerful concept. When used to develop methods, we call this recursion. Recursion allows us to break down large problems into smaller problems whose solutions can be brought together to solve the original problem.

Interestingly, recursion is often a suitable substitute for loops as a means of progressing through the problem solution, but compilers can often convert tail recursive code back into loops, for better performance. All terminating recursive methods involve at least one test that distinguishes the base case from the recursive, and every recursive program must eventually make progress toward a base case to construct a solution.

Mathematical induction provides a means of recursively generating proofs. Perhaps more than most other proof mechanisms, mathematical induction is a useful method for demonstrating a bound on a function, or the correct termination of a method. Since computers are not (yet) able to verify everyday inductive proofs, it is important that they be constructed with appropriate care. Knowing how to correctly base induction on special cases can be tricky and, as we have recently seen, difficult to verify.

In all these areas, practice makes perfect.

Problems

4.1 What is the time complexity associated with accessing a single value in an array? The `Vector` class is clearly more complex than the array. What is the time complexity of accessing an element with the `elementAt` method?

4.2 What is the worst-case time complexity of the `removeElementAt` code in the `Vector` class? What is the best-case time complexity? (You may assume the `Vector` does not get resized during this operation.)

4.3 What is the running time of the following method?

```
public static int reduce(int n)
{
    int result = 0;
    while (n > 1)
    {
        n = n/2;
        result = result+1;
    }
    return result;
}
```

4.4 What is the time complexity of determining the length an n-character null-terminated string? What is the time complexity of determining the length of an n-character counted string?

4.5 What is the running time of the following matrix multiplication method?

```
// square matrix multiplication
// m1, m2, and result are n by n arrays
for (int row = 0; row < n; row++)
{
    for (int col = 0; col < n; col++)
    {
```

```
            int sum = 0;
            for (int entry = 0; entry < n; entry++)
            {
                sum = sum + m1[row][entry]*m2[entry][col];
            }
            result[row][col] = sum;
        }
    }
```

4.6   When discussing symmetry, we investigated a procedure that swapped two values within an array. Is it possible to write a routine that swaps two integer values? If so, provide the code; if not, indicate why.

4.7   For subtle reasons `String` objects cannot be modified. Instead, `Strings` are used as parameters to functions that build new `Strings`. Suppose that `a` is an n-character `String`. What is the time complexity of performing `a=a+"!"`?

4.8   Read Problem 4.7. Suppose that `a` and `b` are n-character `Strings`. What is the complexity of performing `a=a+b`?

4.9⋆   What is the rate of growth (using big-O analysis) of the function $f(n) = n + \log n$? Justify your answer.

4.10   In this text, logarithms are assumed to be in base 2. Does it make a difference, from a complexity viewpoint?

4.11⋆   What is the rate of growth of the function $\frac{1}{n} + 12$? Justify your answer.

4.12⋆   What is the rate of growth of the function $\frac{\sin n}{n}$? Justify your answer.

4.13⋆   Trick question: What is the rate of growth of $\tan n$?

4.14⋆   Suppose n integers between 1 and 366 are presented as input, and you want to know if there are any duplicates. How would you solve this problem? What is the rate of growth of the function $T(n)$, describing the time it takes for you to determine if there are duplicates? (Hint: Pick an appropriate n_0.)

4.15   The first element of a *Syracuse sequence* is a positive integer s_0. The value s_i (for $i > 0$) is defined to be $s_{i-1}/2$ if s_{i-1} is even, or $3s_{i-1} + 1$ if s_{i-1} is odd. The sequence is finished when a 1 is encountered. Write a procedure to print the Syracuse sequence for any integer s_0. It is not immediately obvious that this method should always terminate.

4.16   Rewrite the `sqrt` function of Section 2.1 as a recursive procedure.

4.17   Write a recursive procedure to draw a line segment between (x_0, y_0) and (x_1, y_1) on a screen of pixels with integer coordinates. (Hint: The pixel closest to the midpoint is not far off the line segment.)

4.18   Rewrite the `reduce` method of Problem 4.3 as a recursive method.

4.19   One day you notice that integer multiplication no longer works. Write a recursive procedure to multiply two values a and b using only addition. What is the complexity of this function?

4.20   Modify the "stamp change" problem of Section 4.2.1 to report the number of each type of stamp to be found in the minimum stamp change.

4.21★ Prove that $5^n - 4n - 1$ is divisible by 16 for all $n \geq 0$.

4.22 Prove Observation 4.3, that $\sum_{i=0}^{n} 2^i = 2^{n+1} - 1$.

4.23★ Prove that a function n^c is $O(n^d)$ for any $d \geq c$.

4.24 Show that for any polynomial $\sum_{i=0}^{n} a_i \cdot n^i$ is $O(n^n)$.

4.25★ Prove that $\sum_{i=1}^{n} 2i = n(n+1)$.

4.26★ Prove that $\sum_{i=1}^{n} (2i - 1) = n^2$.

4.27★ Show that for $c \geq 2$ and $n \geq 0$, $\sum_{i=0}^{n} c^i = \frac{c^{n+1}+(c-2)}{c-1} - 1$.

4.28 Prove that $\sum_{i=1}^{n} \log i \leq n \log n$.

4.29 Some artists seek asymmetry. Physicists tell us the universe doesn't always appear symmetric. Why are we unfazed?

4.30 With a colleague, design an interface, including pre- and postconditions. Then, working separately, generate and test two implementations. Bring them together and compare them. How are they similar? What are the significant differences? What bugs were found by reviewing each other's code?

4.31 With a colleague, implement a fresh version of `Lists`. First, agree on the types and names of private fields. Then, going down the list of methods required by the `List` interface, split methods to be implemented between you by assigning every other method to your colleague. Bring the code together and compile it. What types of bugs occur? Did you depend on your colleague's code?

4.32 Consider the implementation of a `Ratio` data type. How does symmetry appear in this implementation?

4.33★ In the `Vector` class, we extend by doubling, but we never discuss reducing by a similar technique. What is a good strategy?

4.34 Consider the following Java method:

```
static public int fido(int n)
// pre: n is a nonnegative integer
// post: result is the nth from the sequence
//     1, 3, 7, 15, 31, 63, 127, ...
{
    int result = 1;
    if (n > 1) result = 1+fido(n-1)+fido(n-1);
    // assertion: the above if condition was tested
    //     fido(n) times while computing result
    return result;
}
```

  a. What does it compute?

  b. Prove or disprove the informal assertion following the `if` statement.

  c. What is the time complexity of the method?

  d. Why is `fido` an appropriate name for this method?

Chapter 5

Sorting

> *"'Come along, children. Follow me.'*
> *Before you could wink an eyelash*
> *Jack, Knak, Lack, Mack, Nack, Ouack, Pack, and Quack*
> *fell into line, just as they had been taught."*
> —Robert McCloskey

COMPUTERS SPEND A CONSIDERABLE AMOUNT of their time keeping data in order. When we view a directory or folder, the items are sorted by name or type or modification date. When we search the Web the results are returned sorted by "applicability." At the end of the month, our checks come back from the bank sorted by number, and our deposits are sorted by date. Clearly, in the grand scheme of things, sorting is an important function of computers. Not surprisingly, data structures can play a significant role in making sorts run quickly. This chapter begins an investigation of sorting methods.

5.1 Approaching the Problem

For the moment we assume that we will be sorting an unordered array of integers (see Figure 5.1a).[1] The problem is to arrange the integers so that every adjacent pair of values is in the correct order (see Figure 5.1b). A simple technique to sort the array is to pass through the array from left to right, swapping adjacent values that are out of order (see Figure 5.2). The exchange of values is accomplished with a utility method:

BubbleSort

```
public static void swap(int data[], int i, int j)
// pre: 0 <= i,j < data.length
// post: data[i] and data[j] are exchanged
{
    int temp;
    temp = data[i];
    data[i] = data[j];
    data[j] = temp;
}
```

---

[1] We focus on arrays of integers to maintain a simple approach. These techniques, of course, can be applied to vectors of objects, provided that some relative comparison can be made between two elements. This is discussed in Section 5.6.

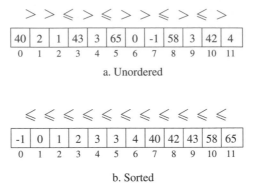

a. Unordered

b. Sorted

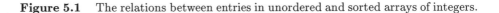

Figure 5.1   The relations between entries in unordered and sorted arrays of integers.

After a single pass the largest value will end up "bubbling" up to the high-indexed side of the array. The next pass will, at least, bubble up the next largest value, and so forth. The sort—called bubble sort—must be finished after $n-1$ passes. Here is how we might write bubble sort in Java:

```
public static void bubbleSort(int data[], int n)
// pre: 0 <= n <= data.length
// post: values in data[0..n-1] in ascending order
{
    int numSorted = 0;      // number of values in order
    int index;              // general index
    while (numSorted < n)
    {
        // bubble a large element to higher array index
        for (index = 1; index < n-numSorted; index++)
        {
            if (data[index] < data[index-1])
                swap(data,index,index-1);
        }
        // at least one more value in place
        numSorted++;
    }
}
```

Observe that the only potentially time-consuming operations that occur in this sort are comparisons and exchanges. While the cost of comparing integers is relatively small, if each element of the array were to contain a long string (for example, a DNA sequence) or a complex object (for example, a Library of Congress entry), then the comparison of two values might be a computationally intensive operation. Similarly, the cost of performing an exchange is to be

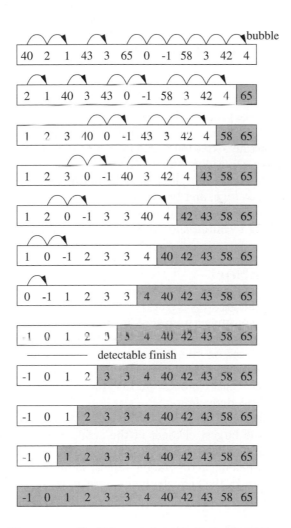

Figure 5.2 The passes of bubble sort: hops indicate "bubbling up" of large values. Shaded values are in sorted order. A pass with no exchanges indicates sorted data.

avoided.[2] We can, therefore, restrict our attention to the number of comparison and exchange operations that occur in sorts in order to adequately evaluate their performance.

In bubble sort each pass of the bubbling phase performs $n - 1$ comparisons and as many as $n - 1$ exchanges. Thus the worst-case cost of performing bubble sort is $O((n - 1)^2)$ or $O(n^2)$ operations. In the best case, none of the compares leads to an exchange. Even in that case, though, the algorithm has quadratic behavior.[3]

Most of us are inefficient sorters. Anyone having to sort a deck of cards or a recipe file is familiar with the feeling that *there must be a better way to do this*. As we shall see, there probably is: most common sorting techniques used in day-to-day life run in $O(n^2)$ time, whereas the best single processor comparison-based sorting techniques are expected to run in only $O(n \log n)$ time. (If multiple processors are used, we can reduce this to $O(\log n)$ time, but that algorithm is beyond the scope of this text.) We shall investigate two sorting techniques that run in $O(n^2)$ time, on average, and two that run in $O(n \log n)$ time. In the end we will attempt to understand what makes the successful sorts successful.

Our first two sorting techniques are based on natural analogies.

5.2   Selection Sort

Children are perhaps the greatest advocates of *selection sort*. Every October, Halloween candies are consumed from best to worst. Whether daily sampling is limited or not, it is clear that choices of the next treat consumed are based on "the next biggest piece" or "the next-most favorite," and so on. Children consume treats in decreasing order of acceptability. Similary, when we select plants from a greenhouse, check produce in the store, or pick strawberries from the farm we seek the best items first.

This selection process can be applied to an array of integers. Our goal is to identify the index of the largest element of the array. We begin by *assuming* that the first element is the largest, and then form a competition among all the remaining values. As we come across larger values, we update the index of the current maximum value. In the end, the index must point to the largest value. This code is idiomatic, so we isolate it here:

SelectionSort

```
int index;        // general index
int max;          // index of largest value
// determine maximum value in array
max = 0;
for (index = 1; index < numUnsorted; index++)
```

---

[2] In languages like Java, where large objects are manipulated through references, the cost of an exchange is usually fairly trivial. In many languages, however, the cost of exchanging large values stored directly in the array is a real concern.

[3] If, as we noted in Figure 5.2, we detected the lack of exchanges, bubble sort would run in $O(n)$ time on data that was already sorted. Still, the average case would be quadratic.

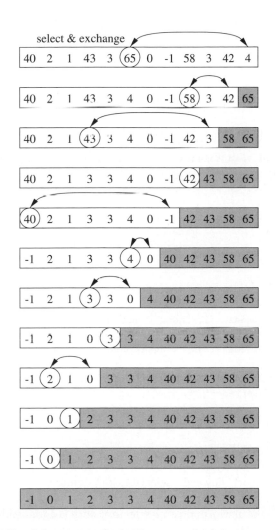

Figure 5.3 Profile of the passes of selection sort: shaded values are sorted. Circled values are maximum among unsorted values and are moved to low end of sorted values on each pass.

```
    {
        if (data[max] < data[index]) max = index;
    }
```

(Notice that the maximum is not updated unless a *larger* value is found.). Now, consider where this maximum value would be found if the data were sorted: it should be clear to the right, in the highest indexed location. This is easily accomplished: we simply swap the last element of the unordered array with the maximum. Once this swap is completed, we know that at least that one value is in the correct location, and we logically reduce the size of problem by one. If we remove the $n-1$ largest values in successive passes (see Figure 5.3) we have selection sort. Here is how the entire method appears in Java:

```
public static void selectionSort(int data[], int n)
// pre: 0 <= n <= data.length
// post: values in data[0..n-1] are in ascending order
{
    int numUnsorted = n;
    int index;      // general index
    int max;        // index of largest value
    while (numUnsorted > 0)
    {
        // determine maximum value in array
        max = 0;
        for (index = 1; index < numUnsorted; index++)
        {
            if (data[max] < data[index]) max = index;
        }
        swap(data,max,numUnsorted-1);
        numUnsorted--;
    }
}
```

Selection sort potentially performs far fewer exchanges than bubble sort: selection sort performs exactly one per pass while bubble sort performs as many as $n-1$. Like bubble sort, however, selection sort demands $O(n^2)$ time based just on comparisons.

Interestingly, the performance of selection sort is independent of the order of the data: if the data are already sorted, it takes selection sort just as long to sort as if the data were unsorted. We can improve on this behavior through a slightly different analogy.

5.3   Insertion Sort

Card players, when collecting a hand, often consider cards one at a time, inserting each into its sorted location. If we consider the "hand" to be the sorted portion of the array, and the "table" to be the unsorted portion, we develop a new sorting technique called *insertion sort*.

In the following Java implementation of insertion sort, the sorted values are kept in the low end of the array, and the unsorted values are found at the high end (see Figure 5.4). The algorithm consists of several "passes" of inserting the lowest-indexed unsorted value into the list of sorted values. Once this is done, of course, the list of sorted values increases by one. This process continues until each of the unsorted values has been incorporated into the sorted portion of the array. Here is the code:

InsertionSort

```java
public static void insertionSort(int data[], int n)
// pre: 0 <= n <= data.length
// post: values in data[0..n-1] are in ascending order
{
    int numSorted = 1;      // number of values in place
    int index;              // general index
    while (numSorted < n)
    {
        // take the first unsorted value
        int temp = data[numSorted];
        // ...and insert it among the sorted:
        for (index = numSorted; index > 0; index--)
        {
            if (temp < data[index-1])
            {
                data[index] = data[index-1];
            } else {
                break;
            }
        }
        // re-insert value
        data[index] = temp;
        numSorted++;
    }
}
```

A total of $n - 1$ passes are made over the array, with a new unsorted value inserted each time. The value inserted may not be a new minimum or maximum value. Indeed, if the array was initially unordered, the value will, on average, end up being inserted near the middle of the previously sorted values. On random data the running time of insertion sort is expected to be dominated by $O(n^2)$ compares and data movements (most of the compares will lead to the movement of a data value).

If the array is initially in order, one compare is needed at every pass to determine that the value is already in the correct location. Thus, the inner loop is executed exactly once for each of $n - 1$ passes. The best case running time performance of the sort is therefore dominated by $O(n)$ comparisons (there are no movements of data within the array). Because of this characteristic, insertion sort is often used when data are very nearly ordered (imagine sorting a phone book after a month of new customers has been appended).

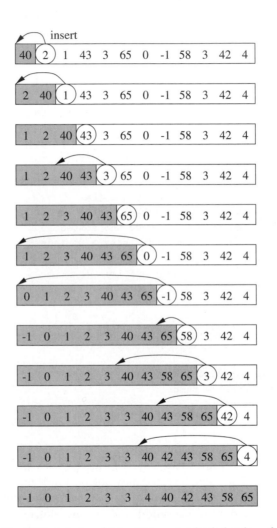

Figure 5.4 Profile of the passes of insertion sort: shaded values form a "hand" of sorted values. Circled values are successively inserted into the hand.

In contrast, if the array was previously in reverse order, the value must be compared with *every* sorted value to find the correct location. As the comparisons are made, the larger values are moved to the right to make room for the new value. The result is that each of $O(n^2)$ compares leads to a data movement, and the worst case running time of the algorithm is $O(n^2)$.

Note that each of these sorts uses a linear ($O(n)$) number of data cells. Not every sorting technique is able to live within this constraint.

5.4   Mergesort

Suppose that two friends are to sort an array of values. One approach might be to divide the deck in half. Each person then sorts one of two half-decks. The sorted deck is then easily constructed by combining the two sorted half-decks. This careful interleaving of sorted lists is called a *merge*.

It is straightforward to see that a merge takes at least $O(n)$ time, because every value has to be moved into the destination deck. Still, within $n - 1$ comparisons, the merge must be finished. Since each of the $n - 1$ comparisons (and potential movements of data) takes at most constant time, the merge is no worse than linear.

There are, of course, some tricky aspects to the merge operation—for example, it is possible that all the cards in one half-deck are smaller than all the cards in the other. Still, the performance of the following merge code is $O(n)$:

MergeSort

```
private static void merge(int data[], int temp[],
                          int low, int middle, int high)
// pre: data[middle..high] are ascending
//      temp[low..middle-1] are ascending
// post: data[low..high] contains all values in ascending order
{
    int ri = low; // result index
    int ti = low; // temp index
    int di = middle; // destination index
    // while two lists are not empty merge smaller value
    while (ti < middle && di <= high)
    {
        if (data[di] < temp[ti]) {
            data[ri++] = data[di++]; // smaller is in high data
        } else {
            data[ri++] = temp[ti++]; // smaller is in temp
        }
    }
    // possibly some values left in temp array
    while (ti < middle)
    {
        data[ri++] = temp[ti++];
    }
    // ...or some values left (in correct place) in data array
}
```

This code is fairly general, but a little tricky to understand (see Figure 5.5). We assume that the data from the two lists are located in the two arrays—in the lower half of the range in `temp` and in the upper half of the range in `data` (see Figure 5.5a). The first loop compares the first remaining element of each list to determine which should be copied over to the result list first (Figure 5.5b). That loop continues until one list is emptied (Figure 5.5c). If `data` is the emptied list, the remainder of the `temp` list is transferred (Figure 5.5d). If the `temp` list was emptied, the remainder of the `data` list is already located in the correct place!

Returning to our two friends, we note that before the two lists are merged each of the two friends is faced with sorting half the cards. How should this be done? If a deck contains fewer than two cards, it's already sorted. Otherwise, each person could recursively hand off half of his or her respective deck (now one-fourth of the entire deck) to a new individual. Once these small sorts are finished, the quarter decks are merged, finishing the sort of the half decks, and the two half decks are merged to construct a completely sorted deck. Thus, we might consider a new sort, called *mergesort*, that recursively splits, sorts, and reconstructs, through merging, a deck of cards. The logical "phases" of mergesort are depicted in Figure 5.6.

```
private static void mergeSortRecursive(int data[],
                                       int temp[],
                                       int low, int high)
// pre: 0 <= low <= high < data.length
// post: values in data[low..high] are in ascending order
{
    int n = high-low+1;
    int middle = low + n/2;
    int i;

    if (n < 2) return;
    // move lower half of data into temporary storage
    for (i = low; i < middle; i++)
    {
        temp[i] = data[i];
    }
    // sort lower half of array
    mergeSortRecursive(temp,data,low,middle-1);
    // sort upper half of array
    mergeSortRecursive(data,temp,middle,high);
    // merge halves together
    merge(data,temp,low,middle,high);
}
```

Note that this sort requires a temporary array to perform the merging. This temporary array is only used by a single merge at a time, so it is allocated once and garbage collected after the sort. We hide this detail with a public wrapper procedure that allocates the array and calls the recursive sort:

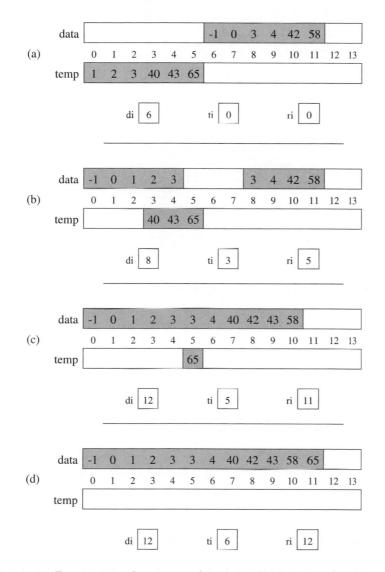

Figure 5.5 Four stages of a merge of two six element lists (shaded entries are participating values): (a) the initial location of data; (b) the merge of several values; (c) the point at which a list is emptied; and (d) the final result.

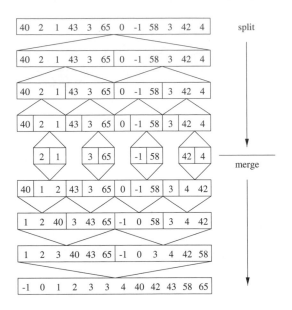

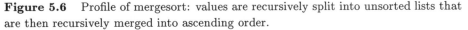

Figure 5.6   Profile of mergesort: values are recursively split into unsorted lists that are then recursively merged into ascending order.

```
public static void mergeSort(int data[], int n)
// pre: 0 <= n <= data.length
// post: values in data[0..n-1] are in ascending order
{
    mergeSortRecursive(data,new int[n],0,n-1);
}
```

Clearly, the depth of the splitting is determined by the number of times that n can be divided in two and still have a value of one or greater: $\log_2 n$. At each level of splitting, every value must be merged into its respective subarray. It follows that at each logical level, there are $O(n)$ compares over all the merges. Since there are $\log_2 n$ levels, we have $O(n \cdot \log n)$ units of work in performing a mergesort.

Mergesort is a common technique for sorting large sets of data that do not fit completely in fast memory. Instead, the data are saved in temporary files that are merged together. When the recursion splits the collection into subsets of a manageable size, they can be sorted using other techniques, if desired.

One of the unappealing aspects of mergesort is that it is difficult to merge two lists without significant extra memory. If we could avoid the use of this extra space without significant increases in the number of comparisons or data movements, then we would have an excellent sorting technique. Our next method demonstrates an $O(n \log n)$ method that requires signficantly less space.

5.5   Quicksort

Since the process of sorting numbers consists of moving each value to its ultimate location in the sorted array, we might make some progress toward a solution if we could move *a single value* to its ultimate location. This idea forms the basis of a fast sorting technique called *quicksort*.

One way to find the correct location of, say, the leftmost value—called a *pivot*—in an unsorted array is to rearrange the values so that all the smaller values appear to the left of the pivot, and all the larger values appear to the right. One method of partitioning the data is shown here. It returns the final location for what was originally the leftmost value:

```
private static int partition(int data[], int left, int right)
// pre: left <= right
// post: data[left] placed in the correct (returned) location
{
    while (true)
    {
        // move right "pointer" toward left
        while (left < right && data[left] < data[right]) right--;
        if (left < right) swap(data,left++,right);
        else return left;
        // move left pointer toward right
        while (left < right && data[left] < data[right]) left++;
        if (left < right) swap(data,left,right--);
        else return right;
    }
}
```

QuickSort

The indices `left` and `right` start at the two ends of the array (see Figure 5.7) and move toward each other until they are equal. The pivot value, being leftmost in the array, is indexed by `left`. Everything to the left of `left` is smaller than the pivot, while everything to the right of `right` is larger. Each step of the main loop compares the left and right values and, if they're out of order, exchanges them. Every time an exchange occurs the variable that references the pivot (`left` or `right`) value is alternated. In any case, the nonpivot variable is moved toward the other. Since, at each step, `left` and `right` move one step closer to each other, within n steps, `left` and `right` are the same, and they point to the current location of the pivot value. Since only smaller values are to the left of the pivot, and larger values are to the right, the pivot must be located in its final location. Values correctly located are shaded in Figure 5.8.

Because the pivot segregates the larger and smaller values, we know that none of these values will appear on the opposite side of the pivot in the final arrangement. This suggests that we can reduce the sorting of a problem of size n to two problems of size approximately $\frac{n}{2}$. To finish the sort, we need only recursively sort the values to the left and right of the pivot. In practice, of course, the splitting of the values is not always optimal (see the placement of

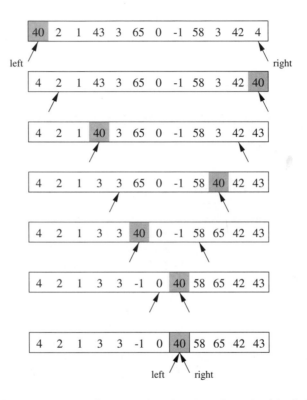

Figure 5.7   The partitioning of an array's values based on the (shaded) pivot value 40. Snapshots depict the state of the data after the **if** statements of the **partition** method.

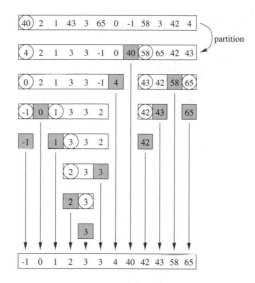

Figure 5.8 Profile of quicksort: leftmost value (the circled *pivot*) is used to position value in final location (indicated by shaded) and partition array into relatively smaller and larger values. Recursive application of partitioning leads to quicksort.

the value 4 in Figure 5.8), but a careful analysis suggests that even with these "tough breaks" quicksort takes only $O(n \log n)$ time.

When either sorted or reverse-sorted data are to be sorted by quicksort the results are disappointing. This is because the pivot value selected (here, the leftmost value) finds its ultimate location at one end of the array or the other. This reduces the sort of n values to $n-1$ values, and the sort requires $O(n)$ passes of an $O(n)$ step partition. The result is an $O(n^2)$ sort. Since nearly sorted data are fairly common, this result is to be avoided.

Notice that picking the leftmost value is not special. If, instead, we attempt to find the correct location for the middle value, then other arrangements of data will cause the degenerate behavior. In short, for any *deterministic* partitioning technique, a degenerate arrangement exists. The key to more consistent performance, then, is a *nondeterministic* partitioning that correctly places a value selected at random (see Problem 5.13). There is, of course, a very unlikely chance that the data are in order *and* the positions selected induce a degenerate behavior, but that chance is small and successive runs of the sorting algorithm on the same data are exceedingly unlikely to exhibit the same behavior. So, although the worst case behavior is still $O(n^2)$, its expected behavior is $O(n \log n)$.

Quicksort is an excellent sort when data are to be sorted with little extra space. Because the speed of partitioning depends on the random access nature of arrays or vectors, quicksort is not suitable when not used with random access structures. In these cases, however, other fast sorts are often possible.

5.6   Sorting Objects

Sorting arrays of integers is suitable for understanding the performance of various sorts, but it is hardly a real-world problem. Frequently, the object that needs to be sorted is an `Object` with many fields, only some of which are actually used in making a comparison.

Let's consider the problem of sorting the entries associated with an electronic phone book. The first step is to identify the structure of a single entry in the phone book. Perhaps it has the following form:

PhoneBook

```
class PhoneEntry
{
    String name;        // person's name
    String title;       // person's title
    int extension;      // telephone number
    int room;           // number of room
    String building;    // office building

    public PhoneEntry(String n, String t, int e,
                      String b, int r)
    // post: construct a new phone entry
    {
        ...
    }

    public int compareTo(PhoneEntry other)
    // pre: other is non-null
    // post: returns integer representing relation between values
    {
        return this.extension - other.extension;
    }
}
```

We have added the `compareTo` method to describe the relation between two entries in the phone book (the shaded fields of Figure 5.9). The `compareTo` method returns an integer that is less than, equal to, or greater than zero when `this` is logically less than, equal to, or greater than `other`. We can now modify any of the sort techniques provided in the previous section to sort an array of phone entries:

```
public static void insertionSort(PhoneEntry data[], int n)
// pre: n <= data.length
// post: values in data[0..n-1] are in ascending order
{
    int numSorted = 1;     // number of values in place
    int index;             // general index
```

0	Dicks, Norman D.	Rep.	55916	2467	Rayburn
1	Dunn, Jennifer	Rep.	57761	432	Cannon
2	Gorton, Slade	Senator	43441	730	Hart
3	Hastings, Doc	Rep.	55816	1323	Longworth
4	McDermott, Jim	Rep.	53106	2349	Rayburn
5	Metcalf, Jack	Rep.	52605	1510	Longworth
6	Murray, Patty	Senator	42621	111	Russell
7	Nethercutt, G. R., Jr.	Rep.	52006	1527	Longworth
8	Smith, Adam	Rep.	58901	1505	Longworth
9	Smith, Linda	Rep.	53536	1317	Longworth
10	White, Rick	Rep.	56311	116	Cannon

Data before sorting

0	Murray, Patty	Senator	42621	111	Russell
1	Gorton, Slade	Senator	43441	730	Hart
2	Nethercutt, G. R., Jr.	Rep.	52006	1527	Longworth
3	Metcalf, Jack	Rep.	52605	1510	Longworth
4	McDermott, Jim	Rep.	53106	2349	Rayburn
5	Smith, Linda	Rep.	53536	1317	Longworth
6	Hastings, Doc	Rep.	55816	1323	Longworth
7	Dicks, Norman D.	Rep.	55916	2467	Rayburn
8	White, Rick	Rep.	56311	116	Cannon
9	Dunn, Jennifer	Rep.	57761	432	Cannon
10	Smith, Adam	Rep.	58901	1505	Longworth

Data after sorting by telephone

Figure 5.9   An array of phone entries for the 105th Congressional Delegation from Washington State, before and after sorting by telephone (shaded).

```
        while (numSorted < n)
        {
            // take the first unsorted value
            PhoneEntry temp = data[numSorted];
            // ...and insert it among the sorted:
            for (index = numSorted; index > 0; index--)
            {
                if (temp.compareTo(data[index-1]) < 0)
                {
                    data[index] = data[index-1];
                } else {
                    break;
                }
            }
            // re-insert value
            data[index] = temp;
            numSorted++;
        }
    }
```

Careful review of this insertion sort routine shows that all the < operators have been replaced by checks for negative `compareTo` values. The result is that the phone entries in the array are ordered by increasing phone number.

If two or more people use the same extension, then the order of the resulting entries depends on the *stability* of the sort. If the sort is stable, then the relative order of the phone entries with identical extensions in the sorted array is the same as their relative order in the unordered array. If the sort is not stable, no guarantee can be made. To ensure that entries are, say, sorted in increasing order by extension and, in case of shared phones, sorted by increasing name, the following `compareTo` method might be used:

```
    public int compareTo(PhoneEntry other)
    // pre: other is non-null
    // post: returns integer representing relation between values
    {
        if (this.extension != other.extension)
            return this.extension - other.extension;
        else return this.name.compareTo(other.name);
    }
```

Correctly specifying the relation between two objects with the `compareTo` method can be difficult when the objects cannot be *totally ordered*. Is it always possible that one athletic team is strictly less than another? Is it always the case that one set contains another? No. These are examples of domains that are *partially ordered*. Usually, however, most types may be totally ordered, and imagining how one might *sort* a collection of objects forces a suitable relation between any pair.

5.7   Vector-Based Sorting

We extend the phone book example one more time, by allowing the `PhoneEntry`s
to be stored in a `Vector`. There are, of course, good reasons to use `Vector` over
arrays, but there are some added complexities that should be considered. Here
is an alternative Java implementation of `insertionSort` that is dedicated to
the sorting of a `Vector` of PhoneEntrys:

```java
protected void swap(int i, int j)
// pre: 0 <= i,j < this.size
// post: elements i and j are exchanged within the vector
{
    Object temp;
    temp = elementAt(i);
    setElementAt(elementAt(j),i);
    setElementAt(temp,j);
}

public void insertionSort()
// post: values of vector are in ascending order
{
    int numSorted = 0;        // number of values in place
    int index;                // general index
    while (numSorted < size())
    {
        // take the first unsorted value
        PhoneEntry temp = (PhoneEntry)elementAt(numSorted);
        // ...and insert it among the sorted:
        for (index = numSorted; index > 0; index--)
        {
            if (temp.compareTo((PhoneEntry)elementAt(index-1)) < 0)
            {
                setElementAt(elementAt(index-1),index);
            } else {
                break;
            }
        }
        // re-insert value
        setElementAt(temp,index);
        numSorted++;
    }
}
```

PhoneBook

Recall that, for `Vectors`, we use the `elementAt` method to fetch a value and
`setElementAt` to store. Since any type of object may be referenced by a vector
entry, we verify the type expected when a value is retrieved from the vector.
This is accomplished through a parenthesized *cast*. If the type of the fetched
value doesn't match type of the cast, the program throws a *class cast exception*.
Here, we cast the result of `elementAt` in the `compareTo` method to indicate that
we are comparing PhoneEntrys.

It is unfortunate that the `insertionSort` has to be specially coded for use with the `PhoneEntry` objects. When we consider ordered structures, we will return to consider more general ways to make use of these sorting mechanisms.

5.8 Conclusions

Sorting is an important and common process on computers. In this chapter we considered several sorting techniques with quadratic running times. Bubble sort approaches the problem by checking and rechecking the relationships between elements. Selection and insertion sorts are based on techniques that people commonly use. Of these, insertion sort is most frequently used; it is easily coded and provides excellent performance when data are nearly sorted.

Two recursive sorting techniques, mergesort and quicksort, use recursion to achieve $O(n \log_2 n)$ running times, which are optimal for comparison-based techniques on single processors. Mergesort works well in a variety of situations, but often requires significant extra memory. Quicksort requires a random access structure, but runs with little space overhead.

We also investigated sorting `Vectors` of objects. This requires the implementation of a `compareTo` method. We will reconsider this topic shortly.

Problems

5.1$\star$ Show that to exchange two integer values it is not strictly necessary to use a third, temporary integer variable. (Hint: Use addition and/or subtraction.)

5.2   We demonstrated that, in the worst case, bubble sort performs $O(n^2)$ operations. We assumed, however, that each pass performed approximately $O(n)$ operations. In fact, pass i performs as many as $O(n - i)$ operations, for $1 \le i \le n - 1$. Show that bubble sort still takes $O(n^2)$ time.

5.3   How does `bubbleSort` (as presented) perform in the best and average cases?

5.4   On any pass of bubble sort, if no exchanges are made, then the relations between all the values are those desired, and the sort is done. Using this information, how fast will bubble sort run in worst, best, and average cases?

5.5   How fast does selection sort run in the best, worst, and average cases?

5.6   How fast does insertion sort run in the best, worst, and average cases? Give examples of best- and worst-case input for insertion sort.

5.7   Running an actual program, count the number of compares needed to sort n values using insertion sort, where n varies (e.g., powers of two). Plot your data. Do the same thing for quicksort. Do the curves appear as theoretically expected? Does insertion sort ever run faster than quicksort? If so, at what point does it run slower?

5.8⋆ Comparing insertion sort to quicksort, it appears that quicksort achieves its speedup without any increase in space. Is that true?

5.9 Using the millisecond timer, determine the length of time it takes to perform an assignment of a nonzero value to an `int`. (Hint: It will take less than a millisecond, so you will have to design several experiments that measure thousands or millions of assignments.)

5.10 Running an actual program, and using the millisecond timer, `System.-currentTimeMillis`, measure the length of time needed to sort arrays of data of various sizes using a sort of your choice. Repeat the experiment but use `Vectors`. Is there a difference? In either case, explain why. (Hint: You may have to develop code along the lines of Problem 5.9.)

5.11⋆ A sort is said to be *stable* if the order of equal values is maintained throughout the sort. Bubble sort is stable, because whenever two equal values are compared, no exchange occurs. Which other sorts are stable (consider insertion sort, selection sort, mergesort, and quicksort)?

5.12⋆ The `partition` function of quicksort could be changed as follows: To place the leftmost value in the correct location, count the number of values that are strictly less than the leftmost value. The resulting number is the correct index for the desired value. Exchange the leftmost value for the value at the indexed location. With all other code left as it is, does this support a correctly functioning quicksort? If not, explain why.

5.13 Modify the `partition` method used by quicksort so that the pivot is randomly selected. (Hint: Before partitioning, consider placing the randomly selected value at the left side of the array.)

5.14 Write a recursive `selectionSort` algorithm. (Hint: Each level of recursion positions a value in the correct location.)

5.15 Write a recursive `insertionSort` algorithm.

5.16⋆ Some of the best-performing sorts depend on the best-performing shuffles. A good shuffling technique rearranges data into any arrangement with equal probability. Design the most efficient shuffling mechanism you can, and argue its quality. What is its performance?

5.17⋆ Write a program called `shuffleSort`. It first checks to see if the data are in order. If they are, the sort is finished. If they aren't, the data are shuffled and the process repeats. What is the best-case running time? Is there a worst-case running time? Why or why not? If each time the data were shuffled they were arranged in a never-seen-before configuration, would this change your answer?

Chapter 6

Lists

*"He's makin' a list
and checkin' it twice!"*
—Haven Gillespie

IMAGINE YOU ARE TO WRITE A ROBUST PROGRAM to handle varying amounts of data. An inventory program is a classic example. The same inventory program might be used to keep track of either tens of items, or millions. To support such applications, the structures that we have seen so far are not ideal. As they reach their capacity they must be expanded. Either this happens manually, as with arrays, or it is automatic, as with `Vector`s. In either case the penalty for growing the structure is not uniformly amortized across the growth of the structure. With `Vector`, for example, every time the structure doubles in size, the cost of adding an element is proportional to the size of the `Vector`.

In this chapter, we develop the concept of a *list*. A list is a *dynamic structure* that grows and shrinks exactly when necessary, and whose elements may be added in constant time. There is some cost for this dynamic behavior, however. While each of the elements of a vector or an array is associated with an index, the elements of a list cannot be *randomly accessed*. Random access may be an unnecessarily expensive feature for some applications. Lists provide an important building block for the design of many effective data structures.

An analogy for lists that may be useful is a child's string of snap-together beads. As we grow the string of beads, we attach and detach new beads on either the front (*head*) or rear (*tail*). Since there are two modifying operations that we can perform (*add* or *remove*) and two ends (*head* or *tail*), there are four operations that modify the ends of the list structure.

If you have never seen these, visit your niece.

In some cases we may wish to perform operations on the internal portion of the list. For example, we may want to test for inclusion (*Is* there a red bead?) or extract an element (*Remove* a red bead!). It is not always clear how we can indicate where to insert a value in the middle of an arbitrarily long list, so we avoid considering that operation—for the moment.[1]

Now, let's see what the Java description of a list looks like:

```
public interface List extends Collection
{
    public Iterator elements();
    // post: returns an iterator allowing
    //    ordered traversal of elements in list
```

List

---

[1] There are good arguments for having such an operation. See Problem 6.9.

```
public int size();
// post: returns number of elements in list

public boolean isEmpty();
// post: returns true iff list has no elements

public void clear();
// post: empties list

public void add(Object value);
// post: value is added to beginning of list (see addToHead)

public void addToHead(Object value);
// post: value is added to beginning of list

public void addToTail(Object value);
// post: value is added to end of list

public Object peek();
// pre: list is not empty
// post: returns first value in list

public Object tailPeek();
// pre: list is not empty
// post: returns last value in list

public Object removeFromHead();
// pre: list is not empty
// post: removes first value from the list

public Object removeFromTail();
// pre: list is not empty
// post: removes the last value from the list

public boolean contains(Object value);
// pre: value is not null
// post: returns true iff list contains an object equal to value

public Object remove(Object value);
// post: removes and returns element equal to value
//       otherwise returns null
}
```

Because this structure is described as an `interface` (as opposed to a `class`) Java understands this to be a *contract* describing the methods that are required of lists. We might think of an interface as being a "structural precondition" describing the outward appearance of any "listlike" class. If we write our code in terms of this interface, we may only invoke methods specified within the contract.

Note that the `List` interface is an extension of the `Collection` interface that we have seen earlier, in Chapter 1.7. Thus, every `List` is also a `Collection`—a structure that supports `add` and `remove` as well as other size-related methods. We will see, over the course of this text, several structures that may serve as `Collections`.

The interface, along with pre- and postconditions, makes many of the *implementation-independent* decisions about the semantics of associated structures. When we develop specific implementations, we determine the *implementation-specific* features of the structure, including its performance. When we compare specific implementations, we compare their performance in terms of space and time. Often, performance can be used to help us select among different implementations for a specific use.

6.1   Example: A Unique Program

As an example of how we might use lists, we write a program that writes out the input with duplicate lines removed. The approach is to store each of the unique lines in a structure (`lines`) as they are printed out. When new lines are read in, they are compared against the existing list of unique, printed lines. If the current line (`current`) is not in the list, it is added. If the current line is in the list, it is ignored.

Unique

```
public static void main(String[] args)
{
    // input is read from System.in
    ReadStream s = new ReadStream(System.in);
    String current;                    // current line
    List lines = new SinglyLinkedList(); // list of unique lines

    // read a list of possibly duplicated lines
    while (!s.eof()) {
        current = s.readLine();
        // check to see if we need to add it
        if (!lines.contains(current)) {
            System.out.println(current);
            lines.add(current);
        }
    }
}
```

In this example we actually construct a particular type of list, a `SinglyLinked-List`. The details of that implementation, discussed in the next section, are not important to us because `lines` is declared to be a generic interface, a `List`. Accessing data through the `lines` variable, we are only allowed to invoke methods found in the `List` interface. On the other hand, if we are able to cast our algorithms in terms of `Lists`, any implementation of a `List` will support our program.

When given input

```
madam
I'm
Adam!
...
Adam!
I'm
Ada!
...
mad
am I...
madam
```

the program generates the following output:

```
madam
I'm
Adam!
...
Ada!
mad
am I...
```

Because there is no practical limit (other than the amount of memory available) on the length of a list, there is no practical limit on the size of the input that can be fed to the program. The list interface does not provide any hint of how the list is actually implemented, so it is difficult to estimate the performance of the program. It is likely, however, that the `contains` method—which is likely to have to consider every existing element of the list—and `add` (a method synonymous with `addToHead`)—which might have to pass over every element to find its correct position—will govern the complexity of the management of this `List`. As we consider implementations of `List`s, we should keep the performance of programs like `Unique` in mind.

6.2   Example: Free-Lists

In situations where a pool of resources is to be managed, it is often convenient to allocate a large number and keep track of those that have not been allocated. This technique is often used to allocate chunks of physical memory that might eventually be allocated to individual applications or printers from a pool that might be used to service a particular type of printing request.

The following application maintains rental contracts for a small parking lot. We maintain each parking space using a simple class, `Space`:

ParkingLot

```
class Space
{   // structure describing parking space
    public final static int COMPACT = 0; // small space
```

```
    public final static int MINIVAN = 1; // medium space
    public final static int TRUCK = 2;   // large space
    protected int number;       // address in parking lot
    protected int size;         // size of space
    public Space(int n, int s)
    // post: construct parking space #n, size s
    {
        number = n;
        size = s;
    }
    public boolean equals(Object other)
    // pre: other is not null
    // post: true iff spaces are equivalent size
    {
        Space that = (Space)other;
        return this.size == that.size;
    }
}
```

The lot consists of 10 spaces of various sizes: 1 large, 6 medium, and 3 small. Renters may rent a space if one of appropriate size can be found on the free list. The **equals** method of the **Space** class determines an appropriate match. The **rented** list maintains **Associations** between names and space descriptions. The following code initializes the free list so that it contains all the parking spaces, while the **rented** list is initially empty:

```
List free = new SinglyLinkedList();   // available
List rented = new SinglyLinkedList(); // rented spaces
for (int number = 0; number < 10; number++)
{
    if (number < 3) // 3 small spaces
        free.add(new Space(number,Space.COMPACT));
    else if (number < 9) // 6 medium spaces
        free.add(new Space(number,Space.MINIVAN));
    else // 1 large space
        free.add(new Space(number,Space.TRUCK));
}
```

The main loop of our program reads in commands from the keyboard—either **rent** or **return**:

```
ReadStream r = new ReadStream();
for (r.skipWhite(); !r.eof(); r.skipWhite())
{
    String command = r.readString(); // rent/return
        ...
}
System.out.println(free.size()+" slots remain available.");
```

Within the loop, when the `rent` command is entered, it is followed by the size of the space needed and the name of the renter. This information is used to construct a contract:

```
Space location;
if (command.equals("rent"))
{   // attempt to rent a parking space
    String size = r.readString();
    Space request;
    if (size.equals("small"))
        request = new Space(0,Space.COMPACT);
    else if (size.equals("medium"))
        request = new Space(0,Space.MINIVAN);
    else request = new Space(0,Space.TRUCK);
    // check free list for appropriate-sized space
    if (free.contains(request))
    {   // a space is available
        location = (Space)free.remove(request);
        String renter = r.readString(); // to whom?
        // link renter with space description
        rented.add(new Association(renter,location));
        System.out.println("Space "+location.number+" rented.");
    } else {
        System.out.println("No space available. Sorry.");
    }
}
```

Notice that when the `contains` method is called on a `List`, a dummy element is constructed to specify the type of object sought. When the dummy item is used in the `remove` command, the actual item removed is returned. This allows us to maintain a single copy of the object that describes a single parking space.

When the spaces are returned, they are returned by name. The contract is looked up and the associated space is returned to the free list:

```
Space location;
if (command.equals("return")){
    String renter = r.readString(); // from whom?
    // template for finding "rental contract"
    Association query = new Association(renter);
    if (rented.contains(query))
    {   // contract found
        Association contract = (Association)rented.remove(query);
        location = (Space)contract.value(); // where?
        free.addToTail(location); // put in free list
        System.out.println("Space "+location.number+" is now free.");
    } else {
        System.out.println("No space rented to "+renter);
    }
}
```

Here is a run of the program:

```
    rent small Alice
Space 2 rented.
    rent large Bob
Space 9 rented.
    rent small Carol
Space 1 rented.
    return Alice
Space 2 is now free.
    return David
No space rented to David
    rent small David
Space 0 rented.
    rent small Eva
Space 2 rented.
    quit
6 slots remain available.
```

Notice that when Alice's space is returned, it is not immediately reused because the free list contains other small, free spaces. The use of `addToHead` instead of `addToTail` would change the reallocation policy of the parking lot.

We now consider a number of implementations of the `List` type.

6.3   Implementation: Singly-Linked Lists

Dynamic memory is allocated using the `new` operator. Java programmers are accustomed to using the `new` operator whenever classes or arrays are to be allocated. The value returned from the `new` operator is a *reference* to the new object. Thus, whenever we need to declare an instance of an array or class, we are actually declaring a reference to one of those objects. Assignment of references provides multiple variables with access to a single, shared instance of an object.

An instance of a class is like a helium-filled balloon. The balloon is the object being allocated. The string on the balloon is a convenient handle that we can use to hold onto with a hand. Anything that holds onto the string is a *reference*. Assignment of references is similar to asking another hand to "hold the balloon I'm holding." To not reference anything (to let go of the balloon) we can assign the reference the value `null`. If nothing references the balloon, then it floats away and we can no longer get access to the instance. When memory is not referenced in any way, it is recycled automatically by a *garbage collector*.

Principle 8   *When manipulating references, draw pictures.*

In this text, we will draw references as arrows pointing to their respective objects (Figure 6.1). When a reference is not referencing anything, we draw it as a dot. Since references can only be in one of two states—pointing to nothing or pointing to an object—these are the only pictures we will ever draw.

Figure 6.1   Pictures of a `null` reference (left) and a non-`null` reference to an instance of a class (right).

---

*First garbage,
now flies!*

One approach to keeping track of arbitrarily large collections of objects is to use a *singly-linked list* to dynamically allocate each chunk of memory "on the fly." As the chunks of memory are allocated, they are linked together to form the entire structure. This is accomplished by packaging with each user object a reference to the next object in the chain. Thus, a list of 10 items contains 10 elements, each of which contains a value as well as another element reference. Each element references the next, and the final element does not reference anything: it is assigned `null` (see Figure 6.2). Here, an implementation of a `SinglyLinkedListElement` contains an additional reference, `nextElement`:

SinglyLinked–
ListElement

```
public class SinglyLinkedListElement
{
    protected Object data; // value stored in this element
    protected SinglyLinkedListElement nextElement; // ref to next

    public SinglyLinkedListElement(Object v,
                                     SinglyLinkedListElement next)
    // post: constructs a new element with value v,
    //       followed by next element
    {
        data = v;
        nextElement = next;
    }

    public SinglyLinkedListElement(Object v)
    // post: constructs a new tail of a list with value v
    {
        this(v,null);
    }

    public SinglyLinkedListElement next()
    // post: returns reference to next value in list
    {
        return nextElement;
    }
```

```
public void setNext(SinglyLinkedListElement next)
// post: sets reference to new next value
{
    nextElement = next;
}

public Object value()
// post: returns value associated with this element
{
    return data;
}

public void setValue(Object value)
// post: sets value associated with this element
{
    data = value;
}
}
```

When a list element is constructed, the value provided is stored away in the object. Here, `nextElement` is a reference to the next element in the list. We access the `nextElement` and `data` fields through `public` methods to avoid accessing protected fields. Notice that, for the first time, we see a self-referential data structure: the `SinglyLinkedListElement` object has a reference to a `SinglyLinkedListElement`. This is a feature common to structures whose size can increase dynamically. This class is declared `public` so that anyone can construct `SinglyLinkedListElements`.

We now construct a new class that *implements* the `List`. For that relation to be complete, it is necessary to provide a complete implementation of each of the methods promised by the interface. Failure to implement *any* of the methods leaves the implementation incomplete, making the class *abstract*.

Our approach will be to maintain, in `head`, a reference to the first element of the list in a protected field (Figure 6.2). This initial element references the second element, and so on. The final element has a `null`-valued `next` reference. If there are no elements, `head` contains a `null` reference (Figure 6.3). We also maintain an integer that keeps track of the number of elements in the list. First, as with all classes, we need to specify protected data and a constructor:

```
protected int count;                      // list size
protected SinglyLinkedListElement head; // ref. to first element

public SinglyLinkedList()
// post: generates an empty list.
{
    head = null;
    count = 0;
}
```

SinglyLinked-
List

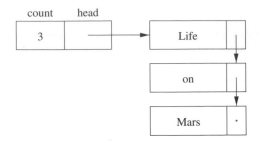

Figure 6.2   A nonempty singly-linked list.

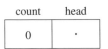

Figure 6.3   An empty singly-linked list.

This code sets the `head` reference to `null` and the `count` field to 0. Notice that, by the end of the constructor, the list is in a consistent state.

Principle 9   *Every public method of an object should leave the object in a consistent state.*

What constitutes a "consistent state" depends on the particular structure, but in most cases the concept is reasonably clear. In the `SinglyLinkedList`, the constructor constructs a list that is empty.

The size-oriented methods are simply written in terms of the `count` identifier. The `size` method returns the number of elements in the list, while the `isEmpty` method returns whether or not `size` would return zero.

```
public int size()
// post: returns the number of elements in list
{
    return count;
}

public boolean isEmpty()
// post: returns true iff the list is empty
{
    return size() == 0;
}
```

There's a great advantage to calling the `size` method to implement `isEmpty`: if we ever change the implementation, we need only change the implementation of `size`.

Both of these methods could avoid referencing the `count` field, by traversing each of the `next` references. In this alternative code we use the analogy of a *finger* referencing each of the elements in the list. Every time the finger references a new element, we increment a counter. The result is the number of elements. This time-consuming process is equivalent to constructing the information stored explicitly in the `count` field.

```
public int size()
// post: returns the number of elements in the list
{
    // number of elements we've seen in list
    int elementCount = 0;
    // reference to potential first element
    SinglyLinkedListElement finger = head;

    while (finger != null) {
        // finger references a new element, count it
        elementCount++;
        // reference possible next element
        finger = finger.next();
    }
    return elementCount;
}

public boolean isEmpty()
// post: returns true iff list has no elements
{
    return size() == 0;
}
```

Note that `isEmpty` does not need to change.[2] It is early verification that the interface for `size` helps to hide the implementation.

The decision between the two implementations has little impact on the user of the class, as long as both implementations meet the postconditions. Since the user is insulated from the details of the implementation, the decision can be made *even after applications have been written*. If, for example, an environment is memory-poor, it might be wise to avoid the use of the `count` field and instead traverse the list to determine the number of elements by counting them. If, however, a machine is slow but memory-rich, then the first implementation would be preferred. Both implementations could be made available, with the user selecting the appropriate design, based on broad guidelines (e.g., memory vs. speed). If this tradeoff does not appear dramatic, you might consider

---

[2] In either case, the method `isEmpty` could be written more efficiently, checking a `null head` reference.

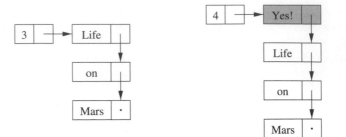

Figure 6.4   A singly-linked list before and after `addToHead`. Shaded value is added to the list. `removeFromHead` reverses this process and returns value.

Problem 6.10. We also discuss space-time tradeoffs in more detail in the next chapter.

Let us now consider the implementation of the methods that manipulate items at the head of the list (see Figure 6.4). First, to add an element at the head of the list, we simply need to create a new `SinglyLinkedListElement` that has the appropriate value, and references the very first element of the list (currently, `head`). The head of the new list is simply a reference to the new element. Finally, we modify the `count` variable to reflect an increase in the number of elements.

```
public void addToHead(Object value)
// post: adds value to beginning of list.
{
    // note the order that things happen:
    // head is parameter, then assigned
    head = new SinglyLinkedListElement(value, head);
    count++;
}
```

To support the `add` method of the `Collection` interface, we have the `add` method simply call `addToHead`.

Removing a value should simply perform the reverse process. We copy the reference[3] to a temporary variable where it can be held for return, and then we simply move the head reference down the list. Once completed, the value is returned.

```
public Object removeFromHead()
// pre: list is not empty
// post: removes and returns value from beginning of list
```

---

[3] Remember: the assignment operator *does not* copy the value, just the reference. If you want a reference to a *new* element, you should use the `new` operator and explicitly create a new object to be referenced.

```
    {
        SinglyLinkedListElement temp = head;
        head = head.next(); // move head down the list
        count--;
        return temp.value();
    }
```

Notice that `removeFromHead` returns a value. Why not? Since `addToHead` "absorbs" a value, `removeFromHead` should do the reverse and "emit" one. Since we think of these two operations as being inverses of each other, it is only natural to have them balance the consumption of objects in this way.

Principle 10 *Symmetry is good.*

One interesting exception to the principle above only occurs in languages like Java, where a garbage collector manages the recycling of dynamic memory. Clearly, `addToHead` must construct a new element to hold the value for the list. On the other hand, `removeFromHead` does not explicitly *get rid* of the element. This is because after `removeFromHead` is finished, there are no references to the element that was just removed. Since there are no references to the object, the garbage collector can be assured that the object can be recycled. All of this makes the programmer a little more lax about thinking about when memory has been logically freed. In languages without garbage collection, a "dispose" operation must be called for any object allocated by a **new** command. Forgetting to dispose of your garbage properly can be a rude shock, causing your program to run out of precious memory. We call this a *memory leak*. Java avoids all of this by collecting your garbage for you.

There's one more method that we provide for the sake of completeness: **peek**.[4] It is a *nondestructive* method that returns a reference to the first value in the list; the list is not modified by this method; we just get access to the data:

```
    public Object peek()
    // pre: list is not empty
    // post: returns the first value in the list
    {
        return head.value();
    }
```

Next, we must write the methods that manipulate the tail of the list (see Figure 6.5). While the interface makes these methods appear similar to those that manipulate the head of the list, our implementation has a natural bias against tail-oriented methods. Access through a single reference to the head of the list makes it difficult to get to the end of a long singly-linked list. More "energy" will have to be put into manipulating items at the tail of the list.

---

[4] The name `peek` is not our favorite choice, but we use it to make the interface for lists similar to the existing Java interfaces. In particular, we will implement a `peek` method when we consider the implementation of `Stacks`. See Principle 6 on page 39.

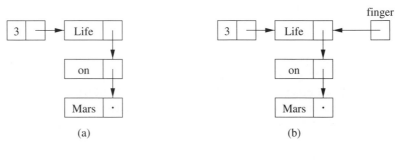

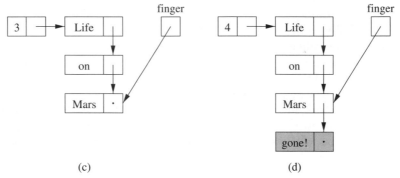

Figure 6.5   The process of adding a new value (shaded) to the tail of a list. The `finger` reference keeps track of progress while searching for the element whose reference must be modified.

Let's see how these methods are implemented:

```
public void addToTail(Object value)
// post: adds value to end of list
{
    // location for the new value
    SinglyLinkedListElement temp =
        new SinglyLinkedListElement(value,null);
    if (head != null)
    {
        // pointer to possible tail
        SinglyLinkedListElement finger = head;
        while (finger.next() != null)
        {
            finger = finger.next();
        }
        finger.setNext(temp);
    } else head = temp;
    count++;
}

public Object removeFromTail()
// pre: list is not empty
// post: last value in list is returned
{
    SinglyLinkedListElement finger = head;
    SinglyLinkedListElement previous = null;
    Assert.pre(head != null,"List is not empty.");
    while (finger.next() != null) // find end of list
    {
        previous = finger;
        finger = finger.next();
    }
    // finger is null, or points to end of list
    if (previous == null)
    {
        // has exactly 1 element
        head = null;
    }
    else
    {
        // pointer to last element is reset.
        previous.setNext(null);
    }
    count--;
    return finger.value();
}
```

Each of these (complex) methods uses the finger-based list traversal technique. We reference each element of the list, starting at the top and moving downward, until we finally reach the tail. At that point we have constructed the desired reference to the end of the list, and we continue as we would have in the head-manipulating methods. We have to be aware of one slight problem that concerns the very simplest case—when the list is empty. If there are no elements, then the finger never becomes non-`null`, and we have to write special code to manipulate the `head` reference.

Two methods potentially work in the context of the middle of lists—`contains` and `remove`. Here, the code becomes particularly tricky because we cannot depend on lists having any values, and, for `remove`, we must carefully handle the boundary cases—when the elements are the first or last elements of the list. Errors in code usually occur at these difficult points, so it is important to make sure they are tested.

Principle 11 *Test the boundaries of your structures and methods.*

Here is the code for these methods:

```
public boolean contains(Object value)
// pre: value is not null
// post: returns true iff value is found in list.
{
    SinglyLinkedListElement finger = head;
    while (finger != null &&
            !finger.value().equals(value))
    {
        finger = finger.next();
    }
    return finger != null;
}

public Object remove(Object value)
// pre: value is not null
// post: removes first element with matching value, if any.
{
    SinglyLinkedListElement finger = head;
    SinglyLinkedListElement previous = null;
    while (finger != null &&
            !finger.value().equals(value))
    {
        previous = finger;
        finger = finger.next();
    }
    // finger points to target value
    if (finger != null) {
        // we found the element to remove
        if (previous == null) // it is first
        {
```

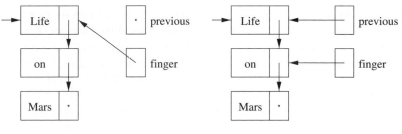

(a)   (b)

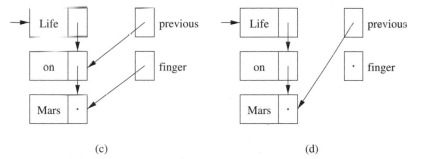

(c)   (d)

Figure 6.6   The relation between `finger` and `previous`. The target element is the head of the list (a), in the middle (b), at the tail (c), or not present (d).

```
        head = finger.next();
    } else {                // it's not first
        previous.setNext(finger.next());
    }
    count--;
    return finger.value();
}
// didn't find it, return null
return null;
}
```

In the `contains` method we call the value's `equals` method to test to see if the values are logically equal. Comparing the values with the == operator checks to see if the references are the same (i.e., that they are, in fact, the same object). We are interested in finding a logically equal object, so we invoke the object's `equals` method.

Some fancy reference manipulation is needed in any routine that removes an element from the list. When we find the target value, the `finger` variable has moved too far down to help with removing the element. By the time `finger` references the element holding the target value, we lose the reference to the previous element—precisely the element that needs to have its **next** reference reset when the value is removed. To avoid this difficulty, we keep another reference, local to the particular method, that is either **null** or references the element just before **finger**. When (and if) we find a value to be removed, the element to be fixed is referenced by **previous** (Figure 6.6). Of course, if **previous** is **null**, we must be removing the first element, and we update the **head** reference. All of this can be very difficult to write correctly, which is another good reason to write it carefully once and reuse the code whenever possible (see Principle 2).

One final method with subtle behavior is the **clear** method. This removes all the elements from the list. In Java, this is accomplished by clearing the reference to the head and adjusting the list size:

```
public void clear()
// post: removes all elements from the list
{
    head = null;
    count = 0;
}
```

All that happens is that **head** stops referencing the list. Instead, it is explicitly made to reference nothing. What happens to the elements of the list? When the garbage collector comes along, it notices that the first element of the former list is not referenced by anything—after all it was only referenced by **head** before. So, the garbage collector collects that first element as garbage. It is pretty *You are what* easy to see that if anything is referenced *only by* garbage, it *is* garbage. Thus, *references you.* the second element (as well as the value referenced by the first element) will be marked as garbage, and so forth. This cascading identification of garbage elements is responsible for recycling all the elements of the list and, potentially, the **Object**s they reference. (If the list-referenced objects are referenced outside of the list, they *may* not be garbage after all!)

We now consider another implementation of the list interface that makes use *Swoon!* of two references per element.

6.4   Implementation: Doubly-Linked Lists

In the last section, we saw indications that some operations can take more "energy" to perform than others, and expending energy takes time. Operations such as modifying the tail of a singly-linked list can take significantly longer than those that modify the head. If we, as users of lists, expect to modify the tail of the list frequently, we might be willing to make our code more complex, or use more space to store our data structure if we could be assured of significant reductions in time spent manipulating the list.

We now consider an implementation of a *doubly-linked list*. In a doubly-linked list, each element points not only to the next element in the list, but also to the previous element. The first and last elements, of course, have **null** **previousElement** and **nextElement** references, respectively.

count	head	tail
0	·	·

Figure 6.7   An empty doubly-linked list.

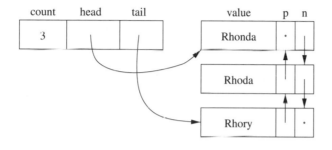

Figure 6.8   A nonempty doubly-linked list.

In addition to maintaining a second reference within each element, we will also consider the addition of a reference to the `tail` of the list. This one reference provides us direct access to the end of the list, and has the potential to improve the `addToTail` and `removeFromTail` methods.

A cursory glance at the resulting data structure identifies that it is more *symmetric* with respect to the head and tail of the list. Writing the tail-related methods can be accomplished by a simple rewriting of the head-related methods. Symmetry is a powerful concept in the design of complex structures; if something is asymmetric, you should step back and ask yourself why.

Principle 12 *Question asymmetry.*

We begin by constructing a `DoublyLinkedListElement` structure that parallels the `SinglyLinkedListElement`. The major difference is the addition of the `previous` reference that refers to the element that occurs immediately before this element in the doubly-linked list. One side effect of doubling the number of references is that we duplicate some of the information.

If we look at two adjacent elements, `Rhonda` and `Rhoda`, in a doubly-linked list, their mutual adjacency is recorded in two references (Figure 6.9): `Rhonda`'s   *Say* that *twice!*
`nextElement` reference refers to `Rhoda`, while `Rhoda`'s `previousElement` reference refers to `Rhonda`. Whenever one of the references is modified, the other must be modified also. When we construct a new `DoublyLinkedListElement`, we set both the `nextElement` and `previousElement` references. If either is non-`null`, a reference in the newly adjacent structure must be updated. *If we fail to do this, the data structure is left in an inconsistent state.*

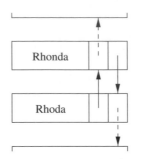

Figure 6.9   Rhonda's next reference duplicates Rhoda's previous reference.

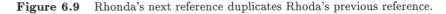

Here's the code:

DoublyLinked-
ListElement

```
protected Object data;
protected DoublyLinkedListElement nextElement;
protected DoublyLinkedListElement previousElement;

public DoublyLinkedListElement(Object v,
                        DoublyLinkedListElement next,
                        DoublyLinkedListElement previous)
// post: constructs new element with list
//       prefix referenced by previous and
//       suffix referenced by next
{
    data = v;
    nextElement = next;
    if (nextElement != null)
        nextElement.previousElement = this;
    previousElement = previous;
    if (previousElement != null)
        previousElement.nextElement = this;
}

public DoublyLinkedListElement(Object v)
// post: constructs a single element
{
    this(v,null,null);
}
```

DoublyLinked-
List

Now we construct the class describing the doubly-linked list, proper. As with any implementation of the list interface, it is necessary for our new **Doubly-LinkedList** to provide code for each method. The constructor simply sets the **head** and **tail** references to **null** and the **count** to zero—the state identifying an empty list:

```
protected int count;
protected DoublyLinkedListElement head;
protected DoublyLinkedListElement tail;

public DoublyLinkedList()
// post: constructs an empty list
{
    head = null;
    tail = null;
    count = 0;
}
```

Many of the fast methods of SinglyLinkedLists, like addToHead, require only minor modifications to maintain the extra references.

```
public void addToHead(Object value)
// pre: value is not null
// post: adds element to head of list
{
    // construct a new element, making it the head
    head = new DoublyLinkedListElement(value, head, null);
    // fix tail, if necessary
    if (tail == null) tail = head;
    count++;
}
```

The payoff for all our extra references comes when we implement methods like those modifying the tail of the list:

```
public void addToTail(Object value)
// pre: value is not null
// post: adds new value to tail of list
{
    // construct new element
    tail = new DoublyLinkedListElement(value, null, tail);
    // fix up head
    if (head == null) head = tail;
    count++;
}

public Object removeFromTail()
// pre: list is not empty
// post: removes value from tail of list
{
    Assert.pre(!isEmpty(),"List is not empty.");
    DoublyLinkedListElement temp = tail;
    tail = tail.previous();
    if (tail == null) {
        head = null;
    } else {
        tail.setNext(null);
```

```
        }
        count--;
        return temp.value();
    }
```

Here, it is easy to see that head- and tail-based methods are textually similar, making it easier to verify that they are written correctly. All the above procedures need to take special care that they handle a list that newly becomes either empty or not empty. In these cases, *both* the **head** and **tail** references must be modified to maintain a consistent view of the list. Some people consider the careful manipulation of these references so time-consuming and error-prone that they dedicate an unused element that permanently resides at the head of the list. It is never seen or modified by the user, and it can simplify the code. Here, for example, are **addToTail** and **removeFromTail** for this type of list:

```
public void addToTail(Object value)
// pre: value is not null
// post: adds new value to tail of list
{
    // construct new element
    tail = new DoublyLinkedListElement(value, null, tail);
    count++;
}

public Object removeFromTail()
// pre: list is not empty
// post: removes value from tail of list
{
    Assert.pre(!isEmpty(),"List is not empty.");
    DoublyLinkedListElement temp = tail;
    tail = tail.previous();
    tail.setNext(null);
    count--;
    return temp.value();
}
```

The reserved-element technique increases the amount of space necessary to store a **DoublyLinkedList** by the size of a single element. The choice is left to the implementor and is another example of a time–space tradeoff.

Returning to our original implementation, we note that **remove** is simplified by the addition of the **previous** reference:

```
public Object remove(Object value)
// pre: value is not null.  List can be empty.
// post: first element matching value is removed from list
{
    DoublyLinkedListElement finger = head;
    while (finger != null &&
           !finger.value().equals(value))
    {
```

```
            finger = finger.next();
        }
        if (finger != null)
        {
            // fix next field of element above
            if (finger.previous() != null)
            {
                finger.previous().setNext(finger.next());
            } else {
                head = finger.next();
            }
            // fix previous field of element below
            if (finger.next() != null)
            {
                finger.next().setPrevious(finger.previous());
            } else {
                tail = finger.previous();
            }
            count--;                // fewer elements
            return finger.value();
        }
        return null;
    }
```

Because every element keeps track of its previous element, there is no difficulty
in finding it from the element that is to be removed. Of course, once the removal
is to be done, several references need to be updated, and they must be assigned
carefully to avoid problems when removing the first or last value of a list.

6.5   Implementation: Circularly-Linked Lists

Careful inspection of the singly-linked list implementation identifies one seemingly unnecessary piece of data: the final reference of the list. This reference is
always null, but takes up as much space as any varying reference. At the same
time, we were motivated to add a tail reference in the doubly-linked list to help
us access either end of the list with equal ease. Perhaps we could use the final
reference of the list as the extra reference we need to keep track of one of the
ends!

*The tail wags
the dog.*

Here's the technique: Instead of keeping track of both a head and a tail
reference, we explicitly keep only the reference to the tail. Since this element
would normally have a null reference, we use that reference to refer, implicitly,
to the head. This implementation marries the speed of the DoublyLinkedList
with the space needed by the SinglyLinkedList. In fact, we are able to make
use of the SinglyLinkedListElement class as the basis for our implementation.
To build an empty list we initialize the tail to null and the count to zero:

```
    protected SinglyLinkedListElement tail;
    protected int count;
```

CircularList

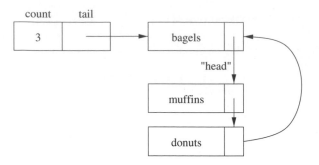

Figure 6.10   A non-empty circularly-linked list.

```
public CircularList()
// pre: constructs a new circular list
{
    tail = null;
    count = 0;
}
```

Whenever access to the head of the list is necessary, we use `tail.next()`, instead.[5] Thus, methods that manipulate the head of the list are only slight modifications of the implementations we have seen before for singly- and doubly-linked lists. Here is how we add a value to the head of the list:

```
public void addToHead(Object value)
// pre: value non-null
// post: adds element to head of list
{
    SinglyLinkedListElement temp =
        new SinglyLinkedListElement(value);
    if (tail == null) { // first value added
        tail = temp;
        tail.setNext(tail);
    } else { // element exists in list
        temp.setNext(tail.next());
        tail.setNext(temp);
    }
    count++;
}
```

---

[5] This longhand even works in the case when there is exactly one element, since its next reference points to itself.

Now, to add an element to the end of the list, we first add it to the head, and then "rotate" the list by moving the `tail` down the list. The overall effect is to have added the element to the tail!

```
public void addToTail(Object value)
// pre: value non-null
// post: adds element to tail of list
{
    // new entry:
    addToHead(value);
    tail = tail.next();
}
```

The "recycling" of the tail reference as a new head reference does not solve all of our problems. Careful thought will demonstrate that the removal of a value from the tail of the list remains a difficult problem. Because we only have access to the tail of the list, and not the value that precedes it, it is difficult to remove the final value. To accomplish this, we must iterate through the structure, looking for an element that refers to the same element as the tail reference.

```
public Object removeFromTail()
// pre: !isEmpty()
// post: returns and removes value from tail of list
{
    Assert.pre(!isEmpty(),"The list is not empty.");
    SinglyLinkedListElement finger = tail;
    while (finger.next() != tail) {
        finger = finger.next();
    }
    // finger now points to second-to-last value
    SinglyLinkedListElement temp = tail;
    if (finger == tail)
    {
        tail = null;
    } else {
        finger.setNext(tail.next());
        tail = finger;
    }
    count--;
    return temp.value();
}
```

There are two approaches to improving the performance of this operation. First, we could reconsider the **previous** links of the doubly-linked list. There's not much advantage to doing this, and if we did, we could then keep the head reference instead of the tail reference. The second technique is to point instead to the element before the tail; that is the subject of Problem 6.11.

6.6   Conclusions

In this chapter we have developed the notion of a list, and three different implementations. One of the features of the list is that as each of the elements is added to the list, the structure is expanded dynamically, using dynamic memory. To aid in keeping track of an arbitrarily large number of chunks of dynamic memory, we allocate, with each chunk, at least one reference for keeping track of logically "near by" memory.

Although the description of the interface for lists is quite detailed, none of the details of any particular implementation show through the interface. This approach to designing data structures makes it less possible for applications to depend on the peculiarities of any particular implementation, making it more likely that implementations can be improved without having to reconsider individual applications.

Finally, as we investigated each of the three implementations, it became clear that there were certain basic tradeoffs in good data structure design. Increased speed is often matched by an increased need for space, and an increase in complexity makes the code less maintainable. We discuss these tradeoffs in more detail in upcoming chapters.

Problems

6.1   When considering a data structure it is important to see how it works in the *boundary cases*. Given an empty `List`, which methods may be called without violating preconditions?

6.2   One method of `Lists` is motivated by symmetry: `tailPeek` looks at the last element of a `List`. Describe the implementation of `tailPeek` for each of the three `List` types we have seen in this chapter.

6.3   From within Java programs, you may access information on the Web using URL's (Uniform Resource Locators). Programmers at MindSlave software (working on their new NetPotato browser) would like to keep track of a potentially large bookmark list of frequently visited URL's. It would be most useful if they had arbitrary access to the values saved within the list. Is a `List` an appropriate data structure? (Hint: If not, why?)

6.4   Write a `List` method, `equals`, that returns true exactly when the elements of two lists are pair-wise equal. Ideally, your implementation should work for any `List` implementation, without change.

6.5   Write a method of `SinglyLinkedList`, called `reverse`, that reverses the order of the elements in the list. This method should be *destructive*—it should modify the list upon which it acts.

6.6   Write a method of `DoublyLinkedList`, called `reverse`, that reverses the order of the elements in the list. This method should be destructive.

6.7   Write a method of `CircularList`, called `reverse`, that reverses the order of the element in the list. This method should be destructive.

6.8 Each of the n references in a singly-linked list are needed if we wish to remove the final element. In a doubly-linked list, are each of the additional n `previous` references necessary if we want to remove the tail of the list in constant time? (Hint: What happens if you have a previous reference that points back a constant number of items. Items "skipped over" by the back reference maintain `null` previous references.)

6.9⋆ Design the best method you can for inserting an object into the middle of a `SinglyLinkedList`.

6.10⋆ Which implementation of the `size` and `isEmpty` methods would you use if:

a. You had the potential for a million-element list. (Consider the problem of keeping track of the alumni for the University of Michigan.)

b. You had the potential for a million small lists. (Consider the problem of keeping track of the dependents for each of a million income-tax returns.)

6.11⋆ One way to make all the circular list operations run quickly is to keep track of the element that points to the last element in the list. If we call this `penultimate`, then the tail is referenced by `penultimate.next`, and the head by `penultimate.next.next`. What are the disadvantages of this?

6.12 Suppose we read n integers $1, 2, \ldots, n$ from the input, in order. Flipping a coin, we add each new value to either the head or tail of the list. Does this shuffle the data? (Hint: See Problem 5.16.)

6.13⋆ Implement the `List` interface using `Vectors`. Why would one consider implementing lists this way?

6.14 Measure the performance of the `addToHead`, `remove`, and `removeFromTail` methods for each of the three implementations (you may include the `ListVector` class from Problem 6.13). Which implementations perform best for small lists? Which implementations perform best for large lists?

6.15 Implement a recursive version of the `size` method for `SinglyLinkedLists`. (Hint: A wrapper may be useful.)

6.16 Implement a recursive version of the `contains` method for `SinglyLinkedLists`.

6.17 Suppose the `add` of the `Unique` program is replaced by `addToTail` and the program is run on (for example) the first chapter of Mark Twain's *Tom Sawyer*. Why does the modified program run as much as 25 percent *faster* than the program using the `add` method? (Hint: Mark Twain didn't write randomly.)

Chapter 7

Linear Structures

" 'Rule Forty-two.
All persons more than a mile high to leave the court.'...
'Well, I shan't go,' said Alice; 'Besides
that's not a regular rule: you just invented it now.'
'It's the oldest rule in the book,' said the King.
'Then it ought to be Number One,' said Alice."
—Lewis Carroll

THE STATE OF SOME STRUCTURES REFLECTS THEIR HISTORY. Many systems—
for example, a line at a ticket booth or, as Alice presumes, the King's book of
rules—modify their state using exactly two operations: *add* and *remove*. As
with most data structures, when values are added and removed the structure
grows and shrinks. *Linear structures*, however, shrink in a predetermined manner: values are removed in an order based only on the order they were added.
All linear structures abide by a very simple interface:

```
public interface Linear extends Store
{
    public void add(Object value);
    // pre: value is non-null
    // post: the value is added to the collection,
    //       the consistent replacement policy not specified.

    public Object peek();
    // pre: structure is not empty
    // post: returns reference to next object to be removed.

    public Object remove();
    // pre: structure is not empty.
    // post: removes an object from store
}
```

Linear

The two structures that we investigate in this chapter—*stacks* and *queues*—are
the most common examples of linear data structures.

7.1 Stacks

Our first linear structure is a *stack*. A stack is a collection of items that exhibit
the behavior that *the last item in is the first item out*. It is a *LIFO* ("lie-foe")

structure. The `add` method pushes an item onto the stack, while `remove` pops off the item that was pushed on most recently. (The traditionally named methods `push` and `pop` are provided as alternatives for `add` and `remove`, respectively. We will use these stack-specific terms when we wish to emphasize the LIFO quality.) A nondestructive operation, `peek`, returns the top element of the `Stack`—the element that would be returned next. Since it is meaningless to `remove` or `peek` a `Stack` that is empty, it is important to have access to the size (e.g., `isEmpty`) methods of a `Store`. Here is the interface that defines what it means to be a `Stack`:

Stack

```
public interface Stack extends Linear
{
    public void add(Object item);
    // post: item is added to stack
    //       will be popped next if no intervening add

    public void push(Object item);
    // post: item is added to stack
    //       will be popped next if no intervening push

    public Object remove();
    // pre: stack is not empty
    // post: most recently added item is removed and returned

    public Object pop();
    // pre: stack is not empty
    // post: most recently pushed item is removed and returned

    public Object peek();
    // pre: stack is not empty
    // post: top value (next to be popped) is returned
}
```

To maintain applications that are consistent with Java's `java.util.Stack` the alternative operations of `push` and `pop` may be preferred.

7.1.1   Example: Simulating Recursion

Earlier we mentioned that tail recursive methods could be transformed to use loops. More complex recursive methods—especially those that perform multiple recursive calls—can be more complex to implement. In this section, we focus on the implementation of an iterative version of the quicksort sorting algorithm. Before we turn to the implementation, we will investigate the calling mechanisms of languages like Java.

Data available to well-designed methods come mainly from two locations: the method's parameters and its local variables. These values help to define the method's current *state*. In addition to the explicit values, implicit parameters also play a role. Let us consider the recursive version of quicksort we saw earlier:

```
private static void quickSortRecursive(int data[], int low, int high)
// pre: low <= high
// post: data[low..high] in ascending order
{
    int pivot;   // the final location of the leftmost value
    if (low >= high) return;
    // place the leftmost value at the correct location (pivot)
    pivot = partition(data,low,high);
      // 1. Sort the smaller values...
    quickSortRecursive(data,low,pivot-1);
      // 2. ...and then sort larger values...
    quickSortRecursive(data,pivot+1,high);
      // 3. Done, return!
}
```

QuickSort

The *flow of control* in most methods is from top to bottom. If the machine stops execution, it is found to be executing one of the statements. In our recursive quicksort, there are three main points of execution: (1) before the first recursive call, (2) before the second recursive call, and (3) just before the return. To focus on what needs to be accomplished, the computer keeps a special reference to the code, called a *program counter*. For the purposes of our exercise, we will assume the program counter takes on the value 1, 2, or 3, depending on its location within the routine.

These values—the parameters, the local variables, and the program counter—reside in a structure called a *call frame*. Whenever a method is called, a new call frame is constructed and filled out with appropriate values. Because many methods may be active at the same time (methods can call each other), there are usually several active call frames. These frames are maintained in a *call stack*. Since the first method to return is the last method called, a stack seems appropriate. Figure 7.1 describe the relationship between the call frames of the call stack and a partial run of quicksort.

Our approach is to construct a stack of frames that describes the progress of the various "virtually recursive" calls to quicksort. Each frame must maintain enough information to simulate the actual call frame of the recursive routine:

```
class callFrame
{
    int pivot;// location of pivot
    int low;  // left index
    int high; // right index
    int PC; // next statment (see #'d comment in recursive code)

    public callFrame(int l, int h)
    // post: generate new call frame with low and high as passed
    {
        low = l; high = h; PC = 1;
    }
}
```

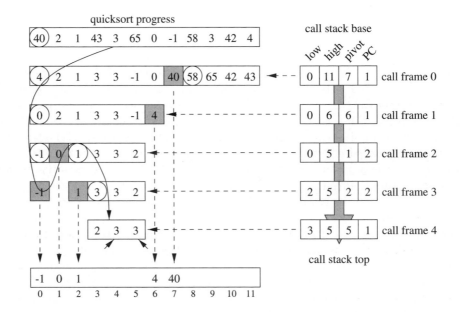

Figure 7.1   A partially complete quicksort and its call stack. The quicksort routine is currently partitioning the three-element subarray containing 2, 3, and 3. The curve indicates the progress of recursion in quicksort to this point.

Just as with real call frames, it's possible for variables to be uninitialized (e.g., `pivot`)! We can consider an iterative version of quicksort:

```
public static void quickSortIterative(int data[], int n)
// pre: n <= data.length
// post: data[0..n-1] in ascending order
{
    Stack callStack = new StackList();
    callStack.push(new callFrame(0,n-1));
    while (!callStack.isEmpty())
    {   // some "virtual" method outstanding
        callFrame curr = (callFrame)callStack.peek();
        if (curr.PC == 1) { // partition and sort lower
            // return if trivial
            if (curr.low >= curr.high) { callStack.pop(); continue; }
            // place the pivot at the correct location
            curr.pivot = partition(data,curr.low,curr.high);
            curr.PC++;
            // sort the smaller values...
            callStack.push(new callFrame(curr.low,curr.pivot-1));
        } else if (curr.PC == 2) { // sort upper
            curr.PC++;
            // sort the larger values....
            callStack.push(new callFrame(curr.pivot+1,curr.high));
        } else { callStack.pop(); continue; } // return
    }
}
```

We begin by creating a new stack initialized with a `callFrame` that simulates first call to the recursive routine. The `low` and `high` variables of the frame are initialized to 0 and $n - 1$ respectively, and we are about to execute statement 1. As long as there is a call frame on the stack, some invocation of quicksort is still executing. Looking at the top frame, we conditionally execute the code associated with each statement number. For example, statement 1 returns (by popping off the top call frame) if `low` and `high` suggest a trivial sort. Each variable is prefixed by `curr` because the local variables reside within the call frame, `curr`. When we would execute a recursive call, we instead increment the "program counter" and push a new frame on the stack with appropriate initialization of local variables. Because each local variable appears in several places on the call stack, recursive procedures appear to have fewer local variables. The conversion of recursion to iteration, then, requires more explicit handling of local storage during execution.

The sort continues until all the call frames are popped off. This happens when each method reaches statement 3, that is, when the recursive quicksort would have returned.

We now discuss two implementations of `Stacks`: one based on a `Vector` and one based on a `List`.

7.1.2   Vector-Based Stacks

Let us consider a traditional stack-based analogy: the storage of trays in a fast-food restaurant. At the beginning of a meal, you are given a tray from a stack. The process of removing a tray is the popping of a tray off the stack. When trays are returned, they are pushed back on the stack.

Now, assume that the side of the tray holder is marked in a rulerlike fashion, perhaps to measure the number of trays stacked. Squinting one's eyes, this looks like a sideways vector:

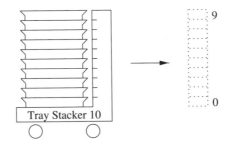

Following our analogy, the implementation of a `Stack` using a `Vector` can be accomplished by aligning the "top" of the `Stack` with the "end" of the `Vector` (see Figure 7.2). We provide two constructors, including one that provides the `Vector` with the initial capacity:

StackVector

```
protected Vector data;

public StackVector()
// post: an empty stack is created
{
    data = new Vector();
}

public StackVector(int size)
// post: an empty stack with initial capacity of size is created
{
    data = new Vector(size);
}
```

To `add` elements on the `Stack`, we simply use the `addElement` of the `Vector`. When an element is to be `removed` from the `Stack` we carefully remove the last element, returning its value.

```
public void add(Object item)
// post: item is added to stack
//       will be popped next if no intervening add
{
    data.addElement(item);
}
```

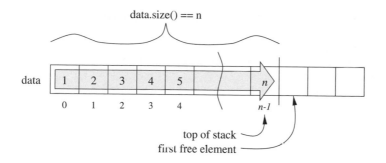

Figure 7.2 A vector-based stack containing n elements. The top of the stack is implied by the length of the underlying vector. The arrow demonstrates direction of growth.

```
public void push(Object item)
// post: item is added to stack
//       will be popped next if no intervening push
{
    add(item);
}

public Object remove()
// pre: stack is not empty
// post: most recently added item is removed and returned
{
    Object result = data.elementAt(size()-1);
    data.removeElementAt(size()-1);
    return result;
}

public Object pop()
// pre: stack is not empty
// post: most recently pushed item is removed and returned
{
    return remove();
}
```

The **add** method appends the element to the end of the vector, extending it if necessary. Notice that if the vector has n elements, this element is written to slot n, increasing the number of elements to $n+1$. Removing an element reverses this process: it removes and returns the last element. (Note the invocation of our principle of symmetry, here. We will depend on this notion in our design of a number of **add** and **remove** method pairs.) The **peek** method is like **removo**, except that the stack is not modified. The size of the stack is easily determined by requesting the same information from the underlying **Vector**. Of course when the `Vector` is empty, so is the `Stack` it supports.[1]

```
public boolean empty()
// post: returns true iff the stack is empty
{
    return size() == 0;
}

public int size()
// post: returns the number of elements in stack
{
    return data.size();
}

public void clear()
// post: removes all elements from stack
{
    data.clear();
}

public boolean isEmpty()
// post: returns true iff the stack is empty
{
    return size() == 0;
}
```

The `clear` method is required because the `Stack` indirectly extends the `Store` interface.

7.1.3   List-Based Stacks

Only the top "end" of the stack ever gets modified. It is reasonable, then, to seek an efficient implementation of a `Stack` using a `SinglyLinkedList`. Because our `SinglyLinkedList` manipulates its head more efficiently than its tail, we align the `Stack` top with the head of the `SinglyLinkedList` (see Figure 7.3).

The `add` method simply performs an `addToHead`, and the `remove` operation performs `removeFromHead`. Since we have implemented the list's `remove` operation so that it returns the value removed, the value can be passed along through the stack's `remove` method.

StackList

```
public void add(Object value)
// post: pushes value onto stack.
//       will be first value popped off.
{
    data.addToHead(value);
}
```

---

[1] The class `java.util.Stack` has an `empty` method that is analogous to our `isEmpty` method. We prefer to use `isEmpty` for consistency.

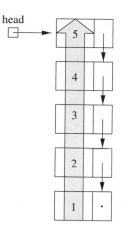

Figure 7.3 A stack implemented using a singly-linked list. The arrow demonstrates the direction of stack growth.

```
public void push(Object value)
// post: pushes value onto stack.
//       will be first value popped off.
{
    add(value);
}

public Object remove()
// pre: !isEmpty()
// post: returns and removes top element of stack
{
    return data.removeFromHead();
}

public Object pop()
// pre: !isEmpty()
// post: returns and removes top element of stack
{
    return remove();
}
```

The remaining methods are simply the obvious wrappers for similar methods from the `SinglyLinkedList`. Because the stack operations are trivial representations of the linked-list operations, their complexities are all the same as the corresponding operations found in linked-lists—each takes constant time.

It should be noted that any structure implementing the `List` interface would be sufficient for implementing a `Stack`. The distinction, however, between the various lists we have seen presented here has focused on providing quick access to the tail of the list. Since stacks do not require access to the tail, the alternative implementations of list structure do not provide any benefit. Thus we use the `SinglyLinkedList` implementation.

7.1.4   Comparisons

Clearly, stacks are easily implemented using the structures we have seen so far. In fact, the complexities of those operations make it difficult to decide which of the classes is better. How can we make the decision?

Let's consider each a little more carefully. First, in terms of time, both underlying structures provide efficient implementations. In addition, both structures provide (virtually) unlimited extension of the structure. Their difference stems from a difference in approach for expanding the structure. In the case of the vector, the structure is responsible for deciding when the structure is extended. Because the structure grows by doubling, the reallocation of memory occurs increasingly less often, but *when* that reallocation occurs, it takes an increasingly long time. So, while the *amortized* cost of dynamically extending vectors is constant time per element, the incremental cost of extending the vector either is zero (if no extension actually occurs) or is occasionally proportional to the size of the vector. Some applications may not be tolerant of this great variation in the cost of extending the structure. In those cases the `StackList` implementation should be considered.

The constant incremental overhead of expanding the `StackList` structure, however, comes at a price. Since each element of the list structure requires a reference to the list that follows, there is a potentially significant overhead in terms of space. If the items stored in the stack are roughly the size of a reference, the overhead is significant. If, however, the size of a reference is insignificant when compared to the size of the elements stored, the increased space use may be reasonable.

7.2   Queues

Most of us have participated in queues—at movie theaters, toll booths, or ice cream shops, or while waiting for a communal bathroom in a large family! A *queue*, like a stack, is an ordered collection of elements with tightly controlled access to the structure. Unlike a stack, however, *the first item in is the first item out*. We call it a *FIFO* ("fie-foe") structure. FIFO's are useful because they maintain the order of the data that run through them.

The primary operations of queues are to *enqueue* and *dequeue* elements. Again, to support the `Linear` interface, we supply the **add** and **remove** methods as alternatives. Elements are added at the *tail* of the structure, where they then pass through the structure, eventually reaching the *head* where they are removed. The interface provides a number of other features we have seen already:

Queue

```
public interface Queue extends Linear
{
    public void add(Object value);
    // post: the value is added to the tail of the structure

    public void enqueue(Object value);
    // post: the value is added to the tail of the structure

    public Object remove();
    // pre: the queue is not empty
    // post: the head of the queue is removed and returned

    public Object dequeue();
    // pre: the queue is not empty
    // post: the head of the queue is removed and returned

    public Object peek();
    // pre: the queue is not empty
    // post: the element at the head of the queue is returned
}
```

As with the `Stack` definition, the `Queue` interface describes necessary characteristics of a class, but not the code to implement it.

7.2.1   Example: Solving a Coin Puzzle

As an example of an application of queues, we consider an interesting coin puzzle (see Figure 7.4). A dime, penny, nickel, and quarter are arranged in decreasing size in each of the leftmost four squares of a five-square board. The object is to reverse the order of the coins and to leave them in the rightmost four slots, in the least number of moves. In each move a single coin moves to the left or right. Coins may be stacked, but only the top coin is allowed to move. When a coin moves, it may not land off the board or on a smaller coin. A typical intermediate legal position is shown in the middle of Figure 7.4. From this point, the nickel may move right and the dime may move in either direction.

We begin by defining a "board state." This object keeps track of the positions of each of the four coins, as well as the series of board states that lead to this state from the start. Its implementation is an interesting problem (see Problem 1.14). We outline its interface here:

CoinPuzzle

```
class State
{
    public static final int DIME=0;     // coins
    public static final int PENNY=1;
    public static final int NICKEL=2;
    public static final int QUARTER=3;
    public static final int LEFT = -1; // directions
    public static final int RIGHT = 1;
```

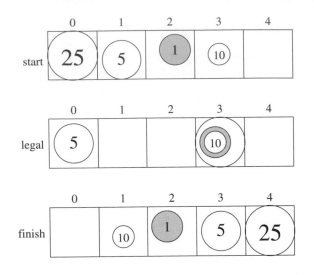

Figure 7.4 A four-coin puzzle. Top and bottom orientations depict the start and finish positions. A typical legal position is shown in the middle.

```
public State()
// post: constuct initial layout of coins

public State(State prior)
// pre: prior is a non-null state
// post: constructs a copy of that state to be successor state

public boolean done()
// post: returns true if state is the finish state

public boolean validMove(int coin, int direction)
// pre: State.DIME <= coin <= State.QUARTER
//      direction = State.left or State.right
// post: returns true if coin can be moved in desired direction

public State move(int coin, int direction)
// pre: coin and direction describe valid move
// post: coin is moved in that direction

public int printMoves()
// post: print moves up to and including this point

public int id()
// post: constuct an integer representing state
//       states of coins are equal iff id's are equal
    }
```

The parameterless constructor builds a board in the initial state, while the one-parameter constructor generates a new state to follow `prior`. The `done` method checks for a state that is in the final position. Coins (identified by constants such as `State.PENNY`) are moved in different directions (e.g., `State.LEFT`), but only if the move is valid. Once the final state is found, the intermediate states leading to a particular board position are printed with `printMoves`.

Once the `State` class has been defined, it is a fairly simple matter to solve the puzzle:

```java
public static void main(String args[])
{
    Queue pool = new QueueList();
    State board = new State();
    BitSet seen = new BitSet(5*5*5*5);
    pool.add(board);
    while (!pool.isEmpty())
    {
        board = (State)pool.remove();
        if (board.done()) break;
        int moveCode = board.id();
        if (seen.contains(moveCode)) continue;
        seen.add(moveCode);
        for (int coin = State.DIME; coin <= State.QUARTER; coin++)
        {
            if (board.validMove(coin,State.LEFT))
                pool.add(board.move(coin,State.LEFT));
            if (board.validMove(coin,State.RIGHT))
                pool.add(board.move(coin,State.RIGHT));
        }
    }
    board.printMoves();
}
```

We begin by keeping a pool of potentially unvisited board states. This queue initially includes the single starting board position. At each stage of the loop an unvisited board position is checked. If it is not the finish position, the boards generated by the legal moves from the current position are added to the state pool. Processing continues until the final position is encountered. At that point, the intermediate positions are printed out.

Because the pool is a FIFO, each unvisited position near the head of the queue must be at least as close to the initial position as those found near the end. Thus, when the final position is found, the distance from the start position (in moves) is a minimum!

A subtle point in this code is the use of the `id` function and the `BitSet`.[2] The `id` function returns a small integer (between 0 and $5^5 - 1$) that uniquely

---

[2] `BitSet`s are part of the `java.util` package, and we provide public implementations of these and other sets in the `structure` package. They are not discussed formally within this text.

identifies the state of the board. These integers are kept in the set. If, in the future, a board position with a previously encountered state number is found, the state can safely be ignored. Without this optimization, it becomes difficult to avoid processing previously visited positions hundreds or thousands of times before a solution is found. We will leave it to the reader to find the solution either manually or automatically. (The fastest solution involves 22 moves.)

We now investigate three different implementations of queues, based on `Lists`, `Vectors`, and arrays. Each has its merits and drawbacks, so we consider them carefully.

7.2.2   List-Based Queues

Drawing upon our various analogies with real life, it is clear that there are *two* points of interest in a queue: the head and the tail. This two-ended view of queues makes the list a natural structure to support the queue. In this implementation, the head and tail of the queue correspond to the head and tail of the list. The major difference is that a queue is restricted to peeking at and removing values from the head and appending elements to the tail. Lists, on the other hand, allow adding and removing values from both ends.

This discussion leads us to the following protected field within the `QueueList` structure:

QueueList

```
protected List data;
```

When we consider the constructor, however, we are forced to consider more carefully what implementation of a list is actually most suitable. While for the stack the `SinglyLinkedList` was ideal, that implementation only provides efficient manipulation of the head of the list. To get fast access to both ends of the list, we are forced to consider either the `DoublyLinkedList` or the `CircularList`. Either would be time-efficient here, but we choose the slightly less space-efficient `DoublyLinkedList` (see Figure 7.5). We now consider our constructor:

```
public QueueList()
// post: constructs a new, empty queue
{
    data = new DoublyLinkedList();
}
```

Notice that, because the `List` structure has unbounded size, the `Queue` structure built atop it is also unbounded. This is a nice feature, since many applications of queues have no easily estimated upper bound.

To add a value to the queue, we simply add an element to the tail of the list. Removing a value from the list provides what we need for the **dequeue** operation.[3]

---

[3] Note, once again, the decision to have **remove** operations symmetric with the **add** operations was the right decision.

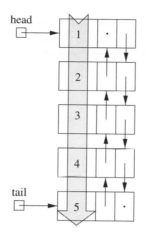

head

tail

Figure 7.5 A Queue implemented using a List. The head of the List corresponds to the head of the Queue.

```
public void add(Object value)
// post: the value is added to the tail of the structure
{
    data.addToTail(value);
}

public void enqueue(Object value)
// post: the value is added to the tail of the structure
{
    add(value);
}

public Object remove()
// pre: the queue is not empty
// post: the element at the head of the queue is removed and returned
{
    return data.removeFromHead();
}

public Object dequeue()
// pre: the queue is not empty
// post: the element at the head of the queue is removed and returned
{
    return remove();
}
```

The needs of the remove operation are satisfied by the removeFromHead operation on a List, so very little code needs to be written. The simplicity of these methods demonstrates how *code reuse* can make the implementation of structures less difficult. This is particularly dramatic when we consider the implementation of the size-related methods of the `QueueList` structure:

```
public Object peek()
// pre: the queue is not empty
// post: the element at the head of the queue is returned
{
    return data.peek();
}

public int size()
// post: returns the number of elements in the queue
{
    return data.size();
}

public void clear()
// post: removes all elements from the queue
{
    data.clear();
}

public boolean isEmpty()
// post: returns true iff the queue is empty
{
    return data.isEmpty();
}
```

Because the `QueueList` is a rewrapping of the `List` structure, the complexity of each of the methods corresponds to the complexity of the underlying `List` implementation. For `DoublyLinkedLists`, most of the operations can be performed in constant time ($O(1)$).

We now consider two implementations that do not use dynamically linked structures for their underpinnings. While these structures have drawbacks, they are useful when space is a concern or when the size of the queue can be bounded above.

7.2.3 Vector-Based Queues

The lure of implementing structures through code reuse can lead to performance problems if the underlying structure is not well considered. Thus, while we have advocated hiding the unnecessary details of the implementation within the object, it is important to have a sense of the *complexity* of the object's methods, if the object is the basis for supporting larger structures.

Principle 13 *Understand the complexity of the structures you use.*

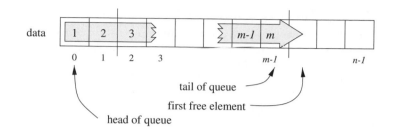

Figure 7.6   A `Queue` implemented atop a `Vector`. As elements are added (enqueued), the `Queue` expands the `Vector`. As elements are removed, the leftmost element is removed, shrinking the `Vector`.

We will return to this issue a number of times. Careful design of data structures sometimes involves careful reconsideration of the performance of structures.

Now, let's consider an implementation of `Queues` using `Vectors`. Recall that a vector is a linear structure whose values can be randomly accessed and modified. We will, again, reconsider the vector as a two-ended structure in our attempt to implement a queue (see Figure 7.6). The head of the queue will be found in the first location of the vector, and the tail of the queue will be found in the last. (The index associated with each element will, essentially, enumerate the order in which they would be removed in the future.)

The constructor creates an empty `QueueVector` by creating an empty `Vector`. When an upper bound can be provided, the second `QueueVector` constructor passes that information along to the `Vector`:

QueueVector

```
protected Vector data;

public QueueVector()
// post: constructs an empty queue
{
    data = new Vector();
}

public QueueVector(int size)
// post: constructs an empty queue of appropriate size
{
    data = new Vector(size);
}
```

Adding an element to the end of the queue is as simple as adding an element to the end of the vector. This is accomplished through the vector method `addElement`.

```
public void add(Object value)
// post: the value is added to the tail of the structure
{
    data.addElement(value);
}

public void enqueue(Object value)
// post: the value is added to the tail of the structure
{
    add(value);
}
```

As with the **remove** method of the **StackVector** class, the **remove** of the **QueueVector** requires a little more finesse. Here, we keep track of the first element of the **Vector**, and then remove it. Finally we return the value we cached away. (This maneuvering reflects an inconsistency in the **Vector** class motivated by the Java implementation.)

```
public Object remove()
// pre: the queue is not empty
// post: the element at the head of the queue is removed and returned
{
    Object result = data.elementAt(0);
    data.removeElementAt(0);
    return result;
}
public Object dequeue()
// pre: the queue is not empty
// post: the element at the head of the queue is removed and returned
{
    return remove();
}
```

As usual, the remaining methods rewrap similar **Vector** methods in the expected way. Because of the restricted nature of this linear structure, we take care not to publicize any features of the **Vector** class that violate the basic restrictions of a **Linear**.

When considering the complexity of these methods, it is important to keep in mind the underlying complexities of the vector. For example, adding a value to the "end" of the vector can be accomplished, on average, in constant time.[4] That method, **addElement**, is so special in its simplicity that it was distinguished from the general **addElementAt** method: the latter operation has time complexity that is expected to be $O(n)$, where n is the length of the vector. The worst-case behavior is $O(n)$—that case is when a value is added at the front of the vector. All the existing elements must be moved to the right to make room for the new value.

---

[4] It can vary considerably, if the vector requires reallocation of memory, but the average time (as we saw in Section 3.5) is still constant time.

A similar situation occurs when we consider the removal of values from a vector. Unfortunately, the case we need to use—removing an element from the beginning of a vector—is precisely the worst case. It requires removing the value and then shifting $n-1$ elements to the left, one slot. That $O(n)$ behavior slows down our `remove` operation, probably by an unacceptable amount. For example, the process of adding n elements to a queue and then dequeuing them takes about $O(n^2)$ time, which may not be acceptable.

Even though the implementation seemed straightforward, we pay a significant price for this code reuse. If we could remove a value from the vector without having to move the other elements, the complexity of these operations could be simplified. We consider that approach in our implementation of the `Queue` interface using arrays of objects.

7.2.4 Array-Based Queues

If we can determine an upper bound for the size of the queue we need, we can gain some efficiency because we need not worry so much about managing the memory we use. Keyboard hardware, for example, often implements a queue of keystrokes that are to be shipped off to the attached processor. The size of that queue can be easily bounded above by, say, several hundred keystrokes. *Fast typists, take note!* Notice, by the way, that this does not limit the number of elements that can run through the queue, only the number of values that can be resident within the queue *simultaneously*.

Once the array has been allocated, we simply place enqueued values in successive locations within the array, starting at location 0. The head of the queue—the location containing the oldest element—is initially found at location 0. As elements are removed, we return the value stored at the head of the queue, and move the head toward the right in the array. All the operations must explicitly store and maintain the size of the queue in a counter. This counter should be a nonnegative number less than the length of the array.

One potential problem occurs when a value is removed from the very end of the array. Under normal circumstances, the head of the queue would move to the right, but we now need to have it "wrap around." One common solution is to use modular arithmetic. When the head moves too far to the right, its value, `head`, is no longer less than the length of the array, `data.length`. After moving the head to the right (by adding 1 to `head`), we simply compute the remainder when dividing by `data.length`. This always returns a valid index for the array, `data`, and it indexes the value "just to the right," in wrap-around fashion (see Figure 7.7). It should be noted, at this point, that remainder computation is "reasonable" for positive values; if `head` were ever to become negative, one must take care to check to see if a negative remainder might occur. If that appears to be a possibility, simply adding `data.length` to the value before remainder computation fixes the problem in a portable way.

Our `QueueArray` implementation, then, requires three values: an array of objects that we allocate once and never expand, the index of the head of the queue, and the number of elements currently stored within the queue.

`QueueArray`

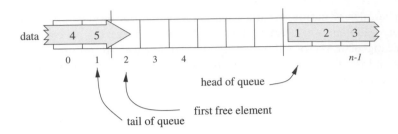

Figure 7.7 A `Queue` implemented atop an array. As elements are added (enqueued), the queue wraps from the back to the front of the array.

```
protected Object data[]; // an array of the data
protected int head; // next dequeue-able value
protected int count; // current size of queue
```

Given an upper bound, the constructor allocates the array and sets the **head** and **count** variables to zero. The initial value of **head** could, actually, be any value between 0 and $size - 1$, but we use zero, for neatness.

42 isn't the ultimate answer, then?

```
public QueueArray(int size)
// post: create a queue capable of holding at most size values
{
    data = new Object[size];
    head = 0;
    count = 0;
}
```

The **add** and **remove** methods appear more complex than their **QueueVector** counterparts, but review of the implementation of the **Vector** class proves their similarity. The **add** method adds a value at the logical end of the queue—the first free slot in the array—in wrap-around fashion. That location is **count** slots to the right of the head of the queue, and is computed using modular arithmetic; **remove** is similar, but carefully moves the **head** to the right. The reader should verify that, in a valid **QueueArray**, the value of **head** will never pass the value of **tail**.

```
public void add(Object value)
// pre: queue is not full
// post: the value is added to the tail of the structure
{
    Assert.pre(!isFull(),"Queue is not full.");
    int tail = (head + count) % data.length;
    data[tail] = value;
    count++;
}
```

```
public void enqueue(Object value)
// pre: queue is not full
// post: the value is added to the tail of the structure
{
    add(value);
}

public Object remove()
// pre: the queue is not empty
// post: the element at the head of the queue is removed and returned
{
    Assert.pre(!isEmpty(),"The queue is not empty.");
    Object value = data[head];
    head = (head + 1) % data.length;
    count--;
    return value;
}

public Object dequeue()
// pre: the queue is not empty
// post: the element at the head of the queue is removed and returned
{
    return remove();
}
```

The peek method just provides quick access to the **head** entry of the array.

```
public Object peek()
// pre: the queue is not empty
// post: the element at the head of the queue is returned
{
    Assert.pre(!isEmpty(),"The queue is not empty.");
    return data[head];
}
```

Because we are directly using arrays, we do not have the luxury of previously constructed size-oriented methods, so we are forced to implement these directly. Again, the cost of an efficient implementation can mean less code reuse—or increased original code and the potential for error.

```
public int size()
// post: returns the number of elements in the queue
{
    return count;
}

public void clear()
// post: removes all elements from the queue
```

```
{
    // we could remove all the elements from the queue
    count = 0;
    head = 0;
}

public boolean isFull()
// post: returns true if the queue is at its capacity
{
    return count == data.length;
}

public boolean isEmpty()
// post: returns true iff the queue is empty
{
    return count == 0;
}
```

Alternative Array Implementations

One aesthetic drawback of the implementation of queues described above is that symmetric operations—**add** and **remove**—do not lead to symmetric code. There are several reasons for this, but we might uncover some of the details by reconsidering the implementations.

Two variables, **head** and **count**, are responsible for *encoding* (in an asymmetric way) the information that might be more symmetrically encoded using two variables, say **head** and **tail**. For the sake of argument, suppose that **head** "points" to the oldest value in the queue, while **tail** points to the oldest value *not* in the queue—the value to the right of the last value in the queue. A simple test to see if the queue is empty is to check to see if **head == tail**. Strangely enough this also appears to be a test to see if the queue is full! Since a nontrivial queue should never be both empty and full at the same time, this problem must be addressed.

Suppose the array has length l. Then both **head** and **tail** have a range of 0 to $l - 1$. They take on l values apiece. Now consider all queues with head values stored beginning at location 0. The **head** is fixed at 0 but **tail** may take on any of the l values between 0 and $l - 1$, inclusive. The queues represented, however, have $l + 1$ potential states: an empty queue, a queue with 1 value, a queue with 2 values, up to a queue with l values. Because there are $l + 1$ queues, they cannot be adequately represented by a pair of variables that can support only l different states. There are several solutions to this conflict that we outline momentarily and discuss in problems at the end of the chapter.

1. A boolean variable, **queueEmpty**, could be added to distinguish between the two states where **head** and **tail** are identical. Code written using this technique is clean and symmetric. The disadvantage of this technique is that more code must be written to maintain the extra variable.

2. An array element logically to the left of the head of the queue can be reserved. The queue is full if there are $l - 1$ values within the queue. Since it would not be possible to add a value when the queue is full, the **tail** and **head** variables would never "become equal" through expansion. The only significant difference is the allocation of an extra reserved cell, and a change in the **isFull** method to see if the tail is just to the logical left of the head. The disadvantage of this technique is that it requires the allocation of another array element. When objects are large, this cost may be prohibitively expensive.[5]

Our actual implementation, of course, provides a third solution to the problem. While we like our solution, data abstraction allows us to hide any changes we might make if we change our minds.

7.3   Example: Solving Mazes

To demonstrate the utility of stacks and queues, we consider the automated solution of a maze. A maze is simply a matrix of cells that are adjacent to one another. The user begins in a special *start cell* and seeks a path of adjacent cells that lead to the *finish cell*.

One general approach to solving a maze (or any other search problem) is to consider unvisited cells as potential tasks. Each unvisited cell represents the task of *finding a path from that cell to the finish*. Some cells, of course, may not be reachable from the start position, so they are tasks we seek to avoid. Other cells lead us on trails from the start to finish. Viewed in this manner, we can use the linear structure to help us solve the problem by keeping track of outstanding tasks—unvisited cells adjacent to visited cells.

In the following program, we make use of two abstract classes, **Position** and **Maze**. A **Position** is used to identify a unique location within a maze. Any **Position** can be transformed into another **Position** by asking it for an adjacent position to the north, south, east, or west. Here is the class:

```
class Position
{
    public Position north()
    // post: returns position above

    public Position south()
    // post: returns position below

    public Position east()
    // post: returns position to right
```

MazeRunner

---

[5] Again, in Java, an **Object** is a small reference to the actual memory used, so the cost is fairly insignificant. In other languages, where instances are stored directly, and not as references, this cost may be prohibitively expensive.

```
        public Position west()
        // post: returns position to left

        public boolean equals(Object other)
        // post: returns true iff objects represent same position
    }
```

The interface for the `Maze` class reads a maze description from a file and generates the appropriate adjacency of cells. We ignore the implementation that is not important to us at this point (it is available online):

```
class Maze
{
    public Maze(String filename)
    // pre: filename is the name of a maze file. # is a wall.
    //      's' marks the start, 'f' marks the finish.
    // post: reads and constructs maze from file <filename>

    public void visit(Position p)
    // pre: p is a position within the maze
    // post: cell at position p is set to be visited

    public boolean isVisited(Position p)
    // pre: p is a position within the maze
    // post: returns true if the position has been visited

    public Position start()
    // post: returns start position

    public Position finish()
    // post: returns finish position

    public boolean isClear(Position p)
    // post: returns true iff p is a clear location within the maze
    }
```

Now, once we have the structures supporting the construction of mazes, we can use a `Linear` structure to organize the search for a solution in a `Maze`:

```
public static void main(String[] arguments)
{
    Maze m = new Maze(arguments[0]); // the maze
    Position goal = m.finish(); // where the finish is
    Position square = null; // the current position
    // a linear structure to manage search
    Linear todo = new StackList();

    // begin by priming the queue(stack) w/starting position
    todo.add(m.start());
    while (!todo.isEmpty()) // while we haven't finished exploring
```

```
####################        ####################
#s#      #f  #    #          #s#      #f...#...#
# ####### #### # # #         #.####### ####.#.#.#
#         # # ### #          #........#..#.###.#
##### ### #       #          ##### ###.#........#
#   # #   ####### ##         #   # #...#######.##
#   # # ### #   # #          #   # #.### #...#..#
#   # # #   # # ## #         #   # #.#..#.#.#.##.#
#   #   #   #     #          #   #...#...#....#
####################        ####################
```

Figure 7.8 A classic maze and its solution found using a stack. Dots indicate locations in the maze visited during the solution process.

```
    {
        // take the top position from the stack and check for finish
        square = (Position)todo.remove();
        if (m.isVisited(square)) continue; // been here before
        if (square.equals(goal)) {
            System.out.println(m); // print solution
            break;
        }
        // not finished
        // visit this location, and add neighbors to pool
        m.visit(square);
        if (m.isClear(square.north())) todo.add(square.north());
        if (m.isClear(square.west()))  todo.add(square.west());
        if (m.isClear(square.south())) todo.add(square.south());
        if (m.isClear(square.east()))  todo.add(square.east());
    }
}
```

We begin by placing the start position on the stack. If, ultimately, the stack is emptied, a solution is impossible. If the stack is not empty, the top position is removed and considered, if not visited. If an unvisited cell is not the finish, the cell is marked visited, and open neighboring cells are added to the stack.

Notice that since the underlying data structure is a Stack, the order in which the neighboring positions are pushed on the stack is the reverse of the order in which they will be considered. The result is that the program prefers to head east before any other direction. This can be seen as it gets distracted by going east at the right border of the maze of Figure 7.8. Because stacks are LIFO structures, the search for a solution prefers to deepen the search rather than investigate alternatives. If a queue was used as the linear structure, the search would expand along a frontier of cells that are equidistant from the start. The solution found, then, would be the most direct route from start to finish, just as in the coin puzzle.

No:
Go west
young Maze!

7.4   Conclusions

In this chapter we have investigated two important linear structures: the `Stack` and the `Queue`. Each implements `add` and `remove` operations. Traditional implementations of `Stacks` refer to these operations as `push` and `pop`, while traditional `Queue` methods are called `enqueue` and `dequeue`. Since these structures are often used to solve similar problems (e.g., search problems), they share a common `Linear` interface.

There are many different ways to implement each of these linear structures, and we have investigated a number—including implementations using arrays. Because of the tradeoffs between speed and versatility, each implementation has its own particular strengths. Still, for many applications where performance is less important, we can select an implementation and use it without great concern because a common interface allows us to freely swap implementations.

We have seen a number of examples that use `Linear` structures to solve complex problems. Since stacks are used to maintain the state of executing methods, we have seen that recursive programs can be converted to iterative programs that maintain an explicit stack. Two explicit search problems—the coin puzzle and the maze—have an obvious relation. Because the coin puzzle searches for a short solution, we use a queue to maintain the pool of goal candidates. For the maze, we chose a stack, but a queue is often just as effective. The coin puzzle can be thought of as a maze whose rules determine the location of the barriers between board positions.

Problems

7.1   Suppose we push each of the first n integers onto a stack, and then perform $\frac{n}{2}$ `pop` operations. What is the state of the stack?

7.2   Suppose we enqueue each of the first n integers into a queue, and then perform $\frac{n}{2}$ `dequeue` operations. What is the state of the queue?

7.3   Suppose you wish to reverse the order of elements of a stack. Using only `Stack` operations, describe how this would be done. How many additional stacks are necessary?

7.4   Suppose you wish to fill a stack with a copy of another, maintaining the order of elements. Using only `Stack` operations, describe how this would be done. How many additional stacks are necessary?

7.5   Suppose you wish to copy a queue into another, preserving the order of elements. Using only `Queue` operations, describe how this would be done.

7.6   Suppose you wish to reverse the order of elements of a queue. Using only `Queue` operations, describe how this would be done. (Hint: While you can't use a stack, you can use something similar.)

7.7⋆   Over time, the elements 1, 2, and 3 are pushed onto the stack in that order. What sequence(s) of popping the elements off the stack is impossible, if any?

7.8 Generalize the solution to Problem 7.7. If elements 1, 2, 3, ..., n are pushed onto a stack in that order, what sequences of popping the elements off the stack are not permissible?

7.9★ Over time, the elements 1, 2, and 3 are added to a queue, in that order. What sequence(s) of removing the elements from the queue is impossible, if any?

7.10 Generalize the solution to Problem 7.9. If elements 1, 2, 3, ..., n are added to a queue in that order, what sequences of removing the elements are not permissible?

7.11 It is conceivable that one linear structure is more general than another. Is it possible to implement a `Queue` using a `Stack`? What is the complexity of each of the `Queue` operations? Is it possible to implement a `Stack` using a `Queue`? What are the complexities of the various `Stack` methods?

7.12 Describe how we might efficiently implement a `Queue` as a pair of `Stacks`, called a "stack pair." (Hint: Think of one of the stacks as the head of the queue and the other as the tail.)

7.13 The implementation of `QueueLists` makes use of a `DoublyLinkedList`. Implement `QueueLists` in a manner that is efficient in time and space using `SinglyLinkedListElement` with a head and tail reference.

7.14 Burger Death needs to keep track of orders placed at the drive-up window. Design a data structure to support their ordering system.

Chapter 8

Iterators

"When I was One,/I had just begun.
When I was Two,/I was nearly new.
When I was Three,/I was hardly Me.
When I was Four,/I was not much more.
When I was Five,/I was just alive.
But now I am Six, I'm clever as clever.
So I think I'll be six now for ever and ever."
—"The End", by Alan Alexander Milne

PROGRAMS MOVE FROM ONE STATE TO ANOTHER. As we have seen, this "state" is composed of the current value of user variables as well as some notion of "where" the computer is executing the program. This chapter discusses *enumerations* and *iterators*—objects that hide the complexities of maintaining the state of a traversal of a data structure.

Ah! Interstate programs!

Consider a program that prints each of the values in a list. It is important to maintain enough information to know exactly "where we are" at all times. This might correspond to a reference to the current value. In other structures it may be less clear how the state of a traversal is maintained. Iterators help us hide these complexities. The careful design of these *control structures* involves, as always, the development of a useful interface that avoids compromising the iterator's implementation or harming the object it traverses.

8.1 Java's Enumeration Interface

Java defines an interface called an Enumeration that provides the user indirect, iterative access to each of the elements of an associated data structure, exactly once. The Enumeration is returned as the result of calling the elements method of various container classes. Every Enumeration provides two methods to the user:

```
public interface Enumeration {
    public boolean hasMoreElements();
    // pre: associated structure, S, is unchanged
    // post: true iff an element of S has yet to be enumerated

    public Object nextElement();
    // pre: S has more unenumerated elements
    // post: returns another element of S, marks it enumerated
}
```

Enumeration

The `hasMoreElements` method returns true if there are unvisited elements of the associated structure. When `hasMoreElements` returns false, the traversal is finished and the `Enumeration` expires. To access an element of the underlying structure, `nextElement` must be called. This method does two things: it returns a reference to the current element and then marks it visited. Typically `hasMoreElements` is the predicate of a `while` loop whose body processes a single element using `nextElement`. Clearly, `hasMoreElements` is an important method, as it provides a test to see if the precondition for the `nextElement` method is met.

The following code prints out a catchy phrase using a `Vector` enumeration:

HelloWorld

```java
public static void main(String args[])
{
    // construct a vector containing two strings:
    Vector v = new Vector();
    v.addElement("Hello");
    v.addElement("world!");

    // construct an enumeration to view values of v
    Enumeration e = v.elements();
    while (e.hasMoreElements())
    {
        // SILLY: v.insertElementAt("silly",1);
        System.out.print(e.nextElement()+" ");
    }
    System.out.println();
}
```

When run, the following immortal words are printed:

```
Hello world!
```

There are some important caveats that come with the use of Java's `Enumeration` construct. First, it is important to avoid modifying the associated structure while the `Enumeration` is active or *live*. Uncommenting the line marked `SILLY` causes the following infinite output to begin:

```
Hello silly silly silly silly silly silly
```

A silly virus vector! Inserting the string `"silly"` as the new second element of the `Vector` causes it to expand each iteration of the loop, making it difficult for the `Enumeration` to detect the end of the `Vector`.

Principle 14 *Never modify a data structure while an associated* `Enumeration` *is live.*

Modifying the structure behind an `Enumeration` can lead to unpredictable results. Clearly, if the designer has done a good job, the implementations of both the `Enumeration` and its associated structure are hidden. Making assumptions about their interaction can be dangerous.

Another subtle aspect of `Enumeration`s is that they do not guarantee a particular traversal order. All that is known is that each element will be visited exactly once before `hasMoreElements` becomes `false`. While we assume that the first example above will print out `Hello world!`, the opposite order may also be possible.

In the next sections, we develop the concept of an *iterator*.

8.2 The `Iterator` Interface

An `Iterator` is an `Enumerator` that traverses an associated data structure in a predictable order. Since this is a *behavior* and not necessarily a characteristic of its *interface*, it cannot be controlled or verified by a Java compiler. Instead, we must assume that developers of `Iterator`s will implement and document their structures in a manner consistent with the following interface:

```
public interface Iterator extends Enumeration
{
    public boolean hasMoreElements();
    // post: returns true if there is more structure to be viewed:
    //       i.e., if value (nextElement) can return a useful value.

    public Object nextElement();
    // pre: traversal has more elements
    // post: returns current value and increments the iterator

    public void reset();
    // post: the iterator is reset to the beginning of the traversal

    public Object value();
    // pre: traversal has more elements
    // post: returns the current value referenced by the iterator
}
```

Iterator

Every `Iterator` is also a Java `Enumeration`. By extending the `Enumeration` interface, we can use an `Iterator` in any context that requires an `Enumeration`. In this text we will depend entirely on the use of `Iterator`s. Along with the extension come two new methods: `reset` and `value`. The `reset` method reinitializes the `Iterator` for another traversal. The ability to traverse a structure multiple times can be useful when an algorithm makes multiple passes through a structure to perform a single logical operation. The same functionality can be achieved by constructing a new `Iterator` between passes. The `value` method of the `Iterator` retrieves a reference to the *current element* of the traversal. The same reference will be returned by the call to `nextElement`. Unlike `nextElement`, however, `value` does not push the traversal forward. This is useful when the current value of an `Iterator` is needed at a point logically distant from the call to `nextElement`.

The use of an `Iterator` leads to the following idiomatic loop for traversing a structure:

HelloWorld

```
public static void main(String args[])
{
    // construct a vector containing two strings:
    Vector v = new Vector();
    Iterator i;
    v.addElement("Hello");
    v.addElement("world!");

    // construct an iterator to view values of v
    for (i = v.elements(); i.hasMoreElements(); i.nextElement())
    {
        System.out.print(i.value()+" ");
    }
    System.out.println();
}
```

The result is the expected `Hello world!`

8.3   Example: `Vector` Iterators

For our first example, we design an `Iterator` to traverse a `Vector` called, not surprisingly, a `VectorIterator`. We do not expect the user to construct `VectorIterators` directly—instead the `Vector` hides the construction and returns the new structure as a generic `Iterator`, as was seen in the `HelloWorld` example. Here is the `elements` method:

Vector

```
public Iterator elements()
// post: returns an iterator (ordered enumeration) allowing one to
//       view elements of vector
{
    return new VectorIterator(this);
}
```

When a `Vector` constructs an `Iterator`, it provides a reference to *itself* (`this`) as a parameter. This reference is used by the `VectorIterator` to recall which `Vector` it is traversing.

We now consider the interface for a `VectorIterator`:

```
class VectorIterator implements Iterator
{
    public VectorIterator(Vector v)
    // post: constructs an initialized iterator associated with v
```

```
    public void reset()
    // post: the iterator is reset to beginning of the traversal

    public boolean hasMoreElements()
    // post: returns true if there is more structure to be traversed

    public Object value()
    // pre: traversal has more elements
    // post: returns the current value referenced by the iterator

    public Object nextElement()
    // pre: traversal has more elements
    // post: increments the iterated traversal
}
```

As is usually the case, the nonconstructor methods of `VectorIterator` exactly
match those required by the `Iterator` interface. Here is how the `VectorIter-
ator` is constructed and initialized:

```
protected Vector theVector;
protected int current;

public VectorIterator(Vector v)
// post: constructs an initialized iterator associated with v
{
    theVector = v;
    reset();
}

public void reset()
// post: the iterator is reset to beginning of the traversal
{
    current = 0;
}
```

The constructor saves a reference to the associated `Vector` and calls `reset`.
This logically attaches the `Iterator` to the `Vector` and makes the first element
(if one exists) current. Calling the `reset` method allows us to place all the
resetting code in one location.

To see if the traversal is finished, we invoke `hasMoreElements`:

```
public boolean hasMoreElements()
// post: returns true if there is more structure to be traversed
{
    return current < theVector.size();
}
```

This routine simply checks to see if the current index is valid. If the index
is less than the size of the `Vector`, then it can be used to retrieve a current
element from the `Vector`. The two value-returning methods are `value` and
`nextElement`:

```
public Object value()
// pre: traversal has more elements
// post: returns the current value referenced by the iterator
{
    return theVector.elementAt(current);
}

public Object nextElement()
// pre: traversal has more elements
// post: increments the iterated traversal
{
    return theVector.elementAt(current++);
}
```

The **value** method simply returns the current element. It may be called arbitrarily many times without pushing the traversal along. The **nextElement** method, on the other hand, returns the same reference, but only after having incremented **current**. The next value in the **Vector** (again, if there is one) becomes the current value.

Since all the **Iterator** methods have been implemented, Java will allow a **VectorIterator** to be used anywhere an **Iterator** is required. In particular, it can now be returned from the **elements** method of the **Vector** class.

Observe that while the user cannot directly construct a **VectorIterator** (it is a nonpublic class), the **Vector** can construct one on the user's behalf. This allows measured control over the agents that access data within the **Vector**. Also, an **Iterator** is a Java **interface**. It is not possible to directly construct an **Iterator**. We can, however, construct any class that implements the **Iterator** interface and use that as we would any instance of an **Iterator**.

Since an **Iterator** extends the **Enumeration** interface, we may use the value returned by **Vector**'s **elements** method as an **Enumeration** to access the data contained within the **Vector**. Of course, treating the **VectorIterator** as an **Enumeration** makes it difficult to call the **Iterator**-specific methods **reset** and **value**.

8.4   Example: List Iterators

The observant reader will note that all classes that implement the **Collection** class (see page 19) are required to provide an **elements** method. Since the **List** interface (see page 100) extends the **Collection** interface, all **Lists** are required to implement an **elements** method. We sketch the details of an **Iterator** over **SinglyLinkedLists** here. Implementations of other **List**-based iterators are similar.

When implmenting the **VectorIterator** it may be desirable to use only methods available through the **Vector**'s public interface to access the **Vector**'s data. Considering the **List** interface—an interface biased toward manipulating the ends of the structure—it is not clear how a traversal might be accomplished

without disturbing the underlying `List`. Since several `Iterators` may be active
on a single `List` at a time, it is important not to disturb the host structure.
As a result, efficient implementations of `ListIterators` must make use of the
protected fields of the `List` object.

The `SinglyLinkedListIterator` implements all of the standard `Iterator`
methods. To maintain its positioning within the `List`, the iterator maintains
two references: the head of the associated list and a reference to the current
node. The constructor and initialization methods appear as follows:

```
protected SinglyLinkedListElement current;
protected SinglyLinkedListElement head;

public SinglyLinkedListIterator(SinglyLinkedListElement t)
// post: returns an iterator that traverses a linked list
{
    head = t;
    reset();
}

public void reset()
// post: resets the iterator to point to the head of the list
{
    current = head;
}
```

SinglyLinked-
ListIterator

When called by the `SinglyLinkedList`'s `elements` method, the protected **head**
reference is passed along. The constructor caches away this value for use in
reset. The **reset** routine is then responsible for initializing **current** to the
value of **head**. The `Iterator` is able to refer to the `SinglyLinkedListElements`
because both structures are in the same package.

The value-returning routines visit each element and "increment" the **current**
reference by following the **next** reference:

```
protected SinglyLinkedListElement current;
protected SinglyLinkedListElement head;

public boolean hasMoreElements()
// post: returns true iff there are unvisited elements
{
    return current != null;
}

public Object nextElement()
// pre: hasMoreElements()
// post: returns value and advances iterator
{
    Object temp = current.value();
    current = current.next();
    return temp;
}
```

The traversal is finished when the `current` reference "falls off" the end of the `List` and becomes `null`.

Observe that the `Iterator` is able to develop references to values that are not accessible through the public interface of the underlying `List` structure. While it is of obvious utility to access the middle elements of the `List`, these references could be used to modify the associated `List` structure. If the objects referred to through the `Iterator` are modified, this underlying structure could become corrupted. One solution to the problem is to return copies or *clones* of the current object, but then the references returned are not really part of the `List`. The best advice is to think of the values returned by the `Iterator` as *read-only*.

Principle 15 *Assume that values returned by iterators are read-only.*

8.5 Example: Filtering Iterators

We now consider the construction of a *filtering iterator*. Instead of traversing structures, a filtering iterator traverses another iterator! As an example, we construct an iterator that returns the unique values of a structure.

Before we consider the implementation, we demonstrate its use with a simple example. In the following code, suppose that `data` is a `Vector` of `String`s, some of which may be duplicates. For example, the `Vector` could represent the text of the Gettysburg Address. The `elements` method of `data` is used to construct a `VectorIterator`. This is, in turn, used as a parameter to the construction of a `UniqueFilter`. Once constructed, the filter can be used as a standard `Iterator`, but only returns the first instance of each `String` appearing in the `Vector`:

UniqueFilter

```
Vector data = new Vector(1000);
   ...
Iterator dataIterator = data.elements();
Iterator ui = new UniqueFilter(dataIterator);
int count=0;

for (ui.reset(); ui.hasMoreElements(); ui.nextElement())
{
    System.out.print(ui.value()+" ");
    if (++count%8==0) System.out.println();
}
System.out.println();
```

The result of the program, when run on the Gettysburg Address, is the following output, which helps increase the vocabulary of this book by nearly 139 words:

```
four score and seven years ago our fathers
brought forth on this continent a new nation
```

```
conceived in liberty dedicated to the proposition that
all men are created equal now we engaged
great civil war testing whether or any so
can long endure met battlefield of have come
dedicate portion field as final resting place for
those who here gave their lives might live
it is altogether fitting proper should do but
larger sense cannot consecrate hallow ground brave living
dead struggled consecrated far above poor power add
detract world will little note nor remember what
say never forget they did us rather be
unfinished work which fought thus nobly advanced task
remaining before from these honored take increased devotion
cause last full measure highly resolve shall not
died vain under God birth freedom government people
by perish earth
```

Fans of compact writing will find this unique.

The UniqueFilter provides the same interface as other iterators. Its constructor, however, takes a "base" Iterator as its parameter:

```
protected Iterator base; // slave iterator
protected List observed;  // list of previous values

public UniqueFilter(Iterator baseIterator)
// pre: baseIterator is a non-null iterator
// post: constructs unique-value filter
//        host iterator is reset
{
    base = baseIterator;
    reset();
}

public void reset()
// post: master and base iterators are reset
{
    base.reset();
    observed = new SinglyLinkedList();
}
```

When the filter is reset, the base iterator is reset as well. We then construct an empty List of words previously observed. As the filter progresses, words encountered are incorporated into the observed list.

The current value is fetched by the value method. It just passes the request along to the base iterator. A similar technique is used with the hasMoreElements method:

```
public boolean hasMoreElements()
// post: returns true if there are more values available
//        from base stream
```

```
{
    return base.hasMoreElements();
}

public Object value()
// pre: traversal has more elements
// post: returns the current value referenced by the iterator
{
    return base.value();
}
```

Finally, the substance of the iterator is found in the remaining method, next-Element:

```
public Object nextElement()
// pre: traversal has more elements
// post: returns current value and increments the iterator
{
    Object current = base.nextElement();
    // record observation of current value
    observed.add(current);
    // now seek next new value
    while (base.hasMoreElements())
    {
        Object possible = base.value();
        if (!observed.contains(possible))
        {   // new value found! leave
            break;
        } else {
            // old value, continue
            base.nextElement();
        }
    }
    return current;
}
```

Because this routine can only be called if there is a current value, we record the current value in the observed list. The method then increments the base iterator until a new, previously unobserved value is produced, or the base iterator runs dry.

Some subtle details are worth noting here. First, while we have used a VectorIterator on a Vector of Strings, the UniqueFilter can be applied, as is, to any type of iterator and can deliver any type of value. All that is required is that the base type support the equals method. Secondly, as the filter iterator progresses, it forces the base iterator to progress, too. Because of this, two filters are usually not applied to the same base iterator, and the base iterator should never be modified while the filter is running.

8.6   Conclusions

We have seen that data structures can sometimes be used to control the way programs focus on and access data. This is made very explicit with Java's `Enumeration` construct that facilitates visiting all the elements of a structure.

When we wish to traverse the elements of a data structure in a predetermined order, we use an `Iterator`. The `Iterator` provides access to the elements of a structure using an interface that extends that of an `Enumeration`. We have also seen that there are weaknesses in the concept of both of these constructs, because they surrender some of the data hiding and access controls that are provided by the associated structure. Careful use of these controlling structures, however, can yield useful tools to make traversal of structures simpler.

Problems

8.1★   Since the `value` method is available to the `Iterator`, the `nextElement` method does not appear to need to return a value. Why does our implementation return the value?

8.2   Write an `Iterator` that works on `Strings`. Each value returned should be an object of type `Character`.

8.3   Write an `Iterator` that returns a stream of `Integers` that are prime.

8.4   Describe an implementation for an iterator associated with `Circular-Lists`.

8.5   Currently, we have seen no iterator implemented for a `Queue`. Implement an `Iterator` for `QueueArray`.

8.6   Currently, we have seen no iterator implemented for a `Stack`. Implement an `Iterator` for `StackVector`. (Recall that the top of the `Vector` is at the end of the `Stack`.)

8.7   Write an `Iterator` that, given a `Vector`, returns a new `Vector` for each of the $n!$ permutations of the original elements.

8.8   Write a filtering iterator, `ReverseIterator`, that reverses the stream of values produced by another `Iterator`. You may assume that the base `Iterator` will eventually have no more elements, but you may not bound the number.

8.9   Write a filtering iterator, `OrderedIterator`, that sorts the stream of values produced by another `Iterator`. You may assume that the base `Iterator` will eventually have no more elements, but you may not bound the number.

8.10   Write a filtering iterator, `ShuffleIterator`, that shuffles the stream of values produced by another `Iterator`. You may assume that the base `Iterator` will eventually have no more elements, but you may not bound the number.

8.11   Write a filtering iterator that takes a base iterator and an `Object` (called `predicate`) with a static `select` method defined. This iterator passes along only those values that generate `true` when passed to the `select` method of the `predicate` `Object`.

Chapter 9

Ordered Structures

WE HAVE MADE NO ASSUMPTIONS about the type of data we store within our structures—so far. Instead, we have assumed only that the data referenced are a subclass of the type `Object`. Recall that *all* classes are subtypes of `Object` in Java, so that is hardly a constraint. Data structures serve a purpose, often helping us perform tasks more complex than "just holding data." For example, we used the `Stack` and `Queue` classes to *guide* a search through search space in the previous chapter.

One important use of data structures is to help keep data in order—the smallest value in the structure might be stored "close to the front," while the largest value would be stored "close to the rear." Once a structure is ordered it becomes potentially useful as a mechanism for sorting. we simply insert our possibly unordered data into the structure, and then extract the values in order. To do this, however, it is necessary to *compare* data values to see if they are in the correct order. In this chapter we will discuss approaches to the various problems associated with maintaining ordered structures.

9.1 Comparable Objects

In languages like C++ it is possible to *override* the comparison operators (<, >, ==, etc.). When two objects are compared using these operators, a user-written method is called. Java does not support overriding of built-in operators. Thus, it is useful to come up with a convention for supporting *comparable* data.

First, let's look closely at the interface for Java's `Object`. Since every class inherits and extends the interface of the `Object` class, each of its methods may be applied to any class. For example, the `equals` method allows us to check if an `Object` is logically equal to another `Object`. In contrast, the == operator compares two *references* to see if they refer to the same *instance* of an object.

By default, the `equals` function returns `true` whenever two objects are "byte-for-byte" equivalent. This is often not the correct comparison, so the class designer should consider rewriting it as a class-specific method.

For our purposes, we wish to require of comparable classes a method that determines the relative order of objects. How do we *require* this? Through an interface! Since an interface is a contract, we simply wrap the `compareTo` method in a new interface, `Comparable`:

Comparable

```
public interface Comparable
{
    public int compareTo(Object item);
    // pre: item is non-null
    // post: returns value<0 if this<item; 0 if =; >0 if this>item
}
```

Pretty simple! Now, if we require that an object be a `Comparable` object, then we know that it may be compared to similarly typed data using the `compareTo` method.

(In versions of Java before 1.2, the `Comparable` interface is part of the `structure` package. In version 1.2 and later, the `Comparable` interface is automatically imported as part of the Java environment's `java.lang` package.)

9.1.1   Example: Comparable Integers

Throughout this text, we will assume that common types, such as `Integers` and `Strings`, are comparable. In versions of Java before 1.2, however, these types do not implement the `Comparable` interface and, as a result, they cannot be compared. In this section we construct a `ComparableInt` class that provides many of the features of the `Integer` class,[1] as well as a method that allows us to compare one "comparable integer" to another. The interface for this class appears as follows:

ComparableInt

```
public class ComparableInt implements Comparable
{
    public ComparableInt(int x)
    // post: construct an integer object that may be compared

    public int compareTo(Object other)
    // pre: other is a non-null ComparableInt
    // post: returns integer relative to 0
    //       describing relation between this and other

    public boolean equals(Object other)
    // pre: other is a ComparableInt
    // post: returns true iff other is logically equal

    public int value()
    // post: returns the value associated with this object
}
```

---

[1] Ideally, this class should be an *extension* of the `java.lang.Integer` class, but that class is declared `final`, meaning it cannot be extended.

A `ComparableInt` is constructed by passing it an integer. This integer is cached away—notice that we cannot tell how—where it can later be used to compare itself with another `ComparableInt`. The private data and the constructor that initializes them appear as follows:

```
protected Integer data; // where the integer is stored

public ComparableInt(int x)
// post: construct an integer object that may be compared
{
    data = new Integer(x);
}
```

We can see, now, that this class has a single protected `Integer` to actually hold the value. This could have been an `int`, but we potentially benefit—as we expand the functionality of a `ComparableInt`—from methods that have already been written for the `Integer` class. For the moment, we will only make use of the `Integer` constructor and `intValue` methods. The `ComparableInt` constructor calls the `Integer` constructor to set the value; the reverse is accomplished with the `value` method.[2]

```
public int value()
// post: returns the value associated with this object
{
    return data.intValue();
}
```

Now, let us turn to the `compareTo` method. Since the `Comparable` interface declares the `compareTo` method to take an `Object` parameter, it is necessary to declare the parameter as `Object`, even though we expect the parameter to be a `ComparableInt`. We could have declared the `compareTo` method to take a `ComparableInt`, but then the method would not have matched the `Comparable` `compareTo` method. Here is what we do:

```
public int compareTo(Object other)
// pre: other is a non-null ComparableInt
// post: returns integer relative to 0
//       describing relation between this and other
{
    Assert.pre(other instanceof ComparableInt,
            "compareTo expects a ComparableInt");
    ComparableInt that = (ComparableInt)other;
    return value() - that.value();
}
```

---

[2] The identifier `value` is used here, instead of using `Integer`'s `intValue`. This naming scheme is somewhat more robust when, for example, we wish to switch between `ComparableInt` and `ComparableDouble` values. Since the object is clearly an integer, the word `int` is hardly necessary in the accessor and works against maintaining portable and robust code.

Before we do anything with the object passed in, we invoke Java's built-in `instanceof` operator. This operator returns `true` when the object on the left can be considered an object of the type on the right. To convey to Java that we require the parameter to be a `ComparableInt` we *cast*, on the right side of the second line, the value of the parameter. This cast simply tells Java to consider `other` to be a `ComparableInt` (an implementation of `Comparable`) for use in the assignment. The third line, then, checks the order of two values: the integer value stored within `this` object is compared to the integer value stored in `that` object.

We now consider the `equals` method:

```
public boolean equals(Object other)
// pre: other is a ComparableInt
// post: returns true iff other is logically equal
{
    Assert.pre(other instanceof ComparableInt,
            "equals expects a ComparableInt");
    ComparableInt that = (ComparableInt)other;
    return value() == that.value();
    // alternatively:
    // return data.equals(otherInt.data);
}
```

What is important here is that the parameter to the `equals` method be declared as an `Object`. If it is not, then the programmer is writing a *new* method, rather than overriding the default method inherited from the `Object` class. Since equivalent `ComparableInts` may refer to different `Integers`, the default byte-by-byte comparison is not appropriate. Failure to implement the `equals` (or `compareTo`) method can lead to very subtle logical errors. We learn:

Principle 16 *Declare parameters of overriding methods with the most general types possible.*

To reiterate, failure to correctly declare these methods as generally as possible makes it unlikely that Java will call the correct method.

9.1.2   Example: Comparable Associations

Let us return now to the idea of an `Association`. An `Association` is a key-value pair, bound together in a single class. For the same reasons that it is sometimes nice to be able to compare integers, it is often useful to compare `Associations`. Recall that when we constructed an `Association` we took great care in defining the `equals` operator to work on just the **key** field of the `Association`. Similarly, when we extend the concept of an `Association` to its `Comparable` equivalent, we will have to be just as careful in constructing the `compareTo` method.

Unlike the `ComparableInt` class, the `ComparableAssociation` can be declared an extension of the `Association` class. The outline of this extension appears as follows:

Comparable-
Association

```
public class ComparableAssociation
    extends Association
    implements Comparable
{

    public ComparableAssociation(Comparable key)
    // pre: key is non-null
    // post: constructs comparable association with null value

    public ComparableAssociation(Comparable key, Object value)
    // pre: key is non-null
    // post: constructs ass'n between comparable key and a value

    public int compareTo(Object other)
    // pre: other is non-null ComparableAssociation
    // post: returns integer representing relation between values
}
```

Notice that there are very few methods. Since `ComparableAssociation` is an *extension* of the `Association` class, all of the methods written for `Association` are available for use with `ComparableAssociations`. The only additions are those above. Because one of the additional methods is the `compareTo` method, it meets the specification of what it means to be `Comparable`; thus we claim it implements the `Comparable` interface.

Let's look carefully at the implementation. First, as with the `Association` class, there are two constructors for `ComparableAssociations`. The first constructor initializes the key and sets the value reference to null, while the second initializes both `key` and `value`:

```
public ComparableAssociation(Comparable key)
// pre: key is non-null
// post: constructs comparable association with null value
{
    this(key,null);
}


public ComparableAssociation(Comparable key, Object value)
// pre: key is non-null
// post: constructs ass'n between comparable key and a value
{
    super(key,value);
}
```

Remember that there are two special methods available to constructors: `this` and `super`. The `this` method calls another constructor with a different set of parameters (if the parameters are not different, the constructor could be recursive!). We write one very general-purpose constructor, and any special-purpose constructors call the general constructor with reconsidered parameter values. The `super` method is a means of calling the constructor for the superclass—the class we are extending—`Association`. The second constructor simply calls the constructor for the superclass. The first constructor calls the second constructor (which, in turn, calls the superclass's constructor) with a `null value` field. All of this is necessary to be able to construct `ComparableAssociations` using the `Association`'s constructors.

Now, the `compareTo` method is a little tricky:

```
public int compareTo(Object other)
// pre: other is non-null ComparableAssociation
// post: returns integer representing relation between values
{
    Assert.pre(other instanceof ComparableAssociation,
                "compareTo expects a ComparableAssociation");
    ComparableAssociation that = (ComparableAssociation)other;
    Comparable thisKey = (Comparable)this.key();
    Comparable thatKey = (Comparable)that.key();

    return thisKey.compareTo(thatKey);
}
```

Because the `compareTo` method must implement the `Comparable` interface, its parameter is an `Object`. In fact, the precondition requires the parameter to be a `ComparableAssociation`. We access the parameter through an intermediate, temporary variable, `that`, that has type `ComparableAssociation`.

Principle 17 *Avoid multiple casts of the same object by assigning the value to a temporary variable.*

Since `ComparableAssociations` are associations with comparable keys, we know that the `key` within the association has a `compareTo` method. Java is not able to figure this out, so we must give it hints, by casting the appropriate `key` references. Casting, here, is essentially a catalyst to get Java to verify that a referenced object has certain type characteristics. In any case, we get access to both `keys` through independent variables. These allow us to make the comparison by calling the `compareTo` method on the comparable objects. Very little logic is directly encoded in these routines; we mostly make use of the prewritten code to accomplish what we need.

In the next few sections we consider features that we can provide to existing data structures, provided that the underlying data are known to be comparable.

9.2 Keeping Structures Ordered

Now that we have developed the notion of comparable data, we can make use of this ordering to organize our structure. Keeping data in order, however, places significant constraints on the type of operations that should be allowed. If a comparable value is added to a structure that orders its elements, the relative position of the new value is determined by the data, not the structure. Since this placement decision is predetermined, ordered structures have little flexibility in their interface. It is not possible, for example, to insert data at random locations. While simpler to use, these operations also tend to be more costly than their unordered counterparts. Typically, the increased *energy* required is the result of an increase in the number of decisions needed to accomplish insertions and removals.

The implementation of the various structures we see in the remainder of this chapter leads to algorithms for sorting, as we will see in Section 9.2.3.

9.2.1 The OrderedStructure Interface

Recall that a `Collection` is any traversable structure that allows us to add and remove elements and perform membership checks (see Section 1.7). Since the `Collection` interface is an extension of the `Store` interface, a `Collection` also requires the usual size-related methods (e.g., `size`, `isEmpty`, `clear`). None of these methods actually requires that the data within the structure be kept in order. To ensure that the structures we create order their data, we make them abide by an extended interface—an `OrderedStructure`:

```
public interface OrderedStructure extends Collection
{
}
```

Ordered-
Structure

Amazingly enough we have accomplished something for nothing! Actually, what is happening is that we are using the *type* to store the fact that the data are kept in sorted order. Implied in this, of course, is that we are working with `Comparable` values.

The emperor wears no clothes!

9.2.2 The Ordered Vector

We can now consider the implementation of an ordered `Vector` of values. Since it implements an `OrderedStructure` we know that the order in which elements are added does not directly determine the order in which they are ultimately removed. Instead, when elements are added to an `OrderedVector` they are kept in ascending order.

Constructing an ordered vector requires little more than allocating the underlying vector:

```
public OrderedVector()
// post: constructs an empty, ordered vector
{
    data = new Vector();
}
```

OrderedVector

Rather obviously, if there are no elements in the underlying `Vector`, then all of the elements are in order. Initially, at least, the structure is in a consistent state. We must always be mindful of consistency.

Because finding the correct location for a value is important to both adding and removing values, we focus on the development of an appropriate search technique for `OrderedVectors`. This process is much like looking up a word in a dictionary, or a name in a phone book (see Figure 9.1). First we look at the value half way through the vector and determine if the value for which we are looking is bigger or smaller than this *median*. If it is smaller, we restart our search with the left half of the structure. If it is bigger, we restart our search with the right half of the `Vector`. Whenever we consider a section of the `Vector` consisting of a single element, the search can be terminated, with the success of the search dependent on whether or not the indicated element contains the desired value. This approach is called *binary search*.

We present here the code for determining the index of a value in an `Ordered-Vector`. Be aware that if the value is not in the vector, the routine returns the ideal location to insert the value, and may be a location that is outside the vector.

```
protected int indexOf(Comparable target)
// pre: target is a non-null comparable object
// post: returns ideal position of value in vector
{
    Comparable midValue;
    int low = 0;  // lowest possible location
    int high = data.size(); // highest possible location
    int mid = (low + high)/2; // low <= mid <= high
    // mid == high iff low == high
    while (low < high) {
        // get median value
        midValue = (Comparable)data.elementAt(mid);
        // determine on which side median resides:
        if (midValue.compareTo(target) < 0) {
            low = mid+1;
        } else {
            high = mid;
        }
        // low <= high
        // recompute median index
        mid = (low+high)/2;
    }
    return low;
}
```

Each iteration through the loop, `low` and `high` determine the bounds of the vector currently being searched. `mid` is computed to be the middle element (if there are an even number of elements being considered, it is the leftmost of the two middle elements). This middle element is compared with the parameter and the bounds are adjusted to further constrain the search. Since the portion of the vector participating in the search is roughly halved each time, the total number of times around the loop is approximately $O(\log_2 n)$. This is a considerable improvement over the implementation of the `indexOf` method for `Vectors` of arbitrary elements—that routine is *linear* in the size of the structure.

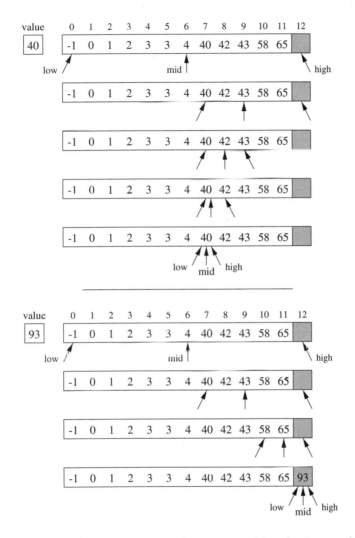

Figure 9.1   Finding the correct location for a comparable value in an ordered array. The top search finds a value in the array; the bottom search fails to find the value, but finds the correct point of insertion. The shaded area is not part of the vector during search.

Notice that `indexOf` is declared as a `protected` member of the class. This makes it impossible for a user to call directly, and makes it more difficult for a user to write code that depends on the underlying implementation. To convince yourself of the utility of this, both `OrderedStructures` of this chapter have exactly the same interface (so these two data types can be interchanged), but they are completely different structures. If the `indexOf` method were made public, then code could be written that makes use of this `Vector`-specific method, and it would be impossible to switch implementations.

Implementation of the `indexOf` method makes most of the nontrivial `OrderedVector` methods more straightforward. The `add` operator simply adds an element to the `Vector` in the location indicated by the `indexOf` operator:

```
public void add(Object value)
// pre: value is non-null
// post: inserts value, leaves vector in order
{
    int position = indexOf((Comparable)value);
    data.insertElementAt(value,position);
}
```

It is interesting to note that the cost of looking up the value is $O(\log n)$, but the `insertElementAt` for relatively "small" values *can* take $O(n)$ time to insert. Thus, the worst (and expected—see Problem 9.12) case time complexity of the `add` operation is $O(n)$, linear in the size of the structure. In reality, for large vectors, the time required to find the index of a value using the `OrderedVector` method is significantly reduced over the time required using the underlying `Vector` method. If the cost of comparing two objects exceeds the cost of assigning one object to another, the use of binary search can be expected to reduce the cost of the `add` operation by as much as a factor of two.

Both `contains` and `remove` can also make use of the `indexOf` operator. First, we consider testing to see if an element is contained by the `OrderedVector`:

```
public boolean contains(Object value)
// pre: value is non-null
// post: returns true if the value is in the vector
{
    int position = indexOf((Comparable)value);
    return (position < size()) &&
            data.elementAt(position).equals(value);
}
```

We simply attempt to find the item in the `Vector`, and if the location returned contains the value we desire, we return `true`; otherwise we return `false`. Since `indexOf` takes $O(\log n)$ time and the check for element equality is constant, the total complexity of the operation is $O(\log n)$. The `Vector` version of the same operation is $O(n)$ time. This is a considerable improvement.

The **return** statement, you will note, returns the result of a *logical and* (**&&**) operator. This is a *short-circuiting* operator: if, after evaluating the left half of the expression, the ultimate value of the expression is known to be false, then the second expression is not evaluated. That behavior is used here to avoid calling the **elementAt** operator with a **position** that might exceed the size of the structure, that is, the length of the **Vector**. This is a feature of many languages, but a potential trap if you ever consider reordering your boolean expressions.

Removing a value from an **OrderedVector** involves finding it within the **Vector** and then explicitly extracting it from the structure:

```
public Object remove(Object value)
// pre: value is non-null
// post: removes one instance of value, if found in vector
{
    if (contains(value)) {
        // we know value is pointed to by indexOf
        int position = indexOf((Comparable)value);
        // since vector contains value, position < size()
        // keep track of the value for return
        Object target = data.elementAt(position);
        // remove the value from the underlying vector
        data.removeElementAt(position);
        return target;
    }
    return null;
}
```

Like **add**, the operation has complexity $O(n)$. But it executes faster than its **Vector** equivalent, **removeElement**.

Note that by keeping the elements sorted, we have made adding and removing an element from the **OrderedVector** relatively symmetric: the expected complexity of each method is $O(n)$. Yet, in the underlying **Vector**, an **addElement** operation takes constant time, while the **removeElement** operation takes $O(n)$ time.

Extracting values in order from an **OrderedStructure** is accomplished by an iterator returned from the **elements** method. Because the elements are stored in the correct order in the **Vector**, the method need only return the value of the **Vector**'s **elements** method:

```
public Iterator elements()
// post: returns an iterator for traversing vector
{
    return data.elements();
}
```

The ease of implementing this particular method reassures us that our layout of values within the vector (in ascending order) is appropriate.

The rest of the `OrderedVector` operators repackage similar operators from the underlying `Vector` class:

```java
public boolean isEmpty()
// post: returns true if the OrderedVector is empty
{
    return data.size() == 0;
}

public void clear()
// post: vector is emptied
{
    data.setSize(0);
}

public int size()
// post: returns the number of elements in vector
{
    return data.size();
}
```

This "repackaging" brings up a point: *Why is it necessary?* If one were to, instead, consider the `OrderedVector` to be an *extension* of the `Vector` class, much of this repackaging would be unnecessary, because each of the repackaged methods could be inherited, and those—like `add`, `contains`, and `remove`—that required substantial reconsideration could be rewritten overriding the methods provided in the underlying `Vector` class.

That's all true! There's one substantial drawback, however, that is uncovered by asking a simple question: *Is an `OrderedVector` suitably used wherever a `Vector` is used?* The answer is: *No!* Consider the following hypothetical code that allocates an `OrderedVector` for use as a `Vector`:

```java
static void main(String args[])
{
    Vector v = new OrderedVector();

    v.addElement("Michael's Pizza");
    v.insertElementAt("Cozy Pizza",1);
    v.insertElementAt("Hot Tomatoes Pizza",0);
}
```

First, `addElement` and `insertElementAt` are not methods for `OrderedVec-tors`. Arguably, the `add` could be renamed to `addElement`.[3] Assuming this could be done, the semantics become problematic. We are inserting elements at specific locations within a `Vector`, but it is really an `OrderedVector`. The

---

[3] This is a substantial reconsideration, since the `add` method is required by the `Collection` and `OrderedStructure` interfaces. Any change to accommodate consistency with `Vectors` would require changes in many other data structures.

values inserted violate the ordering of elements and the postconditions of the add method of the `OrderedVector`.

We now consider a simple application of `OrderedStructures`—sorting.

9.2.3   Example: Sorting

Now that we have seen the implementation of an `OrderedStructure`, we can use these structures to sort comparable values. (Obviously, if values are not comparable, it is hard to see how they might be sorted.) Here is a program to sort integers appearing on the input:

Sort

```
public static void main(String[] args)
{
    ReadStream r = new ReadStream(System.in);
    OrderedStructure o = new OrderedVector();
    // read in integers
    for (r.skipWhite(); !r.eof(); r.skipWhite())
    {
        o.add(new Integer(r.readInt()));
    }
    // and print them out, in order
    Iterator i = o.elements();
    for (i.reset(); i.hasMoreElements(); i.nextElement())
    {
        System.out.println(i.value());
    }
}
```

In this simple program a sequence of numbers is read from the input stream. Each number is placed within an `Integer`,[4] which is then inserted into the `OrderedStructure`, in this case an `OrderedVector`. The insertion of this value into the vector may involve moving, on average, $\frac{n}{2}$ elements out of the way. As the n values are added to the vector, a total of $O(n^2)$ values have to be moved. The overall effect of this loop is to perform insertion sort! Once the values have been inserted in the ordered structure, we can use an iterator to traverse the vector in order and print out the values in order. If the `OrderedVector` is substituted with any structure that meets the `OrderedStructure` interface, similar results are generated, but the performance of the sorting algorithm is determined by the complexity of insertion.

We now turn to a second implementation of the `OrderedStructure` interface built using `List`s.

9.2.4   The Ordered List

Arbitrarily inserting an element into a list is difficult, since it requires moving to the middle of the list to perform the addition. The lists we have developed

---

[4] We assume, at this point, that Java's `Integer` class implements `Comparable`.

are biased toward adding and removing values from their ends. Thus, we choose to use the underlying structure of a `SinglyLinkedList` to provide the basis for our `OrderedList` class. First, we declare the class as an implementation of the `OrderedStructure` interface:

OrderedList

```
public class OrderedList implements OrderedStructure
```

The constructor sets up the structure by calling the **clear** method required by the `Store` interface:

```
protected SinglyLinkedListElement data; // smallest value
protected int count;          // number of values in list

public OrderedList()
// post: constructs an empty ordered list
{
    clear();
}

public void clear()
// post: the ordered list is empty
{
    data = null;
    count = 0;
}
```

Again, the advantage of this technique is that changes to the initialization of the underlying data structure can be made in one place within the code.

To warm up to the methods that we will soon have to write, let's consider implementation of the **contains** method. It uses the "finger" technique from our work with `SinglyLinkedLists`:

```
public boolean contains(Object value)
// pre: value is non-null comparable object
// post: returns true iff contains value
{
    SinglyLinkedListElement finger = data; // target
    Comparable cValue = (Comparable)value; // value sought
    // search down list until we fall off or find bigger value
    while ((finger != null) &&
            (((Comparable)finger.value()).compareTo(cValue) < 0))
    {
        finger = finger.next();
    }
    return finger != null && cValue.equals(finger.value());
}
```

This code is very similar to the **contains** method of the `SinglyLinkedList` class, except that because the list is always kept in order, it can stop searching if it finds an element that is larger than the desired element. This leads to a behavior that is linear in the size of the list, but in the case when a value is not in the list, it terminates—on average—half way down the list. For programs that make heavy use of looking up values in the structure, this can yield dramatic improvements in speed.

Now, let us consider the addition of an element to the `OrderedList`. Since the elements of the `OrderedList` are kept in order constantly, we must be careful to preserve that ordering after we have inserted the value. Here is the code:

```
public void add(Object value)
// pre: value is non-null
// post: value is added to the list, leaving it in order
{
    SinglyLinkedListElement previous = null; // element to adjust
    SinglyLinkedListElement finger = data;   // target element
    Comparable cValue = (Comparable)value;   // the inserted value
    // search for the correct location
    while ((finger != null) &&
            (((Comparable)finger.value()).compareTo(cValue) < 0))
    {
        previous = finger;
        finger = finger.next();
    }
    // spot is found, insert
    if (previous == null) // check for insert at top
    {
        data = new SinglyLinkedListElement(cValue,data);
    } else {
        previous.setNext(
            new SinglyLinkedListElement(cValue,previous.next()));
    }
    count++;
}
```

Here we use the "finger" technique with an additional `previous` reference to help the insertion of the new element. The first loop takes, on average, linear time to find a position where the value can be inserted. After the loop, the `previous` reference refers to the element that will refer to the new element, or is `null`, if the element should be inserted at the head of the list. Notice that we use the `SinglyLinkedListElement` methods to ensure that we reuse code that works, and to make sure that the elements are constructed with reasonable values in their fields.

One of the most common mistakes made is to forget to do important bookkeeping. Remember to increment `count` when inserting a value, and to decrement `count` when removing a value. When designing and implementing structures, it is sometimes useful to look at each method from the point of view of each of the bookkeeping variables that you maintain.

Principle 18 *Consider your code from different points of view.*

Removing a value from the `OrderedList` first performs a check to see if the value is included, and then, if it is, removes it.

```
public Object remove(Object value)
// pre: value is non-null
// post: an instance of value is removed, if in list
{
    SinglyLinkedListElement previous = null; // element to adjust
    SinglyLinkedListElement finger = data;   // target element
    Comparable cValue = (Comparable)value;   // value to remove
    // search for value or fall off list
    while ((finger != null) &&
            (((Comparable)finger.value()).compareTo(cValue) < 0))
    {
        previous = finger;
        finger = finger.next();
    }
    // did we find it?
    if ((finger != null) && cValue.equals(finger.value())) {
        // yes, remove it
        if (previous == null)  // at top?
        {
            data = finger.next();
        } else {
            previous.setNext(finger.next());
        }
        count--;
        // return value
        return finger.value();
    }
    // return nonvalue
    return null;
}
```

When removing the value we return a reference to the value found in the list.

Again, because the `SinglyLinkedListIterator` accepts a `SinglyLinked-ListElement` as its parameter, the implementation of the `OrderedList`'s `elements` method is particularly simple:

```
public Iterator elements()
// post: returns an iterator over ordered list
{
    return new SinglyLinkedListIterator(data);
}
```

The remaining size-related procedures follow those found in the implementation of `SinglyLinkedLists`.

9.2.5   Example: The Modified Parking Lot

In Section 6.2 we implemented a system for maintaining rental contracts for a small parking lot. With our knowledge of ordered structures, we now return to that example to incorporate a new feature—an alphabetical listing of contracts.

As customers rent spaces from the parking office, contracts are added to a generic list of associations between renter names and lot assignments. We now change that structure to reflect a better means of keeping track of this information—an ordered list of comparable associations. This structure is declared as an `OrderedStructure`, but assigned an instance of an `OrderedList`:

Renter— ambiguous noun: (1) one who rents from others, (2) one who rents to others.

```
OrderedStructure rented = new OrderedList(); // rented spaces
```

When a renter fills out a contract, the name of the renter and the parking space information are bound together into a single `ComparableAssociation`:

```
String renter = r.readString();
// link renter with space description
rented.add(new ComparableAssociation(renter,location));
System.out.println("Space "+location.number+" rented.");
```

ParkingLot2

Notice that the renters' name is placed into a `String`. Since `String`s support the `compareTo` method they implement the `Comparable` interface.

At this point, the `rented` structure has all contracts sorted by name. To print these contracts out, we accept a new command, `contracts`:

```
if (command.equals("contracts"))
{   // print out contracts in alphabetical order
    Iterator ci = rented.elements();
    for (ci.reset(); ci.hasMoreElements(); ci.nextElement())
    {   // extract contract from iterator
        ComparableAssociation contract =
            (ComparableAssociation)ci.value();
        // extract person from contract
        String person = (String)contract.key();
        // extract parking slot description from contract
        Space slot = (Space)contract.value();
        // print it out
        System.out.println(person+" is renting "+slot.number);

    }
}
```

An iterator for the `OrderedStructure` is used to retrieve each of the `ComparableAssociation`s, from which we extract and print the renters' names in alphabetical order. If an alternative order were desired, it would be necessary to change the action of the `equals` method of the underlying datatype. Here, since we're using `String`s, that would be difficult. Fortunately, ascending order is usually sufficient.

Here is an example run of the program (the user's input is indented):

```
    rent small Carol
Space 2 rented.
    rent small Alice
Space 1 rented.
    rent large David
Space 9 rented.
    contracts
Alice is renting 1
Carol is renting 2
David is renting 9
    return Alice
Space 1 is now free.
    rent medium Eva
Space 8 rented.
    rent small Bob
Space 0 rented.
    contracts
Bob is renting 0
Carol is renting 2
David is renting 9
Eva is renting 8
    quit
6 slots remain available.
```

Note that, for each of the requests for contracts, the contracts are listed in alphabetical order. This example is particularly interesting since the concept of an ordered structure avoids the need to sort the contracts before they are printed each time and that the interface meshes well with software that doesn't use ordered structures. While running an orderly parking lot can be a tricky business, it is considerably simplified if you understand the subtleties of ordered structures.

9.3   Conclusions

Computers spend considerable amounts of time maintaining ordered data structures. In Java we described an ordering of data values using the comparison operator, `compareTo`. Data that fail to have an operator such as `compareTo` cannot be totally ordered in a predetermined manner. Java enforces the development of an ordering using the `Comparable` interface—an interface that simply requires the implementation of the `compareTo` method.

Once data values may be compared and put in order, it is natural to design a data structure that keeps its values in order. Disk directories, dictionaries, filing cabinets, and zip-code ordered mailing lists are all obvious examples of abstract structures whose utility depends directly on their ability to efficiently maintain a consistently ordered state. Here we extend various unordered structures in a way that allows them to maintain the natural ordering of the underlying data.

Problems

9.1   Describe the contents of an `OrderedVector` after each of the following values has been added: 1, 9, 0, −1, and 3.

9.2   Describe the contents of an `OrderedList` after each of the following values has been added: 1, 9, 0, −1, and 3.

9.3⋆   Suppose duplicate values are added to an `OrderedVector`. Where is the oldest value found (with respect to the newest)?

9.4   Suppose duplicate values are added to an `OrderedList`. Where is the oldest value found (with respect to the newest)?

9.5   Under what conditions would you use an `OrderedVector` over an `OrderedList`?

9.6   At what point does the Java environment complain about your passing of a non-`Comparable` value to an `OrderedVector`?

9.7⋆   Write the `compareTo` method for the `String` class.

9.8⋆   Write the `compareTo` method for a class that is to be ordered by a field, `key`, which is a `double`. Be careful: the result of `compareTo` must be an `int`.

9.9   Write the `compareTo` method for a class describing a person whose name is stored as two `Strings`: `first` and `last`. A person is "less than" another if they appear before the other in a list alphabetized by last name and then first name (as is typical).

9.10⋆   Previous editions of the `structures` package opted for the use of a `lessThan` method instead of a `compareTo` method. The `lessThan` method would return `true` exactly when one value was `lessThan` another. Are these approaches the same, or is one more versatile?

9.11   Show that the expected insertion time of an element into an `OrderedList` is $O(n)$.

9.12   Show that the expected insertion time of an element into an `OrderedVector` is $O(n)$.

9.13   Suppose we extended the definition of an ordered structure to include an `elementAt` method that takes an integer, i. This method returns the ith element of the `OrderedStructure`. What are the best- and worst-case running times for this method on `OrderedVector` and `OrderedList`?

9.14   Your department is interested in keeping track of information about majors. Design a data structure that will maintain useful information for your department. The roster of majors, of course, should be ordered by last name (and then by first, if there are multiple students with the same last name).

Chapter 10

Trees

*"I think that I shall never see
A poem lovely as a binary tree."*
—Bill Amend as Jason Fox

RECURSION IS A BEAUTIFUL APPROACH TO STRUCTURING. We commonly think of recursion as a form of structuring the *control* of programs, but self-reference can be used just as effectively in the structuring of program *data*. In this chapter, we investigate the use of recursion in describing branching structures called *trees*.

Most of the structures we have investigated are *linear*—their natural presentation is in a line. Trees branch. The result is that where there is an inherent ordering in linear structures, we find choices in the way we order the elements of a tree. These "choices" are an indication of the reduced "friction" of the structure and, as a result, trees provide us the fastest ways to solve many problems.

Before we investigate the implementation of trees, we must develop a concise terminology.

10.1 Terminology

A tree is a collection of elements, called *nodes*, and relations between them, called *edges*. Usually, data are stored within the nodes of a tree. We say that two trees are *disjoint* if no node or edge is found common to both. A *trivial tree* has no nodes and thus no data. An isolated node is also a tree.

From these primitives we may recursively construct more complex trees. Let r be a new node and let $\{T_i\}$ be a (possibly empty) set—a *forest*—of distinct trees. A new tree is constructed by making r the root of the tree, and establishing an edge between r and the root of each tree, T_i, in the forest. We depend on drawing trees in a standard orientation—with the root above and the trees below. Figure 10.1g is an aid to understanding this construction.

The *parent* of a node is the unique adjacent node appearing above it (see Figure 10.2). The *root* of a tree is the unique node with no parent. The *ancestors* of a node n are the roots of trees containing n: n, n's parent, n's parent's parent, and so on. The root is the ancestor shared by every node in the tree. A *child* of a node n is any node that has n as its parent. The *descendants* of a node n are those nodes that have n as an ancestor. A *leaf* is a node with no children. Note that n is its own ancestor and descendant. A node m is the *proper ancestor* (*proper descendant*) of a node n if m is an ancestor (descendant) of n, but not vice versa. In a tree T, the descendants of n form the *subtree* of T rooted at n.

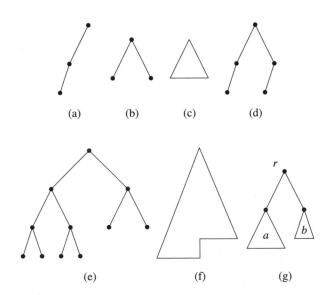

Figure 10.1 Examples of trees. Trees *a* and *b* are three-node trees. Trees are sometimes symbolized abstractly, as in *c*. Tree *b* is *full*, but *d* is not. Tree *e* is not full, but is *complete*. Complete trees are symbolized as in *f*. Abstract tree *g* has root *r* and subtrees *a* and *b*.

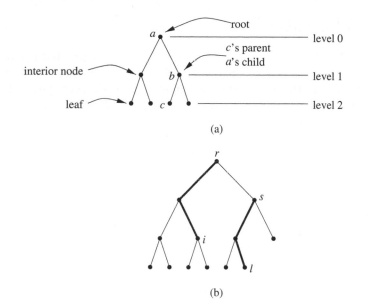

(a)

(b)

Figure 10.2   Anatomy of trees. In (a), a full (and complete) tree. In (b), a complete tree that is not full. Here, the unique path from node i to root r is bold: i has depth 2. Also bold is a longest path from s to a leaf l: s has height 2 and depth 1.

Any node of a tree T that is not a leaf is an *interior node*. Roots can be interior nodes. Nodes m and n are *siblings* if they share a parent. (We will occasionally use the familial terms *cousin*, *uncle*, and *niece* where the meaning is obvious.)

A *path* is the unique shortest sequence of edges from a node n to an ancestor. The *length* of a path is the number of edges it mentions. The *height of a node*, n, in a tree is the length of a longest path between a leaf and n. The *height of a tree* is the height of its root. This is the maximum height of any node in the tree. The *depth* (or *level*) of a node n in its tree T is the length of the path from n to T's root. The sum of a node's depth and height is no greater than the height of the tree.[1] The *degree of a node* n is the number of its children. The *degree of a tree* (or its *arity*) is the maximum degree of any of its nodes. A *binary tree* is a tree with arity less than or equal to 2. A 1-ary binary tree is termed *degenerate*. A node n in a binary tree is *full* if it has degree two. In an *oriented tree* we will call one child the *left child* and the other the *right child*. A *full binary tree* of height h has leaves only on level h, and each of its internal nodes is full. The addition of a node to a full binary tree causes its height to increase. A *complete binary tree* of height h is a full binary tree with 0 or more of the "rightmost" leaves of level h removed.

---

[1] It is less if the node is not on any longest path from the root to a leaf.

10.2   The Interface

Our approach to binary trees is to describe a simple interface that can be used in an implementation-independent manner. This interface makes use of a reference that travels about the tree, called a *cursor*. As with `Iterators`, the cursor allows us to move about the structure, but unlike the `Iterator`, the cursor can be used to direct modifications of the binary tree, including insertions, modifications, and deletions.

Before we discuss many of the details, we investigate what it means to be a `BinaryTree` (right-handed methods have been omitted):

BinaryTree

```java
public class BinaryTree
{
    public BinaryTree()
    // post: creates an empty binary tree

    public void clear()
    // post: removes all nodes from tree

    public void insert(Object value)
    // pre: cursor is null (invalid)
    // post: if tree is empty, value is inserted at root; otherwise
    //         value is inserted where cursor last moved off tree

    public Object remove()
    // pre: cursor is valid and has no children
    // post: leaf is removed; cursor is moved to parent, if any

    public Object value()
    // pre: cursor valid
    // post: returns value of object at cursor

    public void setValue(Object value)
    // pre: cursor valid
    // post: sets value found at cursor

    public void reset()
    // post: moves the cursor to the root, if any

    public boolean valid()
    // post: returns true if the cursor points to a valid node

    public boolean hasLeft()
    // post: returns true iff cursor has left child

    public boolean hasParent()
    // pre: cursor is valid
    // post: returns true iff cursor has parent
```

```
      public boolean isLeftChild()
      // post: returns true if cursor has parent and is left child

      public void moveLeft()
      // pre: cursor is valid
      // post: cursor moves to left child of precursor, or off tree

      public void moveUp()
      // pre: cursor is valid
      // post: cursor moves up to parent of precursor

      public boolean isEmpty()
      // post: returns true iff tree is empty

      public int size()
      // post: returns number of nodes in tree

      public Iterator elements()
      // post: returns inorder traversal of tree
  }
```

Initially, the `BinaryTree` is empty, and the cursor does not point to a valid node. To add a new value to the binary tree we use the `insert` method. This extends the tree by adding a new leaf—the root. Once a tree has nodes, the user *A sprout!* can check whether the cursor references a valid node with the `valid` method. If the node is `valid`, its value may be retrieved with the `value` method or updated with the `setValue` method. When pointing to a valid node, the cursor can be moved left or right (to a child), or up (to a parent). When the cursor "falls off the tree" (becomes invalid) it may be repositioned to the root with the `reset` method. The `clear` method removes all nodes present in the tree. The `remove` method removes the leaf referenced by the tree's cursor.

One novel feature of this interface is the `insert` method. As suggested above, this method inserts a new node into an empty tree. For larger structures we use the cursor to indicate the appropriate location for a newly inserted value: the cursor is first moved "off the tree" by a `moveLeft` or `moveRight`, and then a call is made to `insert` to place the value in the tree at that location. An alternative implementation of insertion methods provides three methods—`insertLeft`, `insertRight`, and `insertRoot`—that handle each of the three cases. The first two methods are cursor-relative, and the last is only a possibility when the tree is empty. We are motivated to go with the first design because

1. The interface is simpler. Fewer methods make a structure more compact and less daunting to users.

2. The design considers usage. Many insertions into binary trees occur at points where the cursor has become invalid. An algorithm attempts to find a suitable location for a value in a tree by searching for it. If none is found, the point of failure is an ideal place for insertion.

3. The usage is consistent. In the alternative design, two of the methods are cursor-relative and depend on a valid cursor. The root-oriented method depends on the cursor being *invalid*. In our design, the `insert` method inserts new values where a cursor is found to be invalid.

We expect, of course, that there will be a tradeoff. In particular, it seems that when the cursor falls off the tree, the tree must remember *how* that happened so that any impending insert can be accomplished correctly. Should we decide later to expand the repertoire of insertion routines, it is fairly easy to see that the alternative implementation can be engineered in terms of our single-method insert (see Problem 10.8).

10.3 Motivating Example: Expression Trees

Most programming languages involve mathematical expressions that are composed of binary operations applied to values. An example from Java is the simple expression R = 1 + (L-1)*2. This expression involves four operators (=, +, -, and *), and 5 values (R, 1, L, 1, and 2). Languages often represent expressions using binary trees. Each value in the expression appears as a leaf, while the operators are internal nodes that represent the reduction of two values to one (for example, L-1 is reduced to a single value for use on the left side of the multiply). The *expression tree* associated with the above expression is shown in Figure 10.3a. We might imagine that the following code constructs the tree and prints −1:

```
BinaryTreeNode v1a,v1b,v2,vL,vR,t;

// set up values 1 and 2, and declare variables
v1a = new BinaryTreeNode(new value(1));
v1b = new BinaryTreeNode(new value(1));
v2 = new BinaryTreeNode(new value(2));
vL = new BinaryTreeNode(new variable("L",0));// L=0
vR = new BinaryTreeNode(new variable("R",0));// R=0

// set up expression
t = new BinaryTreeNode(new operator('-'),vL,v1a);
t = new BinaryTreeNode(new operator('*'),t,v2);
t = new BinaryTreeNode(new operator('+'),v1b,t);
t = new BinaryTreeNode(new operator('='),vR,t);

// evaluate and print expression
System.out.println(eval(t));
```

Once an expression is represented as an expression tree, it may be evaluated by *traversing* the tree in an agreed-upon manner. Standard rules of mathematical precedence suggest that the parenthesized expression (L-1) should be evaluated first. (The L represents a value previously stored in memory.) Once

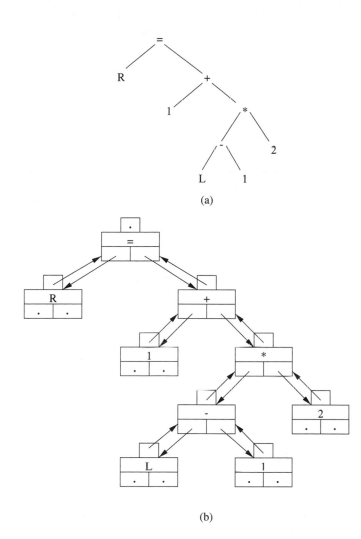

(a)

(b)

Figure 10.3   Expression trees. In (a), an abstract expression tree representing $R = 1 + (L - 1) * 2$. In (b), a possible connectivity of an implementation using references.

the subtraction is accomplished, the result is multiplied by 2. The product is then added to 1. The result of the addition is assigned to R. The assignment operator is treated in a manner similar to other common operators; it just has lower *precedence* (it is evaluated later) than standard mathematical operators. Thus an implementation of binary trees would be aided by a traversal mechanism that allows us to manipulate values as they are encountered.

10.4   Implementation

In this section we consider the implementations of binary trees. As with `List` implementations, we will construct a self-referential `BinaryTreeNode` class. The recursive design motivates implementation of many of the `BinaryTreeNode` operations as recursive methods. However, because the base case of recursion often involves an empty tree—represented by a `null` reference—we are forced to make design decisions that are sometimes at odds with Java's object-oriented approach.

To demonstrate possibilities of alternative implementations, we then develop a wrapper class—called `BinaryTree`—as an object-oriented facade that hides the recursive nature of the underlying structure. In this implementation even the representation of an empty tree is a full-fledged object.

10.4.1   The `BinaryTreeNode` Implementation

Our first step toward the development of a binary tree implementation is to represent an entire subtree as a reference to its root node. The node will maintain a reference to user data and related nodes (the node's parent and its two children) and directly provides methods to maintain a subtree rooted at that node. Here is the interface (again, for brevity, we have omitted right-handed versions of handed operations):

BinaryTree-
Node

```java
public class BinaryTreeNode
{
    protected Object val; // value associated with node
    protected BinaryTreeNode parent; // parent of node
    protected BinaryTreeNode left; // left child of node
    protected BinaryTreeNode right; // right child of node

    public BinaryTreeNode(Object value)
    // post: returns a tree referencing value with two null subtrees

    public BinaryTreeNode(Object value,
                          BinaryTreeNode left,
                          BinaryTreeNode right)
    // post: returns a node referencing value & subtrees

    public BinaryTreeNode left()
    // post: returns reference to left subtree, or null
```

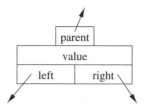

Figure 10.4 The structure of a `BinaryTreeNode`. The parent reference opposes a left or right child reference in parent node.

```
    public BinaryTreeNode parent()
    // post: returns reference to parent node, or null

    public void setLeft(BinaryTreeNode newLeft)
    // post: sets left subtree to newLeft
    //       re-parents newLeft if not null

    protected void setParent(BinaryTreeNode newParent)
    // post: re-parents this node to parent reference, or null

    public Iterator elements()
    // post: returns an inorder traversal of the elements

    public boolean isLeftChild()
    // post: returns true if this is a left child of parent

    public Object value()
    // post: returns value associated with this node

    public void setValue(Object value)
    // post: sets the value associated with this node
}
```

Figure 10.3b depicts the use of `BinaryTreeNodes` in the representation of an entire tree. We visualize the structure of a `BinaryTreeNode` as in Figure 10.4. To construct such a node, we require three pieces of information: a reference to the data that the user wishes to associate with this node, and left and right references to binary tree nodes that are roots of subtrees of this node. The parent reference is determined implicitly from opposing references. The method of constructing the node is as follows:

```
    public BinaryTreeNode(Object value)
    // post: returns a tree referencing value with two null subtrees
```

```
{
    val = value;
    parent = left = right = null;
}

public BinaryTreeNode(Object value,
                      BinaryTreeNode left,
                      BinaryTreeNode right)
// post: returns a node referencing value & subtrees
{
    this(value);
    setLeft(left);
    setRight(right);
}
```

In the three-parameter variant of the constructor we make two calls to "setting" routines. These routines allow one to set the references of the left and right subtrees, but also ensure that the children of this node reference this node as their parent. This is the direct cost of implementing forward and backward references along every link. The return, though, is the considerable simplification of other code within the classes that make use of **BinaryTreeNode** methods.

Principle 19 *Don't let opposing references show through the interface.*

When maintenance of opposing references is left to the user, there is an opportunity for references to become inconsistent. Furthermore, one might imagine implementations with fewer references (it is common, for example, to avoid the parent reference); the details of the implementation should be hidden from the user, in case the implementation needs to be changed.

Here is the code for **setLeft** (**setRight** is similar):

```
public void setLeft(BinaryTreeNode newLeft)
// post: sets left subtree to newLeft
//       re-parents newLeft if not null
{
    if (left != null &&
        (left.parent() == this)) left.setParent(null);
    left = newLeft;
    if (left != null) left.setParent(this);
}
```

If the setting of the left child causes a subtree to be disconnected from this node, and that subtree considers this node to be its parent (it should), we disconnect the node by setting its parent to **null**. We then set the left child reference to the value passed in. Any dereferenced node is explicitly told to set its **parent** reference to **null**. We also take care to set the opposite parent reference by calling the **setParent** method of the root of the associated nontrivial tree. Because we want to maintain consistency between the "downward" child references and the "upward" parent references, we declare **setParent** to be **protected** to make it impossible for the user to refer to directly:

```
protected void setParent(BinaryTreeNode newParent)
// post: re-parents this node to parent reference, or null
{
    parent = newParent;
}
```

It is, of course, useful to be able to access the various references once they have been set. We accomplish this through the accessor functions such as `left`:

```
public BinaryTreeNode left()
// post: returns reference to left subtree, or null
{
    return left;
}
```

Once the node has been constructed, its value can be inspected and modified using the value-based functions that parallel those we have seen with other types:

```
public Object value()
// post: returns value associated with this node
{
    return val;
}

public void setValue(Object value)
// post: sets the value associated with this node
{
    val = value;
}
```

Once the `BinaryTreeNode` class is implemented, we may use it as the basis for our implementation of `BinaryTrees`.

10.4.2 Implementation of the `BinaryTree` Wrapper

The construction of the `BinaryTree` class now becomes more straightforward. Internally, we maintain a reference to the root of the tree, a `BinaryTreeNode`. If the reference is `null`, we consider the tree to be empty.

Maintaining the cursor requires a little more care. Specifically, we use three protected fields: `cursor`, a reference to a current node or `null`; `prior`, which keeps track of the value of the cursor before it fell off the tree; and `wentLeft`, a boolean variable to aid in identifying whether a new node is to be inserted as a left or right child. This last field is `true` if the cursor fell off the tree to the left of a node. Maintenance of these variables demands care, but pays off in the simplicity of external interface.

The construction of a `BinaryTree` simply initializes these variables with values that are consistent with an empty tree. This process is precisely that of the `clear` method, so we reuse that code.

BinaryTree

```
protected BinaryTreeNode root;    // the root of the binary tree
protected BinaryTreeNode cursor;  // pointer to the current node
protected BinaryTreeNode prior;   // cursor's prior value
protected boolean wentLeft;       // cursor result of moving left
protected int size;               // the size of the tree

public BinaryTree()
// post: creates an empty binary tree
{
    clear();
}

public void clear()
// post: removes all nodes from tree
{
    root = null;
    cursor = null;
    prior = null;
    size = 0;
    wentLeft = false;       // arbitrary
}
```

Many methods, like those that manipulate the values referenced by the cursor, are wrappers for similar methods available from the **BinaryTreeNode** class:

```
public Object value()
// pre: cursor valid
// post: returns value of object at cursor
{
    return cursor.value();
}

public void setValue(Object value)
// pre: cursor valid
// post: sets value found at cursor
{
    cursor.setValue(value);
}
```

Next, we consider the manipulation of the cursor. The cursor can be reset to the root (if there is a root) with the **reset** method. Here we set **cursor** to the root of the tree. The value of **prior** is set to **null**. If both the **cursor** and **prior** are set to **null**, then a call to **insert** will generate a new root. The movement methods, **moveLeft**, **moveRight**, and **moveUp**, traverse the tree using similar methods of the **BinaryTreeNode** class. If the **cursor** should fall off the tree, then **prior** and **wentLeft** are updated appropriately, to inform any successive **insert** method how to consistently add a leaf to the structure.

```
public void reset()
// post: moves the cursor to the root, if any
```

```
{
    cursor = root;
    prior = null;
    wentLeft = false; // arbitrary
}

public void moveLeft()
// pre: cursor is valid
// post: cursor moves to left child of precursor, or off tree
{
    prior = cursor;
    wentLeft = true;
    cursor = cursor.left();
}

public void moveUp()
// pre: cursor is valid
// post: cursor moves up to parent of precursor
{
    prior = null;
    cursor = cursor.parent();
}
```

At times it may be useful to check the topology of the tree. The availability of data through the cursor can be checked with valid. The hasLeft, hasRight, and hasParent methods first determine whether the respective movement operations would invalidate the cursor. Each of these involves a check for null references.

```
public boolean valid()
// post: returns true if the cursor points to a valid node
{
    return cursor != null;
}

public boolean hasLeft()
// post: returns true iff cursor has left child
{
    return (cursor != null) && (cursor.left() != null);
}
```

Sometimes it is useful to ascertain whether the cursor's node is a left or right child of its parent. (For example, when a node is removed it is important to know which of the references of the parent node should be updated.) The method simply calls the BinaryTreeNode method, which, in turn, compares the cursor's parent's left reference with the cursor. If they are equal, the cursor is a left child; otherwise it can be assumed to be a right child. When the cursor refers to the root, the cursor is neither a left nor right child. It is interesting to note that these functions cannot be written without making use of protected information—here, the values of references to underlying BinaryTreeNodes.

```
public boolean isLeftChild()
// post: returns true if cursor has parent and is left child
{
    return (cursor != null) && cursor.isLeftChild();
}
```

At this point we are ready to consider insertion of a value into a tree. When insert is called, we should expect that the cursor is null. If the root is null, then the insertion simply constructs a new BinaryTreeNode and updates the root. Otherwise, prior is a reference to the new parent, and wentLeft guides our decision to place the new value as the left or right child of the parent. Once the new value is inserted, the cursor contains a valid reference to the node.

```
public void insert(Object value)
// pre: cursor is null (invalid)
// post: if tree is empty, value is inserted at root; otherwise
//       value is inserted where cursor last moved off tree
{
    Assert.pre(cursor == null,"Insertion does not overwrite value.");
    if (prior == null) {
        Assert.pre(root == null,
                   "Insertion at root only allowed in empty tree.");
        cursor = root = new BinaryTreeNode(value);
    } else {
        if (wentLeft) {
            prior.setLeft(cursor = new BinaryTreeNode(value));
        } else {
            prior.setRight(cursor = new BinaryTreeNode(value));
        }
    }
    size++;
}
```

The process of removing a node reverses the process of insertion:

```
public Object remove()
// pre: cursor is valid and has no children
// post: leaf is removed; cursor is moved to parent, if any
{
    Assert.pre(cursor != null,"Node to be removed exists.");
    Assert.pre(!(hasLeft()||hasRight()),
               "Node to be removed is leaf.");
    Object value = cursor.value();
    if (isLeftChild()) {
        moveUp();
        cursor.setLeft(null);
    } else if (isRightChild()) {
        moveUp();
        cursor.setRight(null);
    } else {
```

```
            root = cursor = prior = null;
        }
        size--;
        return value;
    }
```

As we consider more complex structures, we will see an increasing gap between the design of an interface and the design of the underlying data structure. With binary trees, the design of the interface focuses on providing certain functionalities (e.g., the cursor). In contrast, the design of the `BinaryTreeNode` structure seeks to efficiently implement certain operations (e.g., computation of tree height). If the `BinaryTree` structure were developed as a single unit, one of these design paths would be sacrificed—either the interface would become less user-oriented or the implementation would become more complex.

Principle 20 *Use wrappers to provide a consistent interface to recursive structures.*

One feature that we have not discussed is the implementation of an `Iterator` for the `BinaryTree` class. Not surprisingly a structure with branching (and therefore a choice in traversal order) makes traversal implementation more difficult. In the next section we consider the construction of several `Iterators` for binary trees.

10.5   Traversals

We have seen, of course, there is a great industry in selling calculators that allow users to enter expressions in what appear to be arbitrary ways. For example, some calculators allow users to specify expressions in *infix* form, where keys associated with operators are pressed between operands. Other brands of calculators advocate a *postfix*[2] form, where the operator is pressed only after the operands have been entered. Reconsidering our representation of expressions as trees, we observe that there must be a similar variety in the ways we traverse a `BinaryTree` structure. We consider those here.

When designing iterators for linear structures there are usually few useful choices: start at one end and visit each element until you get to the other end. Many of the linear structures we have seen provide an `elements` method that constructs an iterator for traversing the structure. For binary trees, there is no "obvious" order for traversing the structure. Here are four rather obvious but distinct mechanisms:

Preorder traversal. Each node is visited before any of its children are visited.
    Typically, we visit a node, and then each of the nodes in its left subtree,

---

[2] Reverse Polish Notation (RPN) was developed by Jan Lukasiewicz, an eighteenth century mathematician, and was made popular by Hewlett-Packard in their calculator wars with Texas Instruments in the early 1970s.

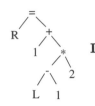

followed by each of the nodes in the right subtree. A preorder traversal of the expression tree in the margin visits the nodes in the order: $=$, R, $+$, 1, $*$, $-$, L, 1, and 2.

Inorder traversal. Each node is visited after all the nodes of its left subtree have been visited and before any of the nodes of the right subtree. The inorder traversal is usually only useful with binary trees, but similar traversal mechanisms can be constructed for trees of arbitrary arity. An inorder traversal of the expression tree visits the nodes in the order: R, $=$, 1, $+$, L, $-$, 1, $*$, and 2. Notice that, while this representation is similar to the expression that actually generated the binary tree, the traversal has removed the parentheses.

Postorder traversal. Each node is visited after its children are visited. We visit all the nodes of the left subtree, followed by all the nodes of the right subtree, followed by the node itself. A postorder traversal of the expression tree visits the nodes in the order: R, 1, L, 1, $-$, 2, $*$, $+$, and $=$. This is precisely the order that the keys would have to be pressed on a "reverse Polish" calculator to compute the correct result.

Levelorder traversal. All nodes of level i are visited before the nodes of level $i + 1$. The nodes of the expression tree are visited in the order: $=$, R, $+$, 1, $*$, $-$, 2, L, and 1. (This particular ordering of the nodes is motivation for another implementation of binary trees we shall consider later, and in Problem 10.13.)

As these are the most common and useful techniques for traversing a binary tree, we will investigate their respective implementations. Traversing `BinaryTree`s involves constructing an iterator that traverses the entire tree of `BinaryTreeNode`s. For this reason, and because the traversal of subtrees proves to be just as easy, we discuss implementations of iterators for `BinaryTreeNode`s.

Most implementations of iterators maintain a linear structure that keeps track of the state of the iterator. In some cases, this auxiliary structure is not strictly necessary (see Problem 10.23) but may reduce the complexity of the implementation and improve its performance.

10.5.1 Preorder Traversal

For a preorder traversal, we wish to traverse each node of the tree before any of its proper descendants (recall the node is a descendant of itself). To accomplish this, we keep a stack of nodes whose right subtrees have not been investigated. In particular, the current node is the topmost element of the stack, and elements stored deeper within the stack are more distant ancestors.

BTPreorder-
Iterator

We develop a new implementation of an `Iterator` that is not declared `public`. Since it will be a member of the `structure` package, it *is* available for use by the classes of the `structure` package, including `BinaryTreeNode`. The `BinaryTreeNode` class will construct and return a reference to the preorder iterator when the `preorderElements` method is called:

```
public Iterator preorderElements()
// post: The elements of the binary tree rooted at node n are
//       traversed in preorder
{
    return new BTPreorderIterator(this);
}
```

Note that the constructor for the iterator accepts a single parameter—the root of the subtree to be traversed. Because the iterator only gives access to values stored within nodes, this is not a breach of the privacy of our binary tree implementation. The actual implementation of the BTPreorderIterator is fairly short:

```
class BTPreorderIterator implements Iterator
{
    protected BinaryTreeNode root; // root of tree to be traversed
    protected Stack todo; // stack of unvisited nodes whose
                          // nontrivial ancestors have been visited

    public BTPreorderIterator(BinaryTreeNode root)
    // post: constructs an iterator to traverse in preorder
    {
        todo = new StackList();
        this.root = root;
        reset();
    }

    public void reset()
    // post: resets the iterator to retraverse
    {
        todo.clear();
        // stack is empty.  Push on the current node.
        if (root != null) todo.push(root);
    }

    public boolean hasMoreElements()
    // post: returns true iff iterator is not finished
    {
        return !todo.isEmpty();
    }

    public Object value()
    // pre: hasMoreElements()
    // post: returns reference to current value
    {
        return ((BinaryTreeNode)todo.peek()).value();
    }

    public Object nextElement()
    // pre: hasMoreElements();
```

```
        // post: returns current value, increments iterator
        {
            BinaryTreeNode old = (BinaryTreeNode)todo.pop();
            Object result = old.value();

            if (old.right() != null) todo.push(old.right());
            if (old.left() != null) todo.push(old.left());
            return result;
        }
    }
```

As we can see, todo is the private stack used to keep track of references to unvisited nodes whose nontrivial ancestors have been visited. Another way to think about it is that it is the frontier of nodes encountered on paths from the root that have not yet been visited. To construct the iterator we initialize the stack. We also keep a reference to the root node; this will help reset the iterator to the correct node (when the root of the traversal is not the root of the tree, this information is vital). We then reset the iterator to the beginning of the traversal.

Resetting the iterator involves clearing off the stack and then pushing the root on the stack to make it the current node. The hasMoreElements method needs only to check to see if there *is* a top node of the stack, and value returns the reference stored within the topmost BinaryTreeNode of the todo stack.

The only tricky method is nextElement. Recall this method returns the value of the current element, and then "increments" the iterator, causing the iterator to reference the next node in the traversal. Since the current node has just been visited, we push on any children of the node—first any right child, then any left. If the node has a left child (see node A of Figure 10.5), that node (A') is the next node to be visited. If the current node (see node B) has only a right child (B'), it will be visited next. If the current node has no children (see node C), the effect is to visit the closest unvisited right cousin or sibling (C').

It is clear that over the life of the iterator each of the n values of the tree is pushed onto and popped off the stack exactly once; thus the total cost of traversing the tree is $O(n)$. A similar observation is possible for each of the remaining iteration techniques.

10.5.2   Inorder Traversal

BTInorder-
Iterator

The most common traversal of trees is inorder. For this reason, the BTInorder-Iterator is the value returned when the elements method is called on a BinaryTreeNode. Again, the iterator maintains a stack of references to nodes. Here, the nodes on the stack are the unvisited ancestors of the current (unvisited) node.

Thus, the implementation of this traversal is similar to the code for other iterators, save the way that the stack is reset and the mechanism provided in the nextElement method:

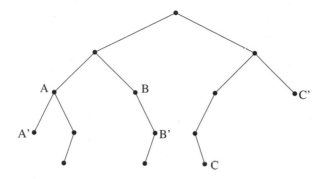

Figure 10.5 Three cases of determining the next current node for preorder traversals. Node A has a left child A' as the next node; node B has no left, but a right child B'; and node C is a leaf and finds its closest, "right cousin," C'.

```
protected BinaryTreeNode root; // root of subtree to be traversed
protected Stack todo; // stack of unvisited ancestors of current

public void reset()
// post: resets the iterator to retraverse
{
    todo.clear();
    // stack is empty.  Push on nodes from root to
    // leftmost descendant
    BinaryTreeNode current = root;
    while (current != null) {
        todo.push(current);
        current = current.left();
    }
}

public Object nextElement()
// pre: hasMoreElements();
// post: returns current value, increments iterator
{
    BinaryTreeNode old = (BinaryTreeNode)todo.pop();
    Object result = old.value();
    // we know this node has no unconsidered left children.
    // if this node has a right child,
    //  we push the right child and its leftmost descendants:
    // else top element of stack is next node to be visited
    if (old.right() != null) {
        BinaryTreeNode current = old.right();
        do {
            todo.push(current);
```

```
                    current = current.left();
                } while (current != null);
            }
            return result;
        }
```

Since the first element considered in an inorder traversal is the leftmost descendant of the root, resetting the iterator involves pushing each of the nodes from the root down to the leftmost descendant on the auxiliary stack.

When the current node is popped from the stack, next element of the traversal must be found. We consider two scenarios:

1. If the current node has a right subtree, the nodes of that tree have not been visited. At this stage we should push the right child, and all the nodes down to and including its leftmost descendant, on the stack.

2. If the node has no right child, the subtree rooted at the current node has been fully investigated, and the next node to be considered is the closest unvisited ancestor of the former current node—the node just exposed on the top of the stack.

As we shall see later, it is common to order the nodes of a binary tree so that left-hand descendants of a node are smaller than the node, which is, in turn, smaller than any of the rightmost descendants. In such a situation, the inorder traversal plays a natural role in presenting the data of the tree in order. For this reason, the `elements` method returns the iterator constructed by the `inorderElements` method.

10.5.3   Postorder Traversal

Traversing a tree in postorder also maintains a stack of uninvestigated nodes. Each of the elements on the stack is a node whose descendants are currently being visited. Since the first element to be visited is the leftmost descendant of the root, the `reset` method must (as with the inorder iterator) push on each of the nodes from the root to the leftmost descendant. (Note that the leftmost descendant need not be a leaf—it does not have a left child, but it may have a right.)

BTPostorder-
Iterator

```
protected BinaryTreeNode root; // root of traversed subtree
protected Stack todo;   // stack of nodes whose descendants
                        // are currently being visited

public void reset()
// post: resets the iterator to retraverse
{
    todo.clear();
    // stack is empty.  push on nodes from root to
    // leftmost descendant
    BinaryTreeNode current = root;
```

```
        while (current != null) {
            todo.push(current);
            if (current.left()!=null)
                current = current.left();
            else
                current = current.right();
        }
    }

    public Object nextElement()
    // pre: hasMoreElements();
    // post: returns current value, increments iterator
    {
        BinaryTreeNode current = (BinaryTreeNode)todo.pop();
        Object result = current.value();
        if (!todo.isEmpty())
        {
            BinaryTreeNode parent = (BinaryTreeNode)todo.peek();
            if (current == parent.left()) {
                current = parent.right();
                while (current != null)
                {
                    todo.push(current);
                    if (current.left() != null)
                        current = current.left();
                    else current = current.right();
                }
            }
        }
        return result;
    }
```

Here a nonleaf node on the stack is potentially exposed twice before becoming current. The first time it may be left on the stack because the element recently popped off was the left child. The right child should now be pushed on. Later the exposed node becomes current because the popped element was its right child.

It is interesting to observe that the stack contains the ancestors of the current node. This stack describes, essentially, the path to the root of the tree. As a result, we could represent the state of the stack by a single reference to the current node.

10.5.4 Levelorder Traversal

A levelorder traversal visits the root, followed by the nodes of level 1, from left to right, followed by the nodes of level 2, and so on. This can be easily accomplished by maintaining a queue of the "next few" nodes to be visited. More precisely, the queue contains the current node, followed by a list of all siblings and cousins to the right of the current node, followed by a list of "nieces

This is the family values traversal.

and nephews" to the left of the current node. After we visit a node, we enqueue
the children of the node. With a little work it is easy to see that these are either
nieces and nephews, or right cousins of the next node to be visited.

BTLevelorder-
Iterator

```
class BTLevelorderIterator implements Iterator
{
    protected BinaryTreeNode root; // root of traversed subtree
    protected Queue todo;  // queue of unvisited relatives

    public BTLevelorderIterator(BinaryTreeNode root)
    // post: constructs an iterator to traverse in levelorder
    {
        todo = new QueueList();
        this.root = root;
        reset();
    }

    public void reset()
    // post: resets the iterator to root node
    {
        todo.clear();
        // stack is empty; push on nodes from root down to the
        // leftmost descendant
        if (root != null) todo.enqueue(root);
    }

    public boolean hasMoreElements()
    // post: returns true iff iterator is not finished
    {
        return !todo.isEmpty();
    }

    public Object value()
    // pre: hasMoreElements()
    // post: returns reference to current value
    {
        return ((BinaryTreeNode)todo.peek()).value();
    }

    public Object nextElement()
    // pre: hasMoreElements();
    // post: returns current value, increments iterator
    {
        BinaryTreeNode current = (BinaryTreeNode)todo.dequeue();
        Object result = current.value();
        if (current.left() != null)
            todo.enqueue(current.left());
        if (current.right() != null)
            todo.enqueue(current.right());
        return result;
```

```
            }
        }
```

To **reset** the iterator, we need only empty the queue and add the root. When the queue is empty, the traversal is finished. When the next element is needed we need only enqueue references to children (left to right). Notice that, unlike the other iterators, this method of traversing the tree is meaningful regardless of the degree of the tree.

10.5.5   Recursion in Iterators

Trees are recursively defined structures, so it would seem reasonable to consider recursive implementations of iterators. The difficulty is that iterators must maintain their state across many calls to **nextElement**. Any recursive approach to traversal would encounter nodes while deep in recursion, and the state of the stack must be preserved.

One way around the difficulties of suspending the recursion is to initially perform the entire traversal, generating a list of values encountered. Since the entire traversal happens "all at once," the list can be constructed using recursion. As the iterator pushes forward, the elements of the list are consumed.

Using this idea, we rewrite the inorder traversal:

Recursive-
Iterators

```
protected BinaryTreeNode root; // root of traversed subtree
protected Queue todo;  // queue of unvisited elements

public BTInorderIteratorR(BinaryTreeNode root)
// post: constructs an iterator to traverse in inorder
{
    todo = new QueueList();
    this.root = root;
    reset();
}

public void reset()
// post: resets the iterator to retraverse
{
    todo.clear();
    enqueueInorder(root);
}

protected void enqueueInorder(BinaryTreeNode current)
// pre: current is non-null
// post: enqueue all values found in tree rooted at current
//       in inorder
{
    if (current == null) return;
    enqueueInorder(current.left());
    todo.enqueue(current);
    enqueueInorder(current.right());
```

```
    }
    public Object nextElement()
    // pre: hasMoreElements();
    // post: returns current value, increments iterator
    {
        BinaryTreeNode current = (BinaryTreeNode)todo.dequeue();
        return current.value();
    }
```

The core of this implementation is the protected method **enqueueInorder**. It simply traverses the tree rooted at its parameter and enqueues every node encountered. Since it recursively enqueues all its left descendants, then itself, and then its right descendants, it is an inorder traversal. Since the queue is a FIFO, the order is preserved and the elements may be consumed at the user's leisure.

For completeness and demonstration of symmetry, here are the pre- and postorder counterparts:

```
    protected void enqueuePreorder(BinaryTreeNode current)
    // pre: current is non-null
    // post: enqueue all values found in tree rooted at current
    //       in preorder
    {
        if (current == null) return;
        todo.enqueue(current);
        enqueuePreorder(current.left());
        enqueuePreorder(current.right());
    }

    protected void enqueuePostorder(BinaryTreeNode current)
    // pre: current is non-null
    // post: enqueue all values found in tree rooted at current
    //       in postorder
    {
        if (current == null) return;
        enqueuePostorder(current.left());
        enqueuePostorder(current.right());
        todo.enqueue(current);
    }
```

It is reassuring to see the brevity of these implementations. Unfortunately, while the recursive implementations are no less efficient, they come at the obvious cost of a potentially long delay whenever the iterator is reset. Still, for many applications this may be satisfactory.

10.6 Property-Based Methods

At this point, we consider the implementation of a number of property-based methods. Properties such as the "height" and "fullness" of a tree are important to guiding updates of a tree structure. Because the binary tree is a recursively defined data type, the proofs of tree characteristics (and the methods that verify them) often have a recursive feel. To emphasize the point, in this section we allow theorems about trees and methods that verify them to intermingle. Again, the methods described here are written for use on `BinaryTreeNodes`, but they are easily adapted for use with `BinaryTree`s.

Our first method makes use of the fact that the root is a common ancestor of every node of the tree. Because of this fact, we can, given a reference to a `BinaryTreeNode`, identify it as the root, or return the root of the tree containing the node's parent.

```
public static BinaryTreeNode root(BinaryTreeNode n)
// post: returns the root of the tree node n
{
    if ((n == null) || (n.parent() == null)) return n;
    else return root(n.parent());
}
```

BinaryTree-
Node

A proof that this method functions correctly could make use of induction, based on the depth of the node involved.

If we count the number of times the `root` routine is recursively called, we compute the number of edges from the node to the root—the depth of the node. Not surprisingly, the code is very similar:

```
public static int depth(BinaryTreeNode n)
// post: returns the depth of a node in the tree
{
    if (n == null) return -1;
    return 1 + depth(n.parent());
}
```

The time it takes is proportional to the depth of the node. For full trees, we will see that this is approximately $O(\log n)$. Notice that in the empty case we return a height of −1. This is consistent with our recursive definition, even if it does seem a little unusual. We could avoid the strange case by avoiding it in the precondition. Then, of course, we would only have put off the work to the calling routine. Often, making tough decisions about base cases can play an important role in making your interface useful. Generally, a method is more robust, and therefore more usable, if you handle as many cases as possible.

Principle 21 *Write methods to be as general as possible.*

Having computed the depth of a node, it follows that we should be able to determine the height of a tree rooted at a particular `BinaryTreeNode`. We know that the height is simply the length of a longest path from the root to a leaf, but we can adapt a self-referential definition: the height of a tree is one more than the height of the tallest subtree. This translates directly into a clean implementation of the height function:

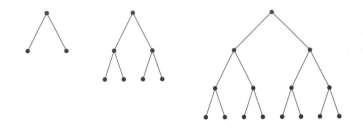

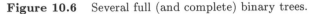

Figure 10.6   Several full (and complete) binary trees.

```
public static int height(BinaryTreeNode n)
// post: returns the height of a node n in its tree
{
    if (n == null) return -1;
    return 1 + Math.max(height(n.left()),height(n.right()));
}
```

This method takes $O(n)$ time to execute on a subtree with n nodes (see Problem 10.10).

At this point, we consider the problem of identifying a tree that is full (see Figure 10.6). Our approach uses recursion:

```
public static boolean isFull(BinaryTreeNode n)
// post: returns true iff the tree rooted at n is full
{
    if (n == null) return true;
    if (height(n.left()) != height(n.right())) return false;
    return isFull(n.left()) && isFull(n.right());
}
```

Again, the method is compact. Unfortunately, detecting this property appears to be significantly more expensive than computing the height. Note, for example, that in the process of computing this function on a full tree, the *height of every node* must be computed from scratch. The result is that the running time of the algorithm on full trees is $O(n \log n)$. Can it be improved upon?

To find the answer, we first prove a series of theorems about the structure of trees, with hope that we can develop an inexpensive way to test for a full tree. Our first result determines the number of nodes that are found in full trees:

Observation 10.1 *A full binary tree of height $h \geq 0$ has $2^{h+1} - 1$ nodes.*

Proof: We prove this by induction on the height of the tree. Suppose the tree has height 0. Then it has exactly one node, which is also a leaf. Since $2^1 - 1 = 1$, the observation holds, trivially.

Our inductive hypothesis is that full trees of height $k < h$ have $2^{k+1} - 1$ nodes. Since $h > 0$, we can decompose the tree into two full subtrees of height $h - 1$, under a common root. Each of the full subtrees has $2^{(h-1)+1} - 1 = 2^h - 1$ nodes, so there are $2(2^h - 1) + 1 = 2^{h+1} - 1$ nodes. This is the result we sought to prove, so by induction on tree height we see the observation must hold for all full binary trees. $\diamond$

This observation suggests that if we can compute the height and size of a tree, we have a hope of detecting a full tree. First, we compute the size of the tree using a recursive algorithm:

```java
public static int size(BinaryTreeNode n)
// post: returns the size of the subtree rooted at n
{
    if (n == null) return 0;
    return size(n.left()) + size(n.right()) + 1;
}
```

This algorithm is similar to the height algorithm: each call to size counts one more node, so the complexity of the routine is $O(n)$. Now we have an alternative implementation of isFull that compares the height of the tree to the number of nodes:

```java
public static boolean isFull(BinaryTreeNode n)
// post: returns true iff the tree rooted at n is full
{
    int h = height(n);
    int s = size(n);
    return s == (1<<(h+1))-1;
}
```

Notice the return statement makes use of shifting 1 $h + 1$ binary places to the left. This efficiently computes 2^{h+1}. The result is that, given a full tree, the function returns true in $O(n)$ steps. Thus, it *is* possible to improve on our previous implementation.

There is one significant disadvantage, though. If you are given a tree with height greater than 100, the result of the return statement cannot be accurately computed: 2^{100} is a large enough number to overflow Java integers. Even reasonably sized trees can have height greater than 100. The first implementation is accurate, even if it is slow. Problem 10.22 considers an efficient and accurate solution.

Redwoods and sequoias come to mind.

We now prove some useful facts about binary trees that help us evaluate performance of methods that manipulate them. First, we consider a pretty result: if a tree has lots of leaves, it must branch in lots of places.

Observation 10.2 *The number of full nodes in a binary tree is one less than the number of leaves.*

Proof: Left to the reader.$\diamond$

With this result, we can now demonstrate that just over half the nodes of a full tree are leaves:

Observation 10.3 *A full binary tree of height $h \geq 0$ has 2^h leaves.*

Proof: In a full binary tree, all nodes are either full interior nodes or leaves. The number of nodes is the sum of full nodes, F, and the number of leaves, L. Since, by Observation 10.2, $F = L - 1$, we know that the count of nodes is $F + L = 2L - 1 = 2^{h+1} - 1$. This leads us to conclude that $L = 2^h$, and that $F = 2^h - 1$. $\diamond$

This result demonstrates that for many simple tree methods (like `size`) half of the time is spent processing leaves. Because complete trees can be viewed as full trees with some rightmost leaves removed, similar results hold for complete trees as well.

10.7   Example: Huffman Compression

Information within machines is stored as a series of `bits`, or 1's and 0's. Because the distribution of the patterns of 1's and 0's is not always uniform, it is possible to compress the bit patterns that are used and reduce the amount of storage that is necessary. For example, consider the following 32 character phrase:

```
If a woodchuck could chuck wood!
```

If each letter in the string is represented by 8 bits (as they often are), the entire string takes 256 bits of storage. Clearly this catchy phrase does not use the full range of characters and so perhaps 8 bits are not needed. In fact, there are 13 distinct characters so 4 bits would be sufficient (4 bits can represent any of 16 values). This would halve the amount of storage required, to 128 bits.

If each character were represented by a unique *variable length* string of bits, further improvements are possible. *Huffman encoding* of characters allows us to reduce the size of this string to only 111 bits by assigning frequently occurring letters (like "o") short representations and infrequent letters (like "a") relatively long representations.

Huffman encodings can be represented by binary trees whose leaves are the characters to be represented. In Figure 10.7 left edges are labeled 0, while right edges are labeled 1. Since there is a unique path from the root to each leaf, there is a unique sequence of 1's and 0's encountered as well. We will use the string of bits encountered along the path to a character as its representation in the compressed output. Note also that no string is a prefix for any other (otherwise one character would be an ancestor of another in the tree). This means that, given the Huffman tree, decoding a string of bits involves simply traversing the tree and writing out the leaves encountered.

The construction of a Huffman tree is an iterative process. Initially, each character is placed in a Huffman tree of its own. The "weight" of the tree is the frequency of its associated character. We then iteratively merge the two

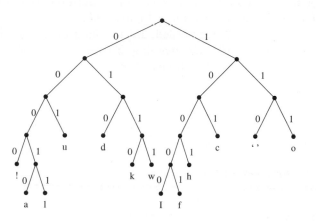

Figure 10.7 The woodchuck Huffman tree. Leaves are labeled with the characters they represent. Paths from root to leaves provide Huffman bit strings.

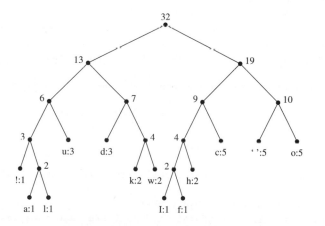

Figure 10.8 The Huffman tree of Figure 10.7, but with nodes labeled by total frequencies of descendant characters.

most lightweight Huffman trees into a single new Huffman tree whose weight is the sum of weights of the subtrees. This continues until one tree remains. One possible tree for our example is shown in Figure 10.8.

Our approach is to use `BinaryTreeNodes` to maintain the structure. This allows the use of recursion and easy merging of trees. Leaves of the tree carry descriptions of characters and their frequencies:

Huffman

```
class leaf
{
    int frequency; // frequency of char
    char ch;     // the character

    public leaf(char c)
    // post: construct character entry with frequency 1

    public boolean equals(Object other)
    // post: return true if leaves represent same character
}
```

Intermediate nodes carry no data at all. Their relation to their ancestors determines their portion of the encoding. The entire tree is managed by a wrapper class, `huffmanTree`:

```
class huffmanTree implements Comparable
{
    BinaryTreeNode root; // root of tree
    int totalWeight;     // weight of tree

    public huffmanTree(leaf e)
    // post: construct a leaf with associated character

    public huffmanTree(huffmanTree left, huffmanTree right)
    // pre: left and right non-null
    // post: merge two trees together and merge their weights

    public int compareTo(Object other)
    // pre: other is not null
    // post: return integer reflecting relation between values

    public boolean equals(Object that)
    // post: return true if this and that are same tree instance

    public void print()
    // post: print out strings associated with characters in tree

    protected void print(BinaryTreeNode r, String representation)
    // post: print out strings associated with chars in tree r,
    //       prefixed by representation
}
```

This class is a `Comparable` because it implements the `compareTo` method. That method allows the trees to be ordered by their total weight during the merging process. The utility method `print` generates our output recursively, building up a different encoding along every path.

We now consider the construction of the tree:

```
public static void main(String args[])
{
    ReadStream r = new ReadStream();
    List freq = new SinglyLinkedList();

    // read data from input
    while (!r.eof())
    {
        char c = r.readChar();
        // look up character in frequency list
        leaf query = new leaf(c);
        leaf item = (leaf)freq.remove(query);
        if (item == null)
        {   // not found, add new leaf
            freq.add(query);
        } else { // found, increment leaf
            item.frequency++;
            freq.add(item);
        }
    }

    // insert each character into a huffman tree
    Iterator li = freq.elements();
    OrderedList trees - new OrderedList();
    for (li.reset(); li.hasMoreElements(); li.nextElement())
    {
        trees.add(new huffmanTree((leaf)li.value()));
    }

    // merge trees in pairs until one remains
    Iterator ti = trees.elements();
    while (trees.size() > 1)
    {
        // construct a new iterator
        ti = trees.elements();
        // grab two smallest values
        huffmanTree smallest = (huffmanTree)ti.nextElement();
        huffmanTree small = (huffmanTree)ti.nextElement();
        // remove them
        trees.remove(smallest);
        trees.remove(small);
        // add bigger tree containing both
        trees.add(new huffmanTree(smallest,small));
    }
```

```
                     // print only tree in list
                     ti  = trees.elements();
                     huffmanTree encoding = (huffmanTree)ti.value();
                     encoding.print();
            }
```

There are three phases in this method: the reading of the data, the construction of the character-holding leaves of the tree, and the merging of trees into a single encoding. Several things should be noted:

1. We store characters in a list. Since this list is likely to be small, keeping it ordered requires more code and is not likely to improve performance.

2. The **huffmanTrees** are kept in an **OrderedList**. Every time we remove values we must construct a fresh iterator and remove the two smallest trees. When they are merged and reinserted, the wrappers for the two smaller trees can be garbage collected. (The next chapter will discuss even better structures for managing these details.)

3. The resulting tree is then printed out. In an application, the information in this tree would have to be included with the compressed text to guide the decompression.

When the program is run on the above input, it generates the following output:

```
Encoding of ! is 0000 (frequency was 1)
Encoding of a is 00010 (frequency was 1)
Encoding of l is 00011 (frequency was 1)
Encoding of u is 001 (frequency was 3)
Encoding of d is 010 (frequency was 3)
Encoding of k is 0110 (frequency was 2)
Encoding of w is 0111 (frequency was 2)
Encoding of I is 10000 (frequency was 1)
Encoding of f is 10001 (frequency was 1)
Encoding of h is 1001 (frequency was 2)
Encoding of c is 101 (frequency was 5)
Encoding of   is 110 (frequency was 5)
Encoding of o is 111 (frequency was 5)
```

Again, the total number of bits that would be used to represent our compressed phrase is only 111, giving us a compression rate of 56 percent. In these days of moving bits about, the construction of efficient compression techniques is an important industry—an industry that depends on the efficient implementation of data structures.

10.8 Conclusions

The tree is a nonlinear structure. Because of branching in the tree, we will find it is especially useful in situations where decisions can guide the process of adding and removing nodes.

Our approach to implementing the binary tree—a tree with degree two or less—is to visualize it as a self-referential structure. This is somewhat at odds with an object-oriented approach. It is, for example, difficult to represent empty self-referential structures in a manner that allows us to invoke methods. To relieve the tension between these two approaches, we design two classes—one class that is self-referential and a wrapper class that carefully manages the self-referential structure in the case when it is empty.

The power of recursion on branching structures is that significant work can be accomplished with very little code. Sometimes, as in our implementation of the `isFull` method, we find ourselves subtly pushed away from an efficient solution because of overzealous use of recursion. Usually we can eliminate such inefficiencies, but we must always verify that our methods act reasonably.

Problems

10.1   Below is a binary tree containing character data.

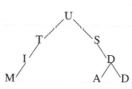

Describe the characters encountered in pre-, post- and inorder traversals.

10.2   In the tree of the preceding problem, what are the ancestors of the leaf D? What are the descendants of the node S? The root of the tree is the common ancestor of what nodes?

10.3   Draw an expression tree for each of the following expressions.

   a. 1

   b. $1 + 5 * 3 - 4/2$

   c. $1 + 5 * (3 - 4)/2$

   d. $(1 + 5) * (3 - 4/2)$

   e. $(1 + (5 * (3 - (4/2))))$

Circle the nodes that are ancestors of the node containing the value 1.

10.4★   What topological characteristics distinguish a tree from a list?

10.5   Write a method that, given two `BinaryTree`s and a node v, constructs a new `BinaryTree` that has v at the root and the two source trees as subtrees. The source trees should be empty when the method is finished.

10.6   Demonstrate how the expression tree associated with the expression $R = 1 + (L - 1) * 2$ can be simplified using first the distributive property and then reduction of constant expressions to constants. Use pictures to forward your argument.

10.7   For each of the methods of `BinaryTree`, indicate which method can be implemented in terms of other `public` methods of that class, or give a reasoned argument why it is not possible. Explain why it is useful to cast methods in terms of other `public` methods, and not base them directly on a particular implementation.

10.8   Implement the alternative `BinaryTree` methods `insertRoot`, `insert-Left`, and `insertRight` in terms of existing `public` methods of `BinaryTree`s (including `insert`).

10.9⋆   Explain why `BinaryTreeNode`s have a `parent` accessor method, but no `setParent` method.

10.10   Prove that efficient computation of the height of a `BinaryTreeNode` must take time proportional to the number of nodes in the tree.

10.11   Write an `equals` method for the `BinaryTree` class. This function should return true if and only if the trees are similarly shaped and refer to equal values (every `Object`, including the `Object`s of the tree, has an `equals` method).

10.12   Write a static method, `clone`, that, given a binary tree, returns a copy of the tree. Because not every object implements the `clone` method, you should *not* copy objects to which the tree refers.

10.13   Design an implementation of `BinaryTree`s that maintains node data in a `Vector`, `data`. In this implementation, element 0 of `data` references the root (if it exists). Every non-`null` element i of `data` finds its left and right children at locations $2i+1$ and $2(i+1)$, respectively. (The inverse of these index relations suggests the parent of a nonroot node at i is found at location $\lfloor (i-1)/2 \rfloor$.) Any element of data that is not used to represent a node should maintain a `null` reference.

10.14   Design an *interface* for general trees—trees with unbounded degree. Make this interface as consistent as possible with `BinaryTree`s when the degree of a tree is no greater than two.

10.15   Implement the general tree structure of Problem 10.14 using `BinaryTreeNode`s. In this implementation, we interpret the left child of a `Binary-TreeNode` to be the leftmost child, and the right child of the `BinaryTreeNode` to be the "leftmost right sibling" of the node.

10.16   Write a preorder iterator for the general tree implemention of Problem 10.15.

10.17   Implement the general tree structure of Problem 10.14 using a tree node of your own design. In this implementation, each node maintains (some sort of) collection of subtrees.

10.18   Write an inorder iterator for the general tree implemention of Problem 10.17.

10.19   Determine the complexity of each of the methods implemented in Problem 10.15.

10.20   Write a static method, `isComplete`, that returns true if and only if the subtree rooted at a `BinaryTreeNode` on which it acts is complete.

10.21⋆   A tree is said to be an *AVL tree* or *height balanced* if, for every node n, the heights of the subtrees of n differ by no more than 1. Write a static `BinaryTreeNode` method that determines if a tree rooted at the referenced node is height balanced.

10.22   The `BinaryTreeNode` method `isFull` takes $O(n \log n)$ time to execute on full trees, which, as we've seen, is not optimal. Careful thought shows that calls to `height` (an $O(n)$ operation) are made more often than is strictly necessary. Write a recursive method `info` that computes two values—the height of the tree and whether or not the tree is full. If `info` makes no call to `height` or `isFull`, its performance is $O(n)$. Verify this on a computer by counting procedure calls. This process is called *strengthening*, an optimization technique that often improves performance of recursive algorithms.

10.23   Demonstrate how, in an inorder traversal, the associated stack can be removed and replaced with a single reference. (Hint: We only need to know the top of the stack, and the elements below the stack top are determined *by* the stack top.)

10.24   Which other traversals can be rewritten by replacing their `Linear` structure with a single reference? How does this change impact the complexity of each of the iterations?

10.25   Suppose the nodes of a binary tree are unique and that you are given the order of elements as they are encountered in a preorder traversal and the order of the elements as they are encountered in a postorder traversal. Under what conditions can you accurately reconstruct the structure of the tree from these two traversal orders?

10.26   Suppose you are to store a k-ary tree where each internal node has k children and (obviously) each leaf has none. If $k = 2$, we see that Observation 10.2 suggests that there is one more leaf than internal node. Prove that a similar situation holds for k-ary trees with only full nodes and leaves: if there are n full nodes, there are $(k - 1)n + 1$ leaves. (Hint: Use induction.)

10.27   Assume that the observation of the previous problem is true and that you are given a k-ary tree with only full nodes and leaves constructed with references between nodes. In a k-ary tree with n nodes, how many references are `null`? Considerable space might be saved if the k references to the children of an internal node were stored in a k-element array, instead of k fields. In leaves, the array needn't be allocated. In an 8-ary tree with only full nodes and leaves (an "octtree") with one million internal nodes, how many bytes of space can be saved using this array technique (assume all references consume four bytes).

Chapter 11

Priority Queues

"'Exactly!' said Mr. Wonka. 'I decided to invite five children to the factory, and the one I liked best at the end of the day would be the winner!'"
—Roald Dahl

SOMETIMES A RESTRICTED INTERFACE IS A FEATURE. The *priority queue*, like an ordered structure, appears to keep its data in order. Unlike an ordered structure, however, the priority queue allows the user only to peek at its smallest element. The priority queue is also similar to the **Linear** structure: values are added to the structure, and they later may be inspected or removed. Unlike their **Linear** counterpart, however, once a value is added to the priority queue it may only be removed if it is the minimum value.[1] It is precisely this restricted interface to the priority queue that allows many of its implementations to run quickly.

Priority queues are used to schedule processes in an operating system, to schedule future events in a simulation, and to generally rank choices that are generated out of order.

Think triage.

11.1 The Interface

Because we will see many contrasting implementations of the priority queue structure, we describe it as abstractly as possible in Java—with an interface:

```
public interface PriorityQueue
{
    public Comparable peek();
    // pre: !isEmpty()
    // post: returns the minimum value in priority queue

    public Comparable remove();
    // pre: !isEmpty()
    // post: returns and removes minimum value from queue

    public void add(Comparable value);
    // pre: value is non-null comparable
```

PriorityQueue

---

[1] We will consider priority queues whose elements are ranked in ascending order. It is, of course, possible to maintain these queues in descending order with only a few modifications.

```
                    // post: value is added to priority queue

                    public boolean isEmpty();
                    // post: returns true iff no elements are in queue

                    public int size();
                    // post: returns number of elements within queue

                    public void clear();
                    // post: removes all elements from queue
                }
```

Because they must be kept in order, the elements of a `PriorityQueue` are `Comparable`. In this interface the smallest values are found near the front of the queue and will be removed soonest.[2] The `add` operation is used to insert a new value into the queue. At any time a reference to the minimum value can be obtained with the `peek` method and is removed with `remove`. The remaining methods are similar to those we have seen before.

Notice that the `PriorityQueue` does not extend any of the interfaces we have seen previously. First, as a matter of convenience, `PriorityQueue` methods consume `Comparable` parameters and return `Comparable` values. Most structures we have encountered manipulate `Objects`. Though similar, the `PriorityQueue` is not a `Queue`. There is, for example, no `dequeue` method. Though this might be remedied, it is clear that the `PriorityQueue` need not act like a first-in, first-out structure. At any time, the value about to be removed is the current minimum value. This value might have been the first value inserted, or it might have just recently "cut in line" before larger values. Still, the priority queue is just as general as the stack and queue since, with a little work, one can associate with inserted values a priority that forces any `Linear` behavior in a `PriorityQueue`. Finally, since the `PriorityQueue` has no `elements` method, it may not be traversed and, therefore, cannot be a `Collection`.

The simplicity of the abstract priority queue makes its implementation relatively straightforward. In this chapter we will consider three implementations: one based on use of an `OrderedStructure` and two based on a novel structure called a *heap*. First, we consider an example that emphasizes the simplicity of our interface.

11.2   Example: Improving the Huffman Code

Huffman

In the Huffman example from the previous chapter we kept track of a pool of trees. At each iteration of the tree-merging phase of the algorithm, the two lightest-weight trees were removed from the pool and merged. There, we used an `OrderedStructure` to maintain the collection of trees:

---

[2] If explicit priorities are to be associated with values, the user may insert a `ComparableAssociation` whose key value is a `Comparable` such as an `Integer`. In this case, the associated value—the data element—need not be `Comparable`.

```
OrderedList trees = new OrderedList();
    ...
// merge trees in pairs until one remains
Iterator ti = trees.elements();
while (trees.size() > 1)
{
    // construct a new iterator
    ti = trees.elements();
    // grab two smallest values
    huffmanTree smallest = (huffmanTree)ti.nextElement();
    huffmanTree small = (huffmanTree)ti.nextElement();
    // remove them
    trees.remove(smallest);
    trees.remove(small);
    // add bigger tree containing both
    trees.add(new huffmanTree(smallest,small));
}
// print only tree in list
ti  = trees.elements();
huffmanTree encoding = (huffmanTree)ti.value();
```

To remove the two smallest objects from the `OrderedStructure`, we must construct an `Iterator` and indirectly remove the first two elements we encounter. This code can be greatly simplified by storing the trees in a `PriorityQueue`. We then remove the two minimum values:

Huffman2

```
PriorityQueue trees = new PriorityVector();
    ...
// merge trees in pairs until one remains
while (trees.size() > 1)
{
    // grab two smallest values
    huffmanTree smallest = (huffmanTree)trees.remove();
    huffmanTree small = (huffmanTree)trees.remove();
    // add bigger tree containing both
    trees.add(new huffmanTree(smallest,small));
}
huffmanTree encoding = (huffmanTree)trees.remove();
```

After the merging is complete, access to the final result is also improved.

A number of interesting algorithms must have access to the minimum of a collection of values, and yet do not require the collection to be sorted. The extra energy required by an `OrderedVector` to keep all the values in order may, in fact, be excessive for some purposes.

11.3   Priority Vectors

Perhaps the simplest implementation of a `PriorityQueue` is to keep all the values in ascending order in a `Vector`. Of course, the constructor is responsible

**Priority-
Vector**

for initialization:

```
protected Vector data;

public PriorityVector()
// post: constructs a new priority queue
{
    data = new Vector();
}
```

From the standpoint of adding values to the structure, the priority queue is very similar to the implementation of the `OrderedVector` structure. In fact, the implementations of the **add** method and the "helper" method **indexOf** are similar to those described in Section 9.2.2. Still, values of a priority queue are removed in a manner that differs from that seen in the `OrderedVector`. They are not removed by value. Instead, **peek** and the parameterless **remove** operate on the **Vector** element that is smallest (leftmost). The implementation of these routines is straightforward:

```
public Comparable peek()
// pre: !isEmpty()
// post: returns the minimum value in the priority queue
{
    return (Comparable)data.elementAt(0);
}

public Comparable remove()
// pre: !isEmpty()
// post: removes and returns minimum value in priority queue
{
    Comparable result = (Comparable)data.elementAt(0);
    data.removeElementAt(0);
    return result;
}
```

The **peek** operation takes constant time. The **remove** operation caches and removes the first value of the **Vector** with a linear time complexity. This cannot be easily avoided since the cost is inherent in the way we use the **Vector** (though see Problem 11.8).

It is interesting to see the evolution of the various types encountered in the discussion of the `PriorityVector`. Although the **Vector** took an entire chapter to investigate, the abstract notion of a vector seems to be a relatively natural structure here. Abstraction has allowed us to avoid considering the minute details of the implementation. For example, we assume that vectors automatically extend themselves. The abstract notion of an `OrderedVector`, on the other hand, appears to be insufficient to directly support the specification of the `PriorityVector`. The reason is that the `OrderedVector` does not support **Vector** operations like **elementAt** and **removeElementAt**. These could, of

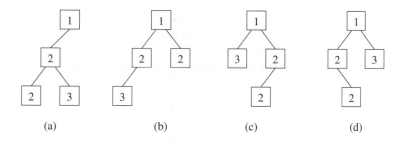

Figure 11.1 Four heaps containing the same values. Note that there is no ordering among siblings. Only heap *b* is complete.

course, be added to the `OrderedVector` interface, but an appeal for symmetry might then suggest implementation of the method `insertElementAt`. This would be a poor decision since it would then allow the user to insert elements out of order.

Principle 22 *Avoid unnaturally extending a natural interface.*

Designers of data structures spend considerable time weighing these design tradeoffs. While it is tempting to make the most versatile structures to support a wide variety of extensions, it surrenders the interface distinctions between structures that often allow for novel, efficient, and safe implementations.

In the next section we discuss a rich class of structures that allow us to maintain a loose ordering among elements. It turns out that even a loose ordering is sufficient to implement priority queues.

11.4 A Heap Implementation

In actuality, it is not necessary to develop a complete ranking of the elements of the priority queue in order to support the necessary operations. It is only necessary to be able to quickly identify the *minimum* value and to maintain a relatively loose ordering of the remaining values. This realization is the motivation for a structure called a *heap*:

Definition 11.1 *A* heap *is a binary tree whose root references the minimum value and whose subtrees are, themselves, heaps.*

An alternate definition is also sometimes useful:

Definition 11.2 *A* heap *is a binary tree whose values are in ascending order on every path from root to leaf.*

We will draw our heaps in the manner shown in Figure 11.1, with the minimum value on the top and the possibly larger values below. Notice that each of the four heaps contains the same values but has a different structure. Clearly, there is a great deal of freedom in the way that the heap can be oriented—for example, exchanging subtrees does not violate the heap property (heaps c and d are mirror images of each other). While not every tree with these four values is a heap, many are (see problems). This flexibility reduces the *friction* associated with constructing and maintaining a valid heap and, therefore, a valid priority queue. When friction is reduced we have the potential for increasing the speed of some operations.

Principle 23 *Seek structures with reduced friction.*

This is completely obvious.

We will say that a heap is a *complete heap* if the binary tree holding the values of the heap is complete. Any set of n values may be stored in a complete heap. (To see this we need only sort the values into ascending order and place them in levelorder in a complete binary tree. Since the values were inserted in ascending order, every child is at least as great as its parent.) The abstract notion of a complete heap forms the basis for the first of two heap implementations of a priority queue.

11.4.1 Vector-Based Heaps

Any complete binary tree (and therefore any complete heap) may be stored compactly in a vector. The method involves traversing the tree in levelorder and mapping the values to successive slots of the vector. When we are finished with this construction we observe the following (see Figure 11.2):

1. The root of the tree is stored in location 0. If non-`null`, this location references the minimum value of the heap.

2. The left child of a value stored in location i is found at location $2i + 1$.

3. The right child of a value stored in location i may be found at the location following the left child, location $2(i + 1) = (2i + 1) + 1$.

4. The parent of a value found in location i can be found at location $\lfloor \frac{i-1}{2} \rfloor$. Since division of integers in Java-like languages throws away the remainder for positive numbers, this expression is written `(i-1)/2`.

These relations may, of course, be encoded as functions. In Figure 11.2 we see the mapping of a heap to a vector, with tree relations indicated by arrows in the vector. Notice that while the vector is not maintained in ascending order, any path from the root to a leaf encounters values in ascending order. If the vector is larger than necessary, slots not associated with tree nodes can maintain a `null` reference.

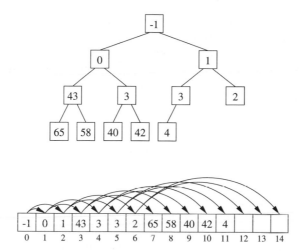

Figure 11.2 An abstract heap (top) and its vector representation. Arrows from parent to child are not physically part of the vector, but are indices computed by the heap's `left-` and `rightChildOf` methods.

With this mapping in mind, we consider the constructor and `static` methods:

```
protected Vector data;

public VectorHeap()
// post: constructs a new priority queue
{
    data = new Vector();
}

public VectorHeap(Vector v)
// post: constructs a new priority queue from an unordered vector
{
    int i;
    data = new Vector(v.size()); // we know ultimate size
    for (i = 0; i < v.size(); i++)
    {   // add elements to heap
        add((Comparable)v.elementAt(i));
    }
}

protected static int parentOf(int i)
// post: returns index of parent of value at i
{
    return (i-1)/2;
}
```

VectorHeap

```
protected static int leftChildOf(int i)
// post: returns index of left child of value at i
{
    return 2*i+1;
}

protected static int rightChildOf(int i)
// post: returns index of right child of value at i
{
    return 2*(i+1);
}
```

The functions `parentOf`, `leftChildOf`, and `rightChildOf` are declared `static` to indicate that they do not actually have to be called on any instance of a heap. Instead, their values are functions of their parameters only.

Principle 24 *Declare object-independent functions* `static`.

Now consider the addition of a value to a complete heap. We know that the heap is currently complete. Ideally, after the addition of the value the heap will remain complete, but will contain one extra value. This realization forces us to commit to inserting a value in a way that ultimately produces a correctly structured heap. Since the first free element of the `Vector` will hold a value, we optimistically insert the new value in that location (see Figure 11.3). If, considering the path from the leaf to the root, the value is in the wrong location, then it must be "percolated upward" to the correct entry. We begin by comparing and, if necessary, exchanging the new value and its parent. If the values along the path are still incorrectly ordered, it must be because of the new value, and we continue to percolate the value upward until either the new value is the root or it is greater than or equal to its current parent. The only values possibly exchanged in this operation are those appearing along the unique path from the insertion point. Since locations that change only become smaller, the integrity of other paths in the tree is maintained.

The code associated with percolating a value upward is contained in the function `percolateUp`. This function takes an index of a value that is possibly out of place and pushes the value upward toward the root until it reaches the correct location. While the routine takes an index as a parameter, the parameter passed is usually the index of the rightmost leaf of the bottom level.

```
protected void percolateUp(int leaf)
// pre: 0 <= leaf < size
// post: takes value at leaf in near-heap,
//       and pushes up to correct location
{
    int parent = parentOf(leaf);
    Comparable value = (Comparable)(data.elementAt(leaf));
    while (leaf > 0 &&
```

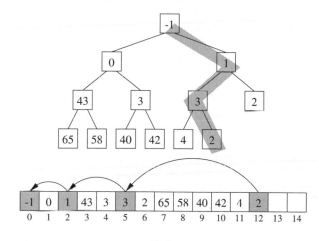

Before

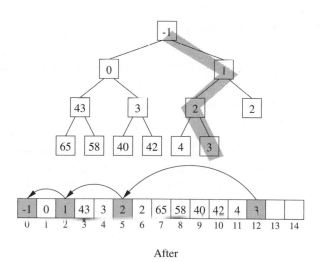

After

Figure 11.3 The addition of a value (2) to a vector-based heap. Above, the value is inserted into a free location known to be part of the result structure. Below, the value is percolated up to the correct location on the unique path to the root.

```
         (value.compareTo((Comparable)(data.elementAt(parent))) < 0))
    {
        data.setElementAt(data.elementAt(parent),leaf);
        leaf = parent;
        parent = parentOf(leaf);
    }
    data.setElementAt(value,leaf);
}
```

Adding a value to the priority queue is then only a matter of appending it to the end of the vector (the location of the newly added leaf) and percolating the value upward until it finds the correct location:

```
public void add(Comparable value)
// pre: value is non-null comparable object
// post: adds value to priority queue
{
    data.addElement(value);
    percolateUp(data.size()-1);
}
```

Let us consider how long it takes to accomplish the addition of a value to the heap. Remember that the tree that we are working with is an n-node complete binary tree, so its height is $\lfloor \log_2 n \rfloor$. Each step of the percolateUp routine takes constant time and pushes the new value up one level. Of course, it may be positioned correctly the first time, but the worst case behavior of inserting the new value into the tree consumes $O(\log n)$ time. This performance is considerably better than the linear behavior of the PriorityVector implementation described earlier. What is the best time? It is constant when the value added is large compared to the values found on the path from the new leaf to the root.

What is the expected time? Be careful!

Next, we consider the removal of the minimum value (see Figures 11.4 and 11.5). It is located at the root of the heap, in the first slot of the vector. The removal of this value leaves an empty location at the top of the heap. Ultimately, when the operation is complete, the freed location will be the rightmost leaf of the bottom level, the last element of the underlying vector. Again, our approach is first to construct a tree that is the correct shape, but potentially not a heap, and then perform transformations on the tree that both maintain its shape and bring the structure closer to being a heap. Thus, when the minimum value is removed, the rightmost leaf on the bottom level is removed and re-placed at the root of the tree (Figure 11.4a–b). At this point, the tree is the correct shape, but it may not be a heap because the root of the tree is potentially too large. Since the subtrees remain heaps, we need to ensure the root of the tree is the minimum value contained in the tree. We first find the minimum child and compare this value with the root (Figure 11.5a). If the root value is no greater, the minimum value is at the root and the entire structure is a heap. If the root is larger, then it is exchanged with the true minimum—the smallest child—pushing the large value downward. At this point, the root of the tree has the correct value. All but one of the subtrees are unchanged, and the shape of

We're "heaping in shape."

the tree remains correct. All that has happened is that a large value has been pushed down to where it may violate the heap property in a subtree. We then perform any further exchanges recursively, with the value sinking into smaller subtrees (Figure 11.5b), possibly becoming a leaf. Since any single value is a heap, the recursion must stop by the time the newly inserted value becomes a leaf.

Here is the code associated with the pushing down of the root:

```
protected void pushDownRoot(int root)
// pre: 0 <= root < size
// post: pushes root down into near-heap
//       constructing heap
{
    int heapSize = data.size();
    Comparable value = (Comparable)data.elementAt(root);
    while (root < heapSize) {
        int childpos = leftChildOf(root);
        if (childpos < heapSize)
        {
            if ((rightChildOf(root) < heapSize) &&
              (((Comparable)(data.elementAt(childpos+1))).compareTo
              ((Comparable)(data.elementAt(childpos))) < 0))
            {
                childpos++;
            }
            // Assert: childpos indexes smaller of two children
            if (((Comparable)(data.elementAt(childpos))).compareTo
                (value) < 0)
            {
                data.setElementAt(data.elementAt(childpos),root);
                root = childpos; // keep moving down
            } else { // found right location
                data.setElementAt(value,root);
                return;
            }
        } else { // at a leaf! insert and halt
            data.setElementAt(value,root);
            return;
        }
    }
}
```

The **remove** method simply involves returning the smallest value of the heap, but only after the rightmost element of the vector has been pushed downward.

```
public Comparable remove()
// pre: !isEmpty()
// post: removes and returns minimum value in queue
{
    Comparable minVal = peek();
```

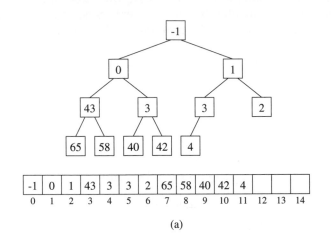

(a)

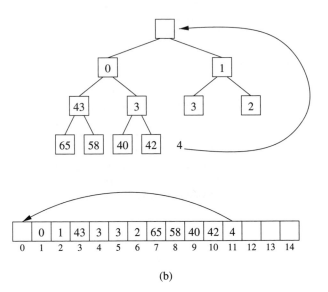

(b)

Figure 11.4 Removing a value from the heap shown in (a) involves moving the rightmost value of the vector to the top of the heap as in (b). Note that this value is likely to violate the heap property but that the subtrees will remain heaps.

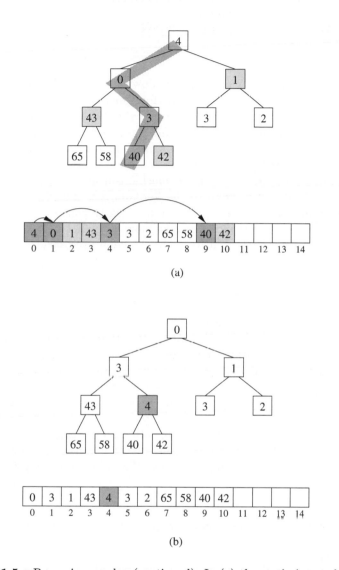

(a)

(b)

Figure 11.5   Removing a value (continued). In (a) the newly inserted value at the root is pushed down along a shaded path following the smallest children (lightly shaded nodes are also considered in determining the path). In (b) the root value finds, over several iterations, the correct location along the path. Smaller values shift upward to make room for the new value.

```
        data.setElementAt(data.elementAt(data.size()-1),0);
        data.setSize(data.size()-1);
        if (data.size() > 1) pushDownRoot(0);
        return minVal;
    }
```

Each level of recursion pushes a large value down into a smaller heap on a path from the root to a leaf. Therefore, the performance of `remove` is $O(\log n)$, an improvement over the behavior of the `PriorityVector` implementation.

Since we have implemented all the required methods of the `PriorityQueue`, the `VectorHeap` implements the `PriorityQueue` and may be used wherever a priority queue is required.

The advantages of the `VectorHeap` mechanism are that, because of the unique mapping of complete trees to the `Vector`, it is unnecessary to explicitly store the connections between elements. Even though we are able to get improved performance over the `PriorityVector`, we do not have to pay a space penalty. The complexity arises, instead, in the code necessary to support the insertion and removal of values.

11.4.2   Example: Heapsort

Any priority queue, of course, can be used as the underlying data structure for a sorting mechanism. When the values of a heap are stored in a `Vector`, an empty location is potentially made available when they are removed. This location could be used to store a removed value. As the heap shrinks, the values are stored in the newly vacated elements of the `Vector`. As the heap becomes empty, the `Vector` is completely filled with values in descending order.

Unfortunately, we cannot make assumptions about the structure of the values initially found in the `Vector`; we are, after all, sorting them. Since the above approach depends on the values being placed in a heap, we must consider one more operation: a constructor that "heapifies" the data found in a `Vector` passed do it:

```
    public VectorHeap(Vector v)
    // post: constructs a new priority queue from an unordered vector
    {
        int i;
        data = new Vector(v.size()); // we know ultimate size
        for (i = 0; i < v.size(); i++)
        {   // add elements to heap
            add((Comparable)v.elementAt(i));
        }
    }
```

The process of constructing a heap from an unordered `Vector` obviously takes the time of n `add` operations, each of which is $O(n)$. The worst-case cost of "heapifying" is, therefore, $O(n \log n)$. (This can be improved—see Problem 11.10.)

Now, the remaining part of the heapsort—removing the minimum values and placing them in the newly freed locations—requires n `remove` operations. This phase also has worst-case complexity $O(n \log n)$. We have, therefore, another sorting algorithm with $O(n \log n)$ behavior and little space overhead.

The feature of a heap that makes the sort so efficient is its short height. The values are always stored in as full a tree as possible and, as a result, we may place a logarithmic upper bound on the time it takes to insert and remove values. In the next section we investigate the use of unrestricted heaps to implement priority queues. These structures have *amortized* cost that is equivalent to heaps built atop vectors.

11.4.3 Skew Heaps

The performance of vector-based heaps is directly dependent on the fact that these heaps are complete. Since complete heaps are a minority of all heaps, it is reasonable to ask if efficient priority queues might be constructed from unrestricted heaps. The answer is yes, if we relax the way we measure performance.

We consider, here, the implementation of heaps using dynamically structured binary trees. A direct cost of this decision is the increase in space. Where a vector stored a single reference, the binary tree node keeps an additional three references. These three references allow us to implement noncomplete heaps in a space-efficient manner (see Problem 11.21). Here are the protected data and the constructor for this structure:

```
protected BinaryTreeNode root;
protected int count;

public SkewHeap()
// post: creates an empty priority queue
{
    root = null;
    count = 0;
}
```

SkewHeap

Notice that we keep track of the size of the heap locally, rather than asking the `BinaryTreeNode` for its size. This is simply a matter of efficiency, but it requires us to maintain the value within the `add` and `remove` procedures. Once we commit to implementing heaps in this manner, we need to consider the implementation of each of the major operators.

The implementation of `peek` simply references the value stored at the root. Its implementation is relatively straightforward:

```
public Comparable peek()
// pre: !isEmpty()
// post: returns the minimum object in queue
{
    return (Comparable)(root.value());
}
```

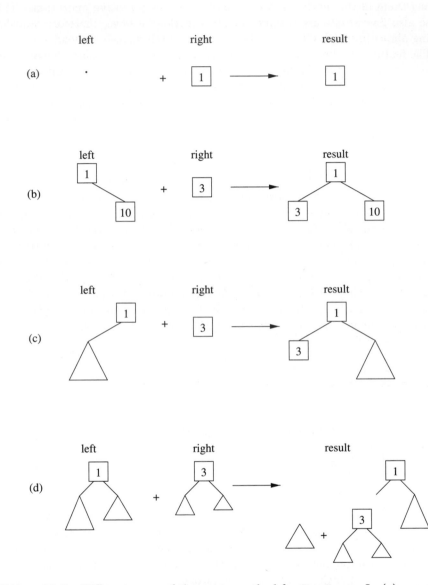

Figure 11.6 Different cases of the `merge` method for `SkewHeap`s. In (a) one of the heaps is empty. In (b) and (c) the right heap becomes the left child of the left heap. In (d) the right heap is merged into what was the right subheap.

Before we consider the implementation of the **add** and **remove** methods, we consider a (seemingly unnecessary) operation, **merge**. This method takes two heaps and merges them together. This is a *destructive* operation: the elements of the participating heaps are consumed in the construction of the result. Our approach will be to make **merge** a recursive method that considers several cases. First, if either of the two heaps participating in the merge is empty, then the result of the merge is the other heap. Otherwise, both heaps contain at least a value—assume that the minimum root is found in the left heap (if not, we can swap them). We know, then, that the result of the merge will be a reference to the root node of the left heap. To see how the right heap is merged into the left we consider two cases:

As with all good things, this will eventually seem necessary.

1. If the left heap has no left child, make the right heap the left child of the left heap (see Figure 11.6b).

2. Otherwise, exchange the left and right children of the left heap. Then merge (the newly made) left subheap of the left heap with the right heap (see Figure 11.6d).

Notice that if the left heap has one subheap, the right heap becomes the left subheap and the merging is finished. Here is the code for the **merge** method:

```
protected static BinaryTreeNode merge(BinaryTreeNode left,
                                       BinaryTreeNode right)
// post: merges two skew heaps into one
{
    if (left == null) return right;
    if (right == null) return left;
    Comparable leftVal = (Comparable)(left.value());
    Comparable rightVal = (Comparable)(right.value());
    BinaryTreeNode result;
    if (rightVal.compareTo(leftVal) < 0)
    {
        result = merge(right,left);
    } else {
        result = left;
        // assertion left side is smaller than right
        // left is new root
        if (result.left() == null)
        {
            result.setLeft(right);
        } else {
            BinaryTreeNode temp = result.right();
            result.setRight(result.left());
            result.setLeft(merge(temp,right));
        }
    }
    return result;
}
```

Once the merge method has been defined, we find that the process of adding a value or removing the minimum is relatively straightforward. To add a value, we construct a new `BinaryTreeNode` containing the single value that is to be added. This is, in essence, a one-element heap. We then merge this heap with the existing heap, and the result is a new heap with the value added:

```
public void add(Comparable value)
// pre: value is non-null object
// post: adds value to priority queue
{
    BinaryTreeNode smallTree = new BinaryTreeNode(value);
    root = merge(smallTree,root);
    count++;
}
```

To remove the minimum value from the heap we must extract and return the value at the root. To construct the smaller resulting heap we detach both subtrees from the root and merge them together. The result is a heap with all the values of the left and right subtrees, but not the root. This is precisely the result we require. Here is the code:

```
public Comparable remove()
// pre: !isEmpty()
// post: returns and removes the minimum object in queue
{
    Comparable result = (Comparable)(root.value());
    root = merge(root.left(),root.right());
    count--;
    return result;
}
```

The remaining priority queue methods for skew heaps are implemented in a relatively straightforward manner.

Because a skew heap has unconstrained topology (see Problem 11.16) it is possible to construct examples of skew heaps with degenerate behavior. For example, adding a new maximum value can take $O(n)$ time. For this reason we cannot put very impressive bounds on the performance of any individual operation. The skew heap, however, is an example of a self-organizing structure: inefficient operations spend some of their excess time making later operations run more quickly. If we are careful, time "charged against" early operations can be *amortized* or redistributed to later operations, which we hope will run very efficiently. This type of analysis can be used, for example, to demonstrate that $m > n$ skew heap operations applied to a heap of size n take no more that $O(m \log n)$ time. On average, then, each operation takes $O(\log n)$ time. For applications that expect to make a significant number of requests of a heap, this performance is appealing.

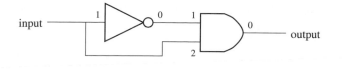

Figure 11.7   A circuit for detecting a rising logic level.

11.5   Example: Circuit Simulation

Consider the electronic digital circuit depicted in Figure 11.7. The two devices shown are *logic gates*. The wires between the gates propagate electrical signals. Typically a zero voltage is called *false* or *low*, while a potential of 10 volts or more is *true* or *high*.

The triangular gate, on the left, is an *inverter*. On its output (pin 0) it "inverts" the logic level found on the input (pin 1): false becomes true and true becomes false. The gate on the right is an *and gate*. It generates a true on pin 0 exactly when both of its inputs (pins 1 and 2) are true.

The action of these gates is the result of a physical process, so the effect of the inputs on the output is delayed by a period of time called a *gate delay*. Gate delays depend on the complexity of the gate, the manufacturing process, and environmental factors. For our purposes, we'll assume the gate delay of the inverter is 0.2 nanosecond (ns) and the delay of the and is 0.8 ns.

The question is: what output is generated when we toggle the input from low to high and back to low several times? To determine the answer we can build the hardware, or simulate it in software. For reasons that will become clear in a moment, simulation will be more useful.

The setup for our simulation will consist of a number of small classes. First, there are a number of components, including an `Inverter`; an `And`; an input, or `Source`; and a voltage sensor, or `Probe`. When constructed, gates are provided gate delay values, and `Sources` and `Probes` are given names. Each of these components has one or more pins to which wires can be connected. (As with real circuits, the outputs should connect only to inputs of other components!) Finally, the voltage level of a particular pin can be set to a particular level. As an example of the interface, we list the `public` methods for the `And` gate:

```
class And extends Component
{
    public And(double delay)
    // pre: delay >= 0.0ns
    // post: constructs and gate with indicated gate delay

    public void set(double time, int pinNum, int level)
    // pre: pinNum = 1 or 2, level = 0/15
```

Circuit

```
         // post: updates inputs and generates events on
         //       devices connected to output
    }
```

Notice that there is a time associated with the **set** method. This helps us document when different events happen in the component. These events are simulated by a comparable **Event** class. This class describes a change in logic level on an input pin for some component. As the simulation progresses, **Events** are created and scheduled for simulation in the future. The ordering of **Events** is based on an event time. Here are the details:

```
    class Event implements Comparable
    {
        protected double time;      // time of event
        protected int level;        // voltage level
        protected Connection c;     // gate/pin

        public Event(Connection c, double t, int l)
        // pre: c is a valid pin on a gate
        // post: constructs event for time t to set pin to level l
        {
            this.c = c;
            time = t;
            level = l;
        }

        public void go()
        // post: informs target component of updated logic on pin
        {
            c.component().set(time,c.pin(),level);
        }

        public int compareTo(Object other)
        // pre: other is non-null
        // post: returns integer representing relation between values
        {
            Event that = (Event)other;
            if (this.time < that.time) return -1;
            else if (this.time == that.time) return 0;
            else return 1;
        }
    }
```

The **Connection** mentioned here is simply a component's input pin.

Finally, to orchestrate the simulation, we use a priority queue to correctly simulate the order of events. The following method simulates a circuit by removing events from the priority queue and setting the logic level on the appropriate pins of the components. The method returns the time of the last event to help monitor the progress of the simulation:

```
public class Circuit
{
    static PriorityQueue eventQueue; // main event queue

    public static double simulate()
    // post: run simulation until event queue is empty
    //       returns final clock time
    {
        double clock = 0.0;
        while (!eventQueue.isEmpty())
        {   // remove next event
            Event e = (Event)eventQueue.remove();
            // keep track of time
            clock = e.time;
            // simulate the event
            e.go();
        }
        System.out.println("-- circuit stable after "+clock+"ns --");
        return clock;
    }
}
```

As events are processed, the logic level on a component's pins are updated.
If the inputs to a component change, new Events are scheduled one gate delay
later for each component connected to the output pin. For Sources and Probes,
we write a message to the output indicating the change in logic level. Clearly,
when there are no more events in the priority queue, the simulated circuit is
stable. If the user is interested, he or she can change the logic level of a Source
and resume the simulation by running the simulate method again.

We are now equipped to simulate the circuit of Figure 11.7. The first portion
of the following code sets up the circuit, while the second half simulates the effect
of toggling the input several times:

```
public static void main(String[] args)
{
    eventQueue = new SkewHeap();
    double time;

    // set up circuit
    Inverter not = new Inverter(0.2);
    And and = new And(0.8);
    Probe output = new Probe("output");
    Source input = new Source("input",not.pin(1));

    input.connectTo(and.pin(2));
    not.connectTo(and.pin(1));
    and.connectTo(output.pin(1));
```

```
        // simulate circuit
        time = simulate();
        input.set(time+1.0,0,15); // first: set input high
        time = simulate();
        input.set(time+1.0,0,0);  // later: set input low
        time = simulate();
        input.set(time+1.0,0,15); // later: set input high
        time = simulate();
        input.set(time+1.0,0,0);  // later: set input low
        simulate();
    }
```

When run, the resulting output is generated:

```
    1.0ns: output now 0 volts
    -- circuit stable after 1.0ns --
    2.0ns: input set to 15 volts
    2.8ns: output now 15 volts
    3.0ns: output now 0 volts
    -- circuit stable after 3.0ns --
    4.0ns: input set to 0 volts
    -- circuit stable after 5.0ns --
    6.0ns: input set to 15 volts
    6.8ns: output now 15 volts
    7.0ns: output now 0 volts
    -- circuit stable after 7.0ns --
    8.0ns: input set to 0 volts
    -- circuit stable after 9.0ns --
```

When the input is moved from low to high, a short "spike" is generated on the output. Moving the input to low again has no impact. The spike is generated by the *rising edge* of a signal, and its width is determined by the gate delay of the inverter. Because the spike is so short, it would have been difficult to detect it using real hardware.[3] Devices similar to this edge detector are important tools for detecting changing states in the circuits they monitor.

11.6   Conclusions

We have seen three implementations of priority queues: one based on a vector that keeps its entries in order and two others based on heap implementations. The vector implementation demonstrates how any ordered structure may be adapted to support the operations of a priority queue.

Heaps form successful implementations of priority queues because they relax the conditions on "keeping data in priority order." Instead of maintaining data in sorted order, heaps maintain a competition between values that becomes

---

[3] This is a very short period of time. During the time the output is high, light travels just over 2 inches!

progressively more intense as the values reach the front of the queue. The cost of inserting and removing values from a heap can be made to be as low as $O(\log n)$.

If the constraint of keeping values in a **Vector** is too much (it may be impossible, for example, to allocate a single large chunk of memory), or if one wants to avoid the uneven cost of extending a vector, a dynamic mechanism is useful. The **SkewHeap** is such a mechanism, keeping data in general heap form. Over a number of operations the skew heap performs as well as the traditional vector-based implementation.

Problems

11.1   Draw the state of a **HeapVector** after each of the values 3, 4, 7, 0, 2, 8, and 6 are added, in that order.

11.2   Consider the heap | 0 | 2 | 1 | 3 | 7 | 4 | 6 | 8 |

1. What does this heap look like, when drawn as a tree?

2. What does this heap look like (in array form) when a value is removed?

11.3   Below is a **SkewHeap**. What does it look like after a value is removed?

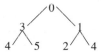

11.4   How might you use priorities to simulate a LIFO structure with a priority queue?

11.5   Is a **VectorHeap** a **Queue**? Is it an **OrderedStructure**?

11.6   How might you use priorities to simulate a FIFO structure with a priority queue?

11.7   Suppose a user built an object whose **compareTo** and **equals** methods were inconsistent. For example, values that were **equals** might also return a negative value for **compareTo**. What happens when these values are added to a **PriorityVector**? What happens when these values are added to a **SkewHeap**?

11.8   We have seen that the cost of removing a value from the **Priority-Vector** takes linear time. If elements were stored in descending order, this could be reduced to constant time. Compare the ascending and descending implementations, discussing the circumstances that suggest the use of one implementation over the other.

11.9   What methods would have to be added to the **OrderedVector** class to make it possible to implement a **PriorityVector** using only a private **Ordered-Vector**?

11.10 Reconsider the "heapifying" constructor discussed in the text. Instead of adding n values to an initially empty heap (at a cost of $O(n \log n)$), suppose we do the following: Consider each interior node of the heap in order of decreasing array index. Think of this interior node as the root of a potential subheap. We know that its subtrees are valid heaps. Now, just push this node down into its (near-)heap. Show that the cost of performing this heapify operation is linear in the size of the `Vector`.

11.11 Design a more efficient version of `HeapVector` that keeps its values in order only when necessary: When values are added, they are appended to the end of the existing heap and a `nonHeap` flag is set to `true`. When values are removed, the `nonHeap` flag is checked and the `Vector` is heapified if necessary. What are the worst-case and best-case running times of the `add` and `remove` operations. (You may assume that you have access to the heapify of the previous problem.)

11.12★ Considered the unordered data: | 4 | 2 | 7 | 3 | 1 | 0 | 5 | 6 |. What does this `Vector` look like after it has been heapified?

11.13 Consider the in-place `Vector`-based heapsort.

  a. A min-heap is particularly suited to sorting data in-place into which order: ascending or descending?

  b. What is the worst-case time complexity of this sort?

  c. What is the best-case time complexity of this sort?

11.14★ Suppose we are given access to a min-heap, but not the code that supports it. What changes to the *comparable data* might we make to force the min-heap to work like a max-heap?

11.15 Suppose we are to find the kth largest element of a heap of n values. Describe how we might accomplish this efficiently. What is the worst-case running time of your method? (Hint: This can be accomplished in linear time.) Notice that if the problem had said "set of n values," we would require a heapify operation like that found in Problem 11.10.

11.16 Demonstrate that any binary tree that has the heap property can be generated by inserting values into a skew heap in an appropriate order. (This realization is important to understanding why an amortized accounting scheme is necessary.)

11.17 Suppose you are given 2^{n-1} distinct values to store in a full heap—a heap that is maintained in a full binary tree. Since there is no ordering between children in a heap, the left and right subheaps can be exchanged. How many equivalent heaps can be produced by only swapping children of a node?

11.18 Given n distinct values to be stored in a heap, how many heaps can store the values? (Difficult.)

11.19 What proportion of the binary trees holding n values are heaps?

11.20 Suppose that n randomly selected (and uniformly distributed) numbers are inserted into a complete heap. Now, select another number and insert it into the heap. What is the expected number of levels the new number will percolate up?

11.21⋆ The mapping strategy that takes a complete binary tree to a vector can actually be used to store general trees, albeit in a space-inefficient manner. The strategy is to allocate enough space to hold the lowest, rightmost leaf, and to maintain null references in nodes that are not currently being used. What is the worst-case vector length needed to store an n-element binary tree?

11.22⋆ Write an `equals` method for a `PriorityVector`. It returns `true` if each pair of corresponding elements removed from the structures would be equal. What is the complexity of the `equals` method. (Hint: You may not need to remove values.)

11.23⋆ Write an `equals` method for a `HeapVector`. It returns `true` if each pair of corresponding elements removed from the structures would be equal. What is the complexity of the `equals` method. (Hint: You may need to remove values.)

11.24 Write an `equals` method for a `SkewHeap`. It returns `true` if each pair of corresponding elements removed from the structures would be equal. What is the complexity of the `equals` method. (Hint: You may need to remove values.)

11.25 Show that the implementation of the `PriorityVector` can be improved by not actually keeping the values in order. Instead, only maintain the minimum value at the left. Demonstrate the implementation of `add` and `remove`.

11.26 Suppose you are a manufacturer of premium-quality video cassette recorders. Your XJ-6 recorder allows the "user" to "program" 4096 different future events to be recorded. Of course, as the time arrives for each event, your machine is responsible for turning on and recording a program.

a. What information is necessary to correctly record an event?

b. Design the data structure(s) needed to support the XJ-6.

Chapter 12
Search Trees

STRUCTURES ARE OFTEN THE SUBJECT OF A SEARCH. We have seen, for example, that binary search is a natural and efficient algorithm for finding values within ordered, randomly accessible structures. Recall that at each point the algorithm compares the value sought with the value in the middle of the structure. If they are not equal, the algorithm performs a similar, possibly recursive search on one side or the other. The pivotal feature of the algorithm, of course, was that the underlying structure was in order. The result was that a value could be efficiently *found* in approximately logarithmic time. Unfortunately, the modifying operations—`add` and `remove`—had complexities that were determined by the linear nature of the vector.

Heaps have shown us that by relaxing our notions of order we can improve on the linear complexities of adding and removing values. These logarithmic operations, however, do not preserve the order of elements in any obviously useful manner. Still, if we were somehow able to totally order the elements of a binary tree, then an algorithmlike binary search might naturally be imposed on this branching structure.

12.1 Binary Search Trees

The *binary search tree* is a binary tree whose elements are kept in order. This is easily stated as a recursive definition.

Definition 12.1 *A binary tree is a* binary search tree *if it is trivial, or if every node is simultaneously greater than or equal to each value in its left subtree, and less than or equal to each value in its right subtree.*

To see that this is a significant restriction on the structure of a binary tree, one need only note that if a maximum of n distinct values is found at the root, all other values must be found in the left subtree. Figure 12.1 demonstrates the many trees that can contain even three distinct values. Thus, if one is not

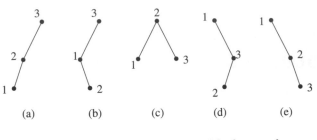

Figure 12.1   Binary search trees with three nodes.

too picky about the value one wants to have at the root of the tree, there are still a significant number of trees from which to choose. This is important if we want to have our modifying operations run quickly: ideally we should be as nonrestrictive about the outcome as possible, in order to reduce the friction of the operation.

One important thing for which to watch is that even though our definition allows duplicate values of the root node to fall on either side, our code will prefer to have them on the left. This preference is arbitrary. If we assume that values equal to the root will be found in the left subtree, but some are actually located in the right, then we might expect inconsistent behavior from methods that search for values. In fact, this is not the case.

To guide access to the elements of a binary search tree, we will consider it an implementation of an `OrderedStructure`, supporting the following methods:

Binary-
SearchTree

```
public class BinarySearchTree implements OrderedStructure
{
    public BinarySearchTree()
    // post: constructs an empty binary search tree

    public boolean isEmpty()
    // post: returns true iff the binary search tree is empty

    public void clear()
    // post: removes all elements from binary search tree

    public int size()
    // post: returns the number of elements in binary search tree

    public void add(Object val)
    // pre: val is non-null
    // post: adds a value to the binary search tree

    public boolean contains(Object val)
    // pre: val is non-null
    // post: returns true iff val is a value found within the tree
```

```
        public Object get(Object val)
        // pre: val is non-null
        // post: returns object found in tree, or null

        public Object remove(Object val)
        // pre: val is non-null
        // post: removes one instance of val, if found

        public Iterator elements()
        // post: returns iterator to traverse BST
    }
```

Unlike the `BinaryTree`, the `BinarySearchTree` provides only one `elements` method. This method provides for an inorder traversal of the tree, which, with some thought, allows access to each of the elements in order.

Maybe even with no thought!

12.2   Example: Tree Sort

Because the `BinarySearchTree` is an `OrderedStructure` it provides the natural basis for sorting. The algorithm of Section 9.2.3 will work equally well here, provided the allocation of the `OrderedStructure` is modified to construct a `BinarySearchTree`. The binary search structure, however, potentially provides significant improvements in performance. If the tree can be kept reasonably short, the cost of inserting each element is $O(\log n)$. Since n elements are ultimately added to the structure, the total cost is $O(n \log n)$.[1] As we have seen in Chapter 10, all of the elements of the underlying binary tree can be visited in linear time. The resulting algorithm has a potential for $O(n \log n)$ time complexity, which rivals the performance of sorting techniques using heaps. The advantage of binary search trees is that the elements need not be removed to determine their order. To attain this performance, though, we must keep the tree as short as possible. This will require considerable attention.

12.3   Implementation

In considering the implementation of a `BinarySearchTree`, it is important to remember that we are implementing an `OrderedStructure`. The methods of the `OrderedStructure` accept and return values that are `Comparable`. The fact that an object is a `Comparable`, of course, only indicates that there is a `compareTo` method—we cannot depend on any other methods to help us control the structure of the tree!

We begin by noticing that a `BinarySearchTree` is little more than a binary tree with an imposed order. As with the `BinaryTree` we maintain a reference

---

[1] This needs to be proved! See Problem 12.11.

to a `BinaryTreeNode` and explicitly keep track of the size of the tree. The constructor need only initialize these two fields to a state consistent with an empty binary search tree:

```
protected BinaryTreeNode root;
protected int count;

public BinarySearchTree()
// post: constructs an empty binary search tree
{
    root = null;
    count = 0;
}
```

As with most implementations of `OrderedStructure`s we develop a method to find the correct location to insert the value, and then use that method as the basis for implementing the public methods—add, contains, and remove. Our approach to the method `locate` is to have it return a reference to the location that identifies the correct point of insertion for the new value. Here is the Java code for the method:

```
protected BinaryTreeNode locate(BinaryTreeNode root,
                                Comparable value)
// pre: root and value are non-null
// post: returned: 1 - existing tree node with the desired value, or
//                 2 - the node to which value should be added
{
    Comparable rootValue = (Comparable)root.value();
    BinaryTreeNode child;

    // found at root: done
    if (rootValue.equals(value)) return root;
    // look left if less-than, right if greater-than
    if (rootValue.compareTo(value) < 0)
    {
        child = root.right();
    } else {
        child = root.left();
    }
    // no child there: not in tree, return this node,
    // else keep searching
    if (child == null) {
        return root;
    } else {
        return locate(child, value);
    }
}
```

The approach of the method parallels binary search. Comparisons are made with the root, which serves as a median value. If the value does not match, then the search is refocused on either the left side of the tree (among smaller values) or the right side of the tree (among larger values). In either case, if the search is about to step off the tree, the current node is returned: if the value were added, it would be a child of the current node.

Once the `locate` method is written, the `contains` method must check to see if the node returned by `locate` actually equals the desired value:

```
public boolean contains(Object val)
// pre: val is non-null
// post: returns true iff val is a value found within the tree
{
    if (root == null) return false;

    BinaryTreeNode possibleLocation = locate(root,(Comparable)val);
    return val.equals(possibleLocation.value());
}
```

It now becomes a fairly straightforward task to add a value. We simply locate the value in the tree using the `locate` function. If the value was not found, `locate` returned a node off of which a leaf with the desired value can be added. If, however, `locate` has found an equivalent value, we must insert the new value as the right child of the predecessor of the node returned by `locate`.[2]

```
public void add(Object val)
// pre: val is non-null
// post: adds a value to the binary search tree
{
    BinaryTreeNode newNode = new BinaryTreeNode(val);

    // add value to binary search tree
    // if there's no root, create value at root
    if (root == null)
    {
        root = newNode;
    } else {
        Comparable value = (Comparable)val;
        BinaryTreeNode insertLocation = locate(root,value);
        Comparable nodeValue = (Comparable)insertLocation.value();
        // The location returned is the successor or predecessor
        // of the to-be-inserted value
        if (nodeValue.compareTo(value) < 0) {
            insertLocation.setRight(newNode);
        } else {
            if (insertLocation.left() != null) {
```

---

[2] With a little thought, it is clear to see that this is a correct location. If there are two copies of a value in a tree, the second value added is a descendant and predecessor (in an inorder traversal) of the located value. It is also easy to see that a predecessor has no right child, and that if one is added, *it* becomes the predecessor.

```
                        // if value is in tree we insert just before
                        predecessor(insertLocation).setRight(newNode);
                    } else {
                        insertLocation.setLeft(newNode);
                    }
                }
            }
            count++;
        }
```

Our **add** code makes use of the protected "helper" function, **predecessor**, which returns a pointer to the node that immediately precedes the indicated root:

```
protected BinaryTreeNode predecessor(BinaryTreeNode root)
// pre: tree is not empty, root node has left child
// post: returns pointer to predecessor of root
{
    Assert.pre(root != null, "No predecessor to middle value.");
    Assert.pre(root.left() != null, "Root has left child.");
    BinaryTreeNode result = root.left();
    while (result.right() != null) {
        result = result.right();
    }
    return result;
}
```

A similar routine can be written for successor, and would be used if we preferred to store duplicate values in the right subtree.

We now approach the problem of removing a value from a binary search tree. Observe that if it is found, it might be an internal node. The "worst case" occurs when the root of a tree is involved, so let us consider that problem.

There are several cases. First (Figure 12.2a), if the root of a tree has no left child, the right subtree can be used as the resulting tree. Likewise (Figure 12.2b), if there is no right child, we simply return the left. A third case (Figure 12.2c) occurs when the left subtree has no right child. Then, the right subtree—a tree with values no smaller than the left root—is made the right subtree of the left. The left root is returned as the result. The opposite circumstance could also be true.

We are, then, left to consider trees with a left subtree that, in turn, contains a right subtree (Figure 12.3). Our approach to solving this case is to seek out the predecessor of the root and make it the new root. Note that even though the predecessor does not have a right subtree, it may have a left. This subtree can take the place of the predecessor as the right subtree of a nonroot node. (Note that this is the result that we would expect if we had recursively performed our node-removing process on the subtree rooted at the predecessor.)

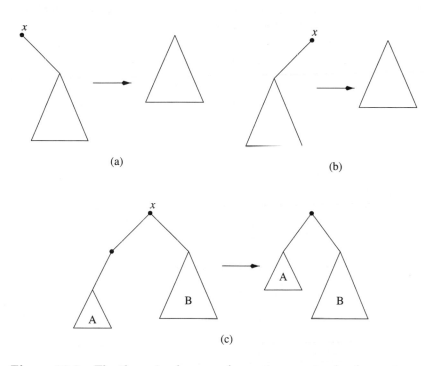

(a)   (b)

(c)

Figure 12.2   The three simple cases of removing a root value from a tree.

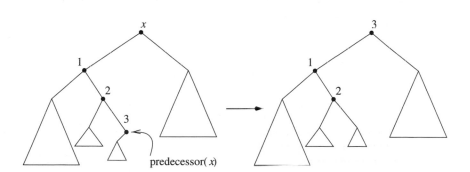

Figure 12.3   Removing the root of a tree with a rightmost left descendant.

Finally, here is the Java code that removes the top `BinaryTreeNode` of a tree and returns the root of the resulting tree:

```java
protected BinaryTreeNode removeTop(BinaryTreeNode topNode)
// pre: tree is not empty
// post: root of tree (topNode) is disconnected from tree and
//        a new root is returned, new root has no parent

{
    // remove topmost BinaryTreeNode from a binary search tree
    BinaryTreeNode left  = topNode.left();
    BinaryTreeNode right = topNode.right();
    // disconnect top node
    topNode.setLeft(null);
    topNode.setRight(null);
    // Case a, no left BinaryTreeNode
    //   easy: right subtree is new tree
    if (left == null) { return right; }
    // Case b, no right BinaryTreeNode
    //   easy: left subtree is new tree
    if (right == null) { return left; }
    // Case c, left node has no right subtree
    //   easy: make right subtree of left
    BinaryTreeNode predecessor = left.right();
    if (predecessor == null)
    {
        left.setRight(right);
        return left;
    }
    // General case, slide down left tree
    //   harder: successor of root becomes new root
    //           parent always points to parent of predecessor
    BinaryTreeNode parent = left;
    while (predecessor.right() != null)
    {
        parent = predecessor;
        predecessor = predecessor.right();
    }
    // Assert: predecessor is predecessor of root
    parent.setRight(predecessor.left());
    predecessor.setLeft(left);
    predecessor.setRight(right);
    return predecessor;
}
```

With the combined efforts of the `removeTop` and `locate` methods, we can now simply locate a value in the search tree and, if found, remove it from the tree. We must be careful to update the appropriate references to rehook the modified subtree back into the overall structure.

Notice that inserting and removing elements in this manner ensures that the inorder traversal of the underlying tree delivers the values stored in the nodes in increasing order. We use this, then, as our preferred iteration method.

```
public Iterator elements()
// post: returns iterator to traverse BST
{
    return new BTInorderIterator(root);
}
```

The remaining methods (`size`, etc.) are implemented in a now-familiar manner.

Each of the time-consuming operations of a `BinarySearchTree` has a worst-case time complexity that is proportional to the height of the tree. It is easy to see that checking for or adding a leaf, or removing a root, involves some of the most time-consuming operations. Thus, for logarithmic behavior, we must be sure that the tree remains as short as possible.

Unfortunately, we have no such assurance. In particular, one may observe what happens when values are inserted in descending order: the tree is heavily skewed to the left. If the same values are inserted in ascending order, the tree can be skewed to the right. If these values are distinct, the tree becomes, essentially, a singly linked list. Because of this behavior, we are usually better off if we shuffle the values beforehand. This causes the tree to become, on average, shorter and more balanced, and causes the expected insertion time to become $O(\log n)$.

Considering that the tree is responsible for maintaining an order among data values, it seems unreasonable to spend time shuffling values before ordering them. In the next section we find out that the process of adding and removing a node can be modified to maintain the tree in a relatively balanced state, with only a little overhead.

12.4   Splay Trees

Because the process of adding a new value to a binary search tree is *deterministic*—it produces the same result tree each time—and because inspection of the tree does not modify its structure, one is stuck with the performance of any degenerate tree constructed. What might work better would be to allow the tree to reconfigure itself when operations appear to be inefficient.

The *splay tree* quickly overcomes poor performance by rearranging the tree's nodes on the fly using a simple operation called a *splay*. Instead of performing careful analysis and optimally modifying the structure whenever a node is added or removed, the splay tree simply moves the referenced node to the top of the tree. The operation has the interesting characteristic that the average depth of the ancestors of the node to be splayed is approximately halved. As with skew heaps, the performance of a splay tree's operators, when amortized over many operations, is logarithmic.

Splay: to spread outward.

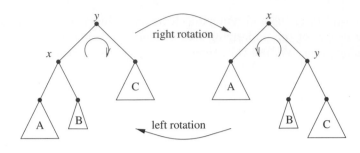

Figure 12.4   The relation between rotated subtrees.

The basis for the splay operation is a pair of operations called *rotations* (see Figure 12.4). Each of these rotations replaces the root of a subtree with one of its children. A right rotation takes a left child, x, of a node y and reverses their relationship. This induces certain obvious changes in connectivity of subtrees, but in all other ways, the tree remains the same. In particular, there is no structural effect on the tree above the original location of node y. A left rotation is precisely the opposite of a right rotation; these operations are inverses of each other.

Finally, a right handed method!

The code for rotating a binary tree about a node is a method of the **Binary-TreeNode** class. We show, here, **rotateRight**; a similar method performs a left rotation.

BinaryTree-Node

```
protected void rotateRight()
// pre: this node has a left subtree
// post: rotates local portion of tree so left child is root
{
    BinaryTreeNode parent = parent();
    BinaryTreeNode newRoot = left();
    boolean wasChild = parent != null;
    boolean wasLeftChild = isLeftChild();

    // hook in new root (sets newRoot's parent, as well)
    setLeft(newRoot.right());

    // puts pivot below it (sets this's parent, as well)
    newRoot.setRight(this);

    if (wasChild) {
        if (wasLeftChild) parent.setLeft(newRoot);
        else              parent.setRight(newRoot);
    }
}
```

For each rotation accomplished, the nonroot node moves upward by one

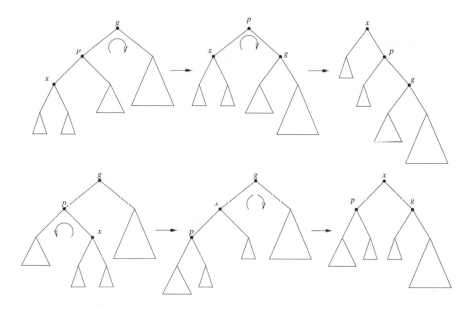

Figure 12.5   Two of the rotation pairs used in the splaying operation. The other cases are mirror images of those shown here.

level. Making use of this fact, we can now develop an operation to splay a tree at a particular node. It works as follows:

- If x is the root, we are done.

- If x is a left (or right) child of the root, rotate the tree to the right (or left) about the root. x becomes the root and we are done.

- If x is the left child of its parent p, which is, in turn, the left child of its grandparent g, rotate right about g, followed by a right rotation about p (Figure 12.5, top). A symmetric pair of rotations is possible if x is a left child of a left child. After double rotation, continue splay of tree at x with this new tree.

- If x is the right child of p, which is the left child of g, we rotate left about p, then right about g (Figure 12.5, bottom). Similarly if x is the left child of a right child. Again, continue the splay at x in the new tree.

After the splay has been completed, the node x is located at the root of the tree. Should the node x be immediately accessed again (a strong possibility), the tree is clearly optimized to handle this situation. It is *not* the case that the tree becomes more balanced (see the top of Figure 12.5). Clearly, if the tree is splayed at an extremal value, the tree is likely to be extremely unbalanced. An interesting feature, however, is that the depth of the nodes on the original path from x to the root of the tree is, on average, halved. Since the average depth of these nodes is halved, they clearly occupy locations closer to the top of the tree where they may be more efficiently accessed.

To guarantee that the splay has an effect on all operations, we simply perform each of the binary search tree operations as before, but we splay the tree at the node accessed or modified during the operation. In the case of **remove**, we splay the tree at the parent of the value removed.

12.5   Splay Tree Implementation

Because the splay tree supports the binary search tree interface, we extend the **BinarySearchTree** data structure. Methods written for the **SplayTree** hide or *override* existing code inherited from the **BinarySearchTree**.

SplayTree

```
public class SplayTree extends BinarySearchTree
{
    public SplayTree()
    // post: construct a new splay tree

    public void add(Object val)
    // pre: val is non-null
    // post: adds a value to the binary search tree

    public boolean contains(Object val)
    // pre: val is non-null
    // post: returns true iff val is a value found within the tree

    public Object get(Object val)
    // pre: val is non-null
    // post: returns object found in tree, or null

    public Object remove(Object val)
    // pre: val is non-null
    // post: removes one instance of val, if found

    protected void splay(BinaryTreeNode splayedNode)
    // pre: splayedNode is non-null node within tree
    // post: splayed node becomes root

    public Iterator elements()
    // post: returns iterator that traverses tree nodes in order
}
```

As an example of how the splay operation is incorporated into the existing binary tree code, we look at the **contains** method. Here, the root is reset to the value of the node to be splayed, and the splay operation is performed on the tree. The postcondition of the splay operation guarantees that the splayed node will become the root of the tree, so the entire operation leaves the tree in the correct state.

```
public boolean contains(Object val)
// pre: val is non-null
// post: returns true iff val is a value found within the tree
{
    if (root == null) return false;

    BinaryTreeNode possibleLocation = locate(root,(Comparable)val);
    if (val.equals(possibleLocation.value())) {
        splay(root = possibleLocation);
        return true;
    } else {
        return false;
    }
}
```

One difficulty with the splay operation is that it potentially modifies the structure of the tree. For example, the `contains` method—a method normally considered nondestructive—potentially changes the underlying topology of the tree. This makes it difficult to construct iterators that traverse the `SplayTree` since the user may use the value found from the iterator in a read-only operation that inadvertently modifies the structure of the splay tree. This *can* have disastrous effects on the state of the iterator. A way around this difficulty is to have the iterator keep only that state information that is necessary to help reconstruct—with help from the structure of the tree—the complete state of our traditional nonsplay iterator. In the case of the `SplayTreeIterator`, we keep track of two references: a reference to an "example" node of the tree and reference to the current node inspected by the iterator. The example node helps recompute the root whenever the iterator is reset. To determine what nodes would have been stored in the stack in the traditional iterator—the stack of unvisited ancestors of the current node—we consider each node on the (unique) path from the root to the current node. Any node whose left child is also on the path is an element of our "virtual stack." In addition, the top of the stack maintains the current node (see Figure 12.6).

It can also wreck your day.

The constructor sets the appropriate underlying references and resets the iterator into its initial state. Because the `SplayTree` is dynamically restructuring, the "root" value passed to the constructor may not always be the root of the tree. Still, one can easily find the root of the current tree, given a node: follow parent pointers until one is `null`. Since the first value visited in an inorder traversal is the leftmost descendant, the reset method travels down the leftmost branch (logically pushing values on the stack) until it finds a node with no left child.

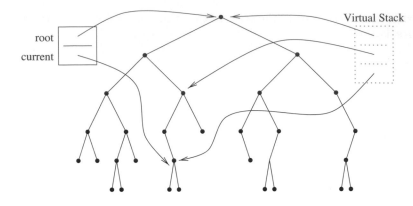

Figure 12.6 A splay tree iterator, the tree it references, and the contents of the "virtual stack" driving the iterator.

```
protected BinaryTreeNode tree; // node of splay tree, root computed
protected BinaryTreeNode current; // current node
// In this iterator, the "stack" normally used is implied by
// looking back up the path from the current node.  Those nodes
// for which the path goes left are on the stack

public SplayTreeIterator(BinaryTreeNode root)
// pre: root is the root of the tree to be traversed
// post: constructs a new iterator to traverse splay tree
{
    this.tree = root;
    reset();
}

public void reset()
// post: resets iterator to smallest node in tree
{
    current = tree;
    if (current != null) {
        while (current.parent() != null) current = current.parent();
        while (current.left() != null) current = current.left();
    }
}
```

The current node points to, by definition, an unvisited node that is, logically, on the top of the outstanding node stack. Therefore, the **hasMoreElements** and **value** methods may access the current value immediately.

```
public boolean hasMoreElements()
// post: returns true if there are unvisited nodes
{
    return current != null;
}

public Object value()
// pre: hasMoreElements()
// post: returns current value
{
    return current.value();
}
```

All that remains is to move the iterator from one state to the next. The **nextElement** method first checks to see if the current (just visited) element has a right child. If so, **current** is set to the leftmost descendant of the right child, effectively popping off the current node and pushing on all the nodes physically linking the current node and its successor. When no right descendant exists, the subtree rooted at the current node has been completely visited. The next node to be visited is the node under the top element of the virtual stack—the closest ancestor whose left child is also an ancestor of the current node. Here is how we accomplish this in Java:

```
public Object nextElement()
// pre: hasMoreElements()
// post: returns current element and increments iterator
{
    Object result = current.value();
    if (current.right() != null) {
        current = current.right();
        while (current.left() != null)
        {
            current = current.left();
        }
    } else {
        // we're finished with current's subtree.  We now "pop" off
        // nodes until we come to the parent of a leftchild ancestor
        // of current
        boolean lefty;
        do
        {
            lefty = current.isLeftChild();
            current = current.parent();
        } while (current != null && !lefty);
    }
    return result;
}
```

The iterator is now able to maintain its position through splay operations.

Again, the behavior of the splay tree is logarithmic when amortized over a number of operations. Any particular operation may take more time to execute, but the time is usefully spent rearranging nodes in a way that tends to make the tree shorter.

From a practical standpoint, the overhead of splaying the tree on every operation may be hard to justify if the operations performed on the tree are relatively random. On the other hand, if the access patterns tend to generate degenerate binary search trees, the splay tree can improve performance.

12.6   Conclusions

A binary search tree is the product of imposing an order on the nodes of a binary tree. Each node encountered in the search for a value represents a point where a decision can be accurately made to go left or right. If the tree is short and fairly balanced, these decisions have the effect of eliminating a large portion of the remaining candidate values.

The binary search tree is, however, a product of the history of the insertion of values. Since every new value is placed at a leaf, the internal nodes are left untouched and make the structure of the tree fairly static. The result is that poor distributions of data can cause degenerate tree structures that adversely impact the performance of the various search tree methods.

To combat the problems of unbalanced trees, various rotation-based optimizations are possible. In splay trees, rotations are used to force a recently accessed value and its ancestors closer to the root of the tree. The effect is often to shorten degenerate trees, resulting in an amortized logarithmic behavior. A remarkable feature of this implementation is that there is no space penalty: no accounting information needs to be maintained in the nodes.

Problems

12.1⋆   What distinguishes a binary search tree from a binary tree?

12.2   Draw all three-node integer-values trees whose nodes are visited in the order 1-2-3 in an inorder traversal. Which are binary search trees?

12.3   Draw all three-node integer-valued trees whose nodes are visited in the order 1-2-3 in a preorder traversal. Which are binary search trees?

12.4   Draw all three-node integer-valued trees whose nodes are visited in the order 1-2-3 in a postorder traversal. Which are binary search trees?

12.5   Redraw the following binary search tree after the root has been removed.

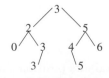

12.6   Redraw the tree shown in Problem 12.5 after the leaf labeled 3 is removed.

12.7   Redraw the tree shown in Problem 12.5 after it is splayed at the leaf labeled 3.

12.8⋆   The `locate` methods from `OrderedVector`s and `BinarySearchTree`s are very similar. They have, for example, similar best-case behaviors. Explain why their behaviors differ in the worst case.

12.9⋆   Prove that if values are distinct any binary search tree can be constructed by appropriately ordering insertion operations.

12.10   In splay trees rotations are performed, possibly reversing the parent–child relationship between two equal values. It is now possible to have a root node with a right child that is equal. Explain why this will not cause problems with each of the current methods `locate`, `add`, and `remove`.

12.11⋆ Describe the topology of a binary search tree after the values 1 through n have been inserted in order. How long does the search tree take to construct?

12.12   Describe the topology of a splay tree after the values 1 through n have been inserted in order. How long does the splay tree take to construct?

12.13⋆ Because the `remove` method of binary search trees "prefers" to replace a node with its predecessor, one expects that a large number of `remove`s will cause the tree to lean toward the right. Describe a scheme to avoid this problem.

12.14   Suppose n distinct values are stored in a binary tree. It is noted that the tree is both a min-heap and a binary search tree. What does the tree look like?

12.15   As we have seen, the splay tree requires the construction of an iterator that stores a single reference to the tree, rather than an unlimited number of references to ancestors. How does this reduction in space utilization impact the running time of the iterator?

12.16⋆ Write an `equals` method for binary search trees. It should return `true` if both trees contain equal values.

12.17   Having answered the previous problem, is it possible to accurately use the same method for splay trees?

12.18   Write a `clone` method for binary search trees. The result of the `clone` should be equal to the original. Carefully argue the utility of your approach.

12.19   Prove that the expected time to perform the `nextElement` method of the splay tree iterator is constant time.

Chapter 13

Dictionaries

WE HAVE SEEN THAT AN *association* ESTABLISHES A LINK between a *key* and a *value*. An *associative array* or *dictionary* is a structure that allows a disjoint set of keys to become associated with an arbitrary set of values. The convenience of an associative array is that the values used to index the elements need not be orderable and their range need not be known ahead of time. Furthermore, there is no upper bound on the size of the structure. It is able to maintain an arbitrary number of different pieces of information simultaneously. The analogy with a dictionary of words is not completely correct, because the dictionary of words is ordered; `Dictionary` structures need not be ordered.

13.1 The Interface

In Java, a `Dictionary` can be found within the `java.util` package. Each `Dictionary` structure must have the following interface:

```
public interface Dictionary extends Store
{
    public Object put(Object key, Object value);
    // pre: key is non-null
    // post: puts key-value pair in Dictionary, returns old value

    public boolean contains(Object value);
    // pre: value is non-null
    // post: returns true iff the dictionary contains the value

    public boolean containsKey(Object key);
    // pre: key is non-null
    // post: returns true iff the dictionary contains the key

    public Object remove(Object key);
    // pre: value is non-null
    // post: removes an object "equal" to value within dictionary
```

Dictionary

```
public Object get(Object key);
// pre: key is non-null
// post: returns value associated with key, in dictionary

public Iterator keys();
// post: returns iterator for traversing keys in dictionary

public Iterator elements();
// post: returns iterator for traversing values in dictionary

public int size();
// post: returns number of elements in dictionary
}
```

The **put** method places a new key–value pair within the **Dictionary**. If the key was already used to index a value, that association is replaced with a new association between the key and value. In any case, the **put** method returns the **value** replaced or **null**. The **get** method allows the user to retrieve the value from the **Dictionary**, provided the key. If the key is not used to index an element of the **Dictionary**, a **null** value is returned. Because this **null** value is not distinguished from a stored value that is **null**, it is common to predicate the call to **get** with a call to the **containsKey** method. This method returns **true** if a key matching the parameter can be found within the **Dictionary**. Sometimes, like human associative memory, it is useful to check to see if a *value* is found in the array. This can be accomplished with the **contains** method.

Aside from the fact that the keys of the values stored within the **Dictionary** should be distinct, there are no other constraints on their type. In particular, the keys of a **Dictionary** need only be accurately compared using the **equals** method. For this reason, it is important that a reasonable equality test be provided for the key type.

Two iterators are provided for **Dictionary**s. One, generated by the **elements** method, returns a stream of the values found within the **Dictionary**. The other, constructed by a call to **keys**, is useful for inspecting each of the keys. Because keys might not implement the **Comparable** class, there is no obvious ordering of the elements. Still, the **Iterator** generated by the **keys** method returns the keys in the same order that **elements** returns the stream of associated values. The pair of iterators can, therefore, be used to reconstruct the key–value pairings.

13.2   Unit Cost Dictionaries: Hash Tables

Clearly a collection of associations is a useful approach to filling the needs of the dictionary. The costs associated with the various structures vary considerably. For **Vectors**, the cost of looking up data has, on average, **Linear** time complexity. Because of limits associated with being linear, all the **Linear** structures have similar performance. When data can be ordered, then sorting the elements of the **Linear** structure improves the performance in the case of **Vectors**: this makes sense because **Vectors** are random access structures whose intermediate values can be accessed given an index.

When we considered binary search trees—a structure that also stores **Comparable** values—we determined the values could be found in logarithmic time. At each stage, the search space can be reduced by a factor of two. The difference between logarithmic and linear algorithms is very dramatic. For example, a balanced **BinarySearchTree** or an ordered **Vector** might find one number in a million in 20 or fewer compares. In an unordered **Vector** the expected number of compares increases to 500,000.

Is it possible to improve on this behavior? With hash tables, the answer is, amazingly, yes. With appropriate care, the hash table can provide access to an arbitrary element in roughly constant time. By "roughly," we mean that as long as sufficient space is provided, each potential key can be reserved an undisturbed location with probability approaching one.

How is this possible? The technique is, actually, rather straightforward. Here is an example of how hashing occurs in real life:

I was just going to say that.

> We head to a local appliance store to pick up a new freezer. When we arrive, the clerk asks us for *the last two digits* of our home telephone number! Only then does the clerk ask for our last name. Armed with that information, the clerk walks directly to a bin in a warehouse of hundreds of appliances and comes back with the freezer in tow.

The technique used by the appliance store was *hashing*. The last two digits of the phone number of the future owner identified a "bin" or *bucket* that contained the object. If two or more items were located in the bin, the name could be used to further distinguish the order.

An alternative approach to the "addressing" of the bins might be to identify each bin with the first letter of the name of the customer. This, however, has a serious flaw, in that it is likely that there will be far more names that begin with S than begin with, say, K. Even when the entire name is used, the names of customers are unlikely to be evenly distributed. These techniques for addressing bins are less likely to uniquely identify the desired parcel.

That would be a large number of bins!

The success of the phone number technique stems from generating an identifier associated with each customer that is both random and evenly distributed.[1]

13.2.1   Open Addressing

We now implement a hash table, modeled after the **Hashtable** of Java's **java.-util** package. All elements in the table are stored in a fixed-length array whose

---

[1] Using the last two digits of the telephone number makes for an evenly distributed set of values. It is *not* the case that the first two digits of the exchange would be useful, as that is not always random. In our town, where the exchange begins with 45, no listed phones have extensions beginning with 45.

length is, ideally, prime. Initialization ensures that each slot within the array is set to `null`. Eventually, slots will contain references to associations between keys and values. We use an array for speed, but a `Vector` would be a logical alternative.

Hashtable

```
protected static Association reserved =
                new Association("reserved",null);
protected Association data[];
protected int count;
protected int capacity;
protected final double loadFactor = 0.6;

public Hashtable(int initialCapacity)
// pre: initialCapacity > 0
// post: constructs a new Hashtable
//       holding initialCapacity elements
{
    data = new Association[initialCapacity];
    capacity = initialCapacity;
    count = 0;
}

public Hashtable()
// post: constructs a new Hashtable
{
    this(997);
}
```

The key and value management methods depend on a function, `locate`, that finds a good location for a value in the structure. First, we use an index-producing function that "hashes" a value to a slot or *bucket* (see Figure 13.1). In Java, every `Object` has a function, called `hashCode`, that returns an integer to be used for precisely this purpose. For the moment, we'll assume the hash code is the alphabet code ($a = 0$, $b = 1$, etc.) of the first letter of the word. The hash code for a particular key (2 for the word "crystal") is used as an index to the first slot to be considered for storing or locating the value in the table. If the slot is empty, the value can be stored there. If the slot is full, it is possible that another value already occupies that space (consider the insertion of "marigold" in Figure 13.1). When the keys of the two objects do not match, we have a *collision*. A *perfect hash function* guarantees that (given prior knowledge of the set of potential keys) no collisions will occur. When collisions do occur, they can be circumvented in several ways. With *open addressing*, a collision is resolved by generating a new hash value, or *rehashing*, and reattempting the operation at a new location.

Slots in the hash table logically have two states—empty (`null`) or full (a reference to an object)—but there is a third possibility. When values are removed, we replace the value with a *reserved* value that indicates that the location potentially impacts the lookup process for other cells during insertions. That

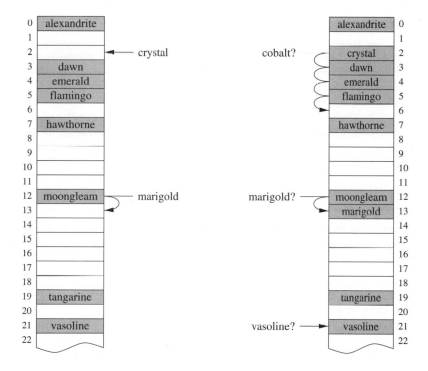

Figure 13.1 Hash functions. On the left, values are hashed into the first available slot, possibly after rehashing. On the right, the lookup process uses a similar approach to possibly find values.

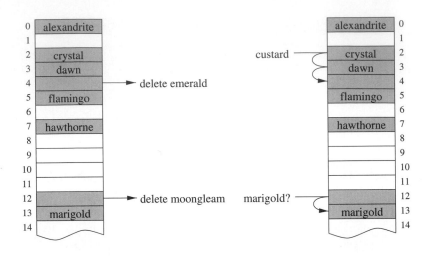

Figure 13.2 On left, deletion of a value leaves a shaded "reserved" cell as a place-holder. On right, a reserved cell is considered empty during insertion, and full during lookup.

association is represented by the empty shaded cell on the left of Figure 13.2. Each time we come across the reserved value in the search for a particular value in the array (right side of Figure 13.2), we continue the search as though there had been a collision. We keep the first reserved location in mind as a possible location for an insertion, if necessary. In the figure, this slot is used by the inserted value "custard."

When large numbers of different-valued keys hash or rehash to the same locations, the effect is called *clustering* (see Figure 13.3). *Primary clustering* is when several keys hash to the same initial location and rehash to slots with potential collisions with the same set of keys. *Secondary clustering* occurs when keys that initially hash to different locations eventually rehash to the same sequence of slots.

In this simple implementation we use *linear-probing* (demonstrated in Figures 13.1–13.3). Any rehashing of values occurs a constant distance from the last hash location. The linear-probing approach causes us to wrap around the array and find the next available slot. It does not solve either primary or secondary clustering, but it is easy to implement and quick to compute. To avoid secondary clustering a related technique, called *double hashing*, uses a second hash function to determine the magnitude of the constant offset (see Figure 13.4). This is not easily accomplished on arbitrary keys since we are provided only one `hashCode` function. In addition, multiples and factors of the hash table size (including 0) must also be avoided to keep the `locate` function from going into an infinite loop. Still, when implemented correctly, the performance of double hashing can provide significant improvements over linear-probing.

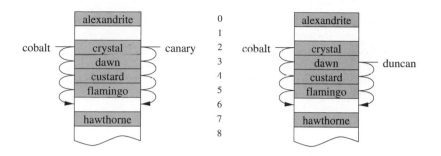

Figure 13.3 On left, *primary clustering* occurs when two values that hash to the same slot continue to compete during rehashing. On right, rehashing causes keys that initially hash to different slots to compete.

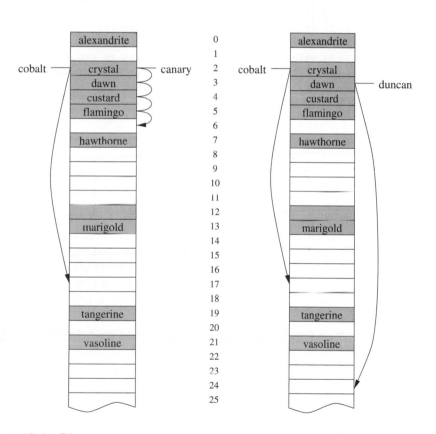

Figure 13.4 The keys of Figure 13.3 are rehashed by an offset determined by the alphabet code ($a = 1$, $b = 2$, etc.) of the *second* letter. No clustering occurs, but strings must have two letters!

We now discuss our implementation of hash tables. First, we consider the locate function. Its performance is important to the efficiency of each of the public methods.

```
protected int locate(Object key)
// pre: key is non-null
// post: returns ideal index of key in table
{
    // compute an initial hash code
    int hash = Math.abs(key.hashCode() % capacity);
    // keep track of first unused slot, in case we need it
    int firstReserved = -1;
    while (data[hash] != null)
    {
        if (data[hash] == reserved) {
            // remember reserved slot if we fail to locate value
            if (firstReserved == -1) firstReserved = hash;
        } else  {
            // value located? return the index in table
            if (key.equals(data[hash].key())) return hash;
        }
        // linear probing; other methods would change this line:
        hash = (1+hash)%capacity;
    }
    // return first empty slot we encountered
    if (firstReserved == -1) return hash;
    else return firstReserved;
}
```

To measure the difficulty of finding an empty slot by hashing, we use the *load factor*, α, computed as the ratio of the number of values stored within the table to the number of slots used. For open addressing, the load factor cannot exceed 1. As we shall see, to maintain good performance the load factor should be kept as low as possible. Our maximum allowable load factor is a constant loadFactor. Exceeding this value causes the array to be expanded (using method rehash).

When a value is added, we simply locate the appropriate slot and insert a new association. If the ideal slot already has a value (it must have an equal key), we return the replaced association. If we replace the reference to an empty cell with the reserved association, we return null instead.

```
public Object put(Object key, Object value)
// pre: key is non-null object
// post: key-value pair is added to hash table
{
    if (loadFactor*capacity <= (1+count)) {
        rehash();
    }
    int hash = locate(key);
```

```
        Association a = data[hash];
        if (a == null || a == reserved)
        {   // logically empty slot; just add association
            data[hash] = new Association(key,value);
            count++;
            return null;
        } else {
            // full slot; add new and return old value
            Object oldValue = a.value();
            a.setValue(value);
            return oldValue;
        }
    }
```

The get function works similarly—we simply return the value from within the key-located association or null, if no association could be found.

```
public Object get(Object key)
// pre: key is non-null Object
// post: returns value associated with key, or null
{
    int hash = locate(key);
    Association a = data[hash];
    if (a == null || a == reserved) return null;
    return data[hash].value();
}
```

The containsKey method is similar. To verify that a value is within the table we build contains from the elements iterator:

```
public boolean contains(Object value)
// pre: value is non-null Object
// post: returns true iff hash table contains value
{
    Iterator i = elements();
    for (;i.hasMoreElements();i.nextElement())
    {
        // the value we seek?
        if (i.value() != null &&
            i.value().equals(value)) return true; // yes!
    }
    // no value found
    return false;
}

public boolean containsKey(Object key)
// pre: key is a non-null Object
// post: returns true if key appears in hash table
{
    int hash = locate(key);
```

```
        return data[hash] != null && data[hash] != reserved;
    }
```

The `contains` method is quite expensive and should be used sparingly.

To remove a value from the `Hashtable`, we locate the correct slot for the value and remove the association. In its place, we leave a reserved mark to maintain consistency in `locate`.

```
public Object remove(Object key)
// pre: key is non-null Object
// post: removes key-value pair associated with key
{
    int hash = locate(key);
    Association a = data[hash];
    if (a == null || a == reserved) {
        return null;
    }
    count--;
    Object oldValue = a.value();
    data[hash] = reserved; // in case anyone depends on us
    return oldValue;
}
```

Our approach to constructing the two iterators (`elements` and `keys`) is to build a single iterator (a `HashtableIterator`) that traverses the `Hashtable` and returns the `Associations`. Once constructed, the association-based iterator can be used to generate the key- and value-based iterators.

The protected iterator is similar to the `Vector` iterator. A current index points to the cell of the current non-`null` (and nonreserved) association. When the iterator is incremented, then the underlying array is searched from the current point forward to find the next non-`null` entry. The iterator must eventually inspect every element of the structure, even if very few of the elements are currently used.[2]

Given an iterator that returns `Associations`, we can construct two different public filtering iterators, a `ValueIterator` and a `KeyIterator`. Each of these maintains a protected internal "slave" iterator and returns, as the iterator is incremented, values or keys associated with the respective elements. This design is much like the design of the `UniqueFilter` of Section 8.5. The following code, for example, implements the `ValueIterator`:

ValueIterator

```
class ValueIterator implements Iterator
{
    protected Iterator slave;
```

---

[2] The performance of this method could be improved by linking the contained associations together. This would, however, incur an overhead on the `add` and `remove` methods that may not be desirable.

```
        public ValueIterator(Iterator slave)
        // pre: slave is an iterator returning Association elements
        // post: creates a new iterator returning associated values
        {
            this.slave = slave;
        }

        public boolean hasMoreElements()
        // post: returns true if current value is valid
        {
            return slave.hasMoreElements();
        }

        public Object nextElement()
        // pre: hasMoreElements()
        // post: returns current value and increments iterator
        {
            Association pair = (Association)slave.nextElement();
            return pair.value();
        }
    }
```

Once these iterators are defined, then the **elements** method of the **Hashtable** is relatively easy to express. We simply construct a new **ValueIterator** that uses the **HashtableIterator** as a source for **Associations**:

```
public Iterator elements()
// post: returns iterator to traverse hash table
{
    return new ValueIterator(new HashtableIterator(data));
}
```

Hashtable

The **keys** method is similar but constructs a **KeyIterator** instead. While the **ValueIterator** and **KeyIterator** are protected, they may be accessed publicly when their identity has been removed by the **elements** and **keys** methods, respectively.

This is a form of identity laundering.

13.2.2   External Chaining

Open addressing is a satisfactory method for handling hashing of data, if one can be assured that the hash table will not get too full. When open addressing is used on nearly full tables, it becomes increasingly difficult to find an empty slot to store a new value.

One approach to avoiding the complexities of open addressing—reserved associations and table extension—is to handle collisions in a fundamentally different manner. *External chaining* solves the collision problem by inserting all elements that hash to the same bucket into a single collection of values. Typically, this collection is a singly linked list. The success of the hash table depends heavily on the fact that the average length of the linked lists (the *load factor* of the table) is small, and that the inserted objects are uniformly distributed. When the objects are uniformly distributed, then the *deviation* in list size is kept small, and no list is much longer than any other.

The process of locating the correct slot in an externally chained table involves simply computing the initial `hashCode` for the key and "modding" by the table size. Once the appropriate bucket is located, we verify that the collection is constructed and the value in the collection is updated. Because our `List` classes do not allow the retrieval of internal elements, we may have to remove and reinsert the appropriate association.

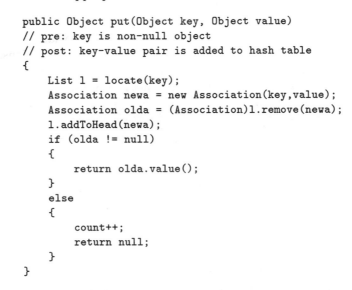

Chained-
HashTable

```
public Object put(Object key, Object value)
// pre: key is non-null object
// post: key-value pair is added to hash table
{
    List l = locate(key);
    Association newa = new Association(key,value);
    Association olda = (Association)l.remove(newa);
    l.addToHead(newa);
    if (olda != null)
    {
        return olda.value();
    }
    else
    {
        count++;
        return null;
    }
}
```

Most of the other methods are implemented in a similar manner: they locate the appropriate bucket to get a `List`, they search for the association within the `List` to get the association, and then they manipulate the key or value of the appropriate association.

One method, `contains`, essentially requires the iteration over two dimensions of the hash table. One loop searches for non-`null` buckets in the hash table—buckets that contain associations in collections—and an internal loop that explicitly iterates across the `List` (the `containsKey` method can directly use the `contains` method provided with the collection). This is part of the price we must pay for being able to store arbitrarily large numbers of keys in each bucket of the hash table.

```
public boolean contains(Object value)
// pre: value is non-null Object
// post: returns true iff hash table contains value
{
    Iterator elements = elements();

    while (elements.hasMoreElements())
    {
```

```
        if (value.equals(elements.nextElement())) return true;
    }
    return false;
}
```

At times the implementations appear unnecessarily burdened by the interfaces of the underlying data structure. For example, once we have found an appropriate `Association` to manipulate, it is difficult to modify the key. This is reasonable, though, since the value of the key is what helped us locate the bucket containing the association. If the key could be modified we could insert a key that was inconsistent with its bucket's location.

Another subtle issue is the selection of the collection class associated with the bucket. Since linked lists have poor linear behavior for most operations, it might seem reasonable to use more efficient collection classes—for example, tree-based structures—for storing data with common hash codes. The graph of Figure 13.5 demonstrates the performance of various ordered structures when asked to construct collections of various sizes. It is clear to see that while `SplayTree`s provide better ultimate performance, the simple linear structures are more efficient when the structure size is in the range of expected use in chained hash tables (see Figure 13.6). When the average collection size gets much larger than this, it is better to increase the size of the hash table and reinsert each of the elements (this is accomplished with the `Hashtable` method, `rehash`).

13.2.3 Generation of Hash Codes

Because any object might eventually be stored within a hash table, and because data abstraction hides the details of implementation, it is important for implementors to provide a `hashCode` method for their classes whenever possible.

Principle 25 *Provide a method for hashing the objects you implement.*

When a `hashCode` method *is* provided, it is vital that the method return the same `hashCode` for any pair of objects that are identified as the same under the `equals` method. If this is not the case, then values indexed by equivalent keys can be stored in distinct locations within the hash table. This can be confusing for the user, and often incorrect.

Principle 26 *Equivalent objects should return equal hash codes.*

The generation of successful hash codes can be tricky. Consider, for example, the generation of hash codes for `String`s. Recall that the purpose of the hash code generation function is to generate uniformly distributed indices into the hash table.

Most of the approaches for hashing strings involve manipulations of the characters that make up the string. Fortunately, when a character is cast as an integer, the internal representation (often the ASCII encoding) is returned,

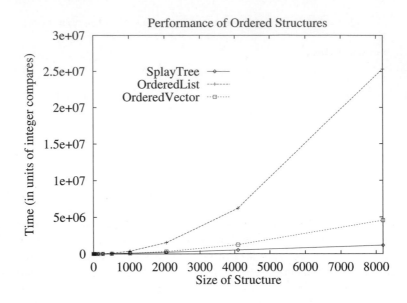

Figure 13.5   The time required to construct large ordered structures from random values.

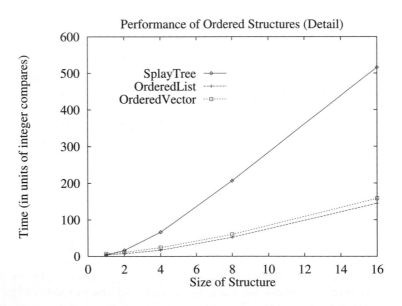

Figure 13.6   The time required to construct small ordered structures from random values.

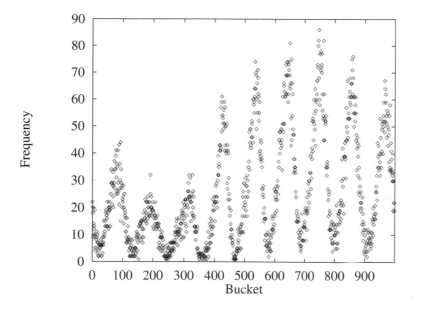

Figure 13.7 Numbers of words from the Unix spelling dictionary hashing to each of the 997 buckets of a default hash table, if sum of characters is used to generate hash code.

usually an integer between 0 and 255. Our first approach, then, might be to use the first character of the string (as we did in our figures). This has rather obvious disadvantages: the first letters of strings are not uniformly distributed, and there isn't any way of generating hash codes greater than 255.

Our next approach would be to sum all the letters of the string. This is a simple method that generates large magnitude hash codes if the strings are long. The main disadvantage of this technique is that if letters are transposed, then the strings generate the same hash values. For example, the string `"dab"` has $100 + 97 + 98 = 295$ as its sum of ASCII values, as does the string `"bad"`. The string `"bad"` and `"bbc"` are also equivalent under this hashing scheme. Figure 13.7 is a histogram of the number of words that hash, using this method, to each slot of a 997 element hash table. The periodic peaks demonstrate the fact that some slots of the table are heavily preferred over others. The performance of looking up and modifying values in the hash table will vary considerably, depending on the slot that targeted by the hash function. Clearly, it would be useful to continue our search for a good mechanism.

Another approach might be to weight each character of the string by its position. To ensure that even very short strings have the potential to generate large hash values, we can provide exponential weights: the hash code for an l character string, s, is

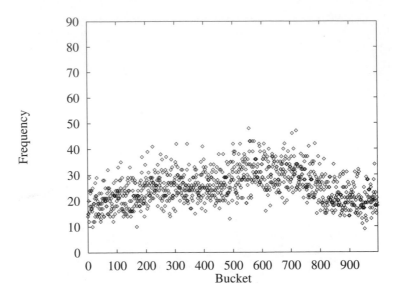

Figure 13.8 Frequency of dictionary words hashing to each of 997 buckets if characters are weighted by powers of 2 to generate hash code.

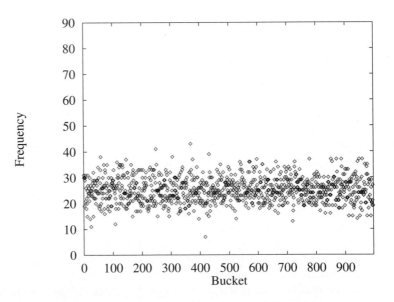

Figure 13.9 Frequency of words from dictionary hashing to each of 997 buckets if hash code is generated by weighting characters by powers of 256.

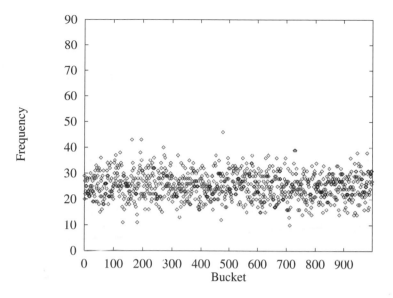

Figure 13.10 Frequency of words from dictionary hashing to each of 997 buckets, using the Java `String` hash code generation.

$$\sum_{i=0}^{l-1} s[i]c^i$$

where c is usually a small integer value. When c is 2, each character is weighted by a power of two, and we get a distribution similar to that of Figure 13.8. While this is closer to being uniform, it is clear that even with exponential behavior, the value of $c = 2$ is too small: not many words hash to table elements with large indices. When $c = 256$ the hash code represents the first few characters of the string exactly (see Figure 13.9). Java currently hashes with $c = 31$.

The hashing mechanism used by Java `Strings` in version 1.1 of the JDK (see Figure 13.10) used a combination of weightings that provided a wide range of values for short strings and was efficient to compute for longer strings. Unfortunately, the constant time algorithm was not suitable for distinguishing between long and nearly identical strings often found, say, in URL's. This novel technique was abandonded in JDK 1.2.

Many of the data structures we have investigated are classes that contain multiple objects of unspecified type. When constructing hash codes for collection classes, it is best to return a composition of hash codes of the contained elements. Each of the techniques used to generate hash codes from a composition of characters of strings can be used to compose hash codes of objects in collection classes.

Method	Successful	Unsuccessful
Linear-probes	$\frac{1}{2}\left(1 + \frac{1}{(1-\alpha)}\right)$	$\frac{1}{2}\left(1 + \frac{1}{(1-\alpha)^2}\right)$
Double hashing	$\frac{1}{\alpha}\log\frac{1}{(1-\alpha)}$	$\frac{1}{1-\alpha}$
External chaining	$1 + \frac{1}{2}\alpha$	$\alpha + e^{\alpha}$

Figure 13.11 Performance of hashing methods, as a function of α, the load factor. The number of association compares needed to locate the correct value or to demonstrate that the value cannot be found.

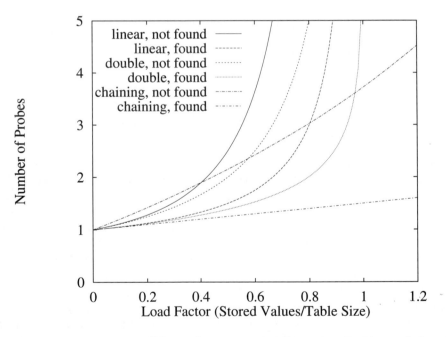

Figure 13.12 The shape of the performance curves for various hashing techniques. Our hash table implementation uses linear-probing.

13.2.4 Analysis

For open addressing, the load factor, α, obviously cannot exceed 1. As the load factor approaches 1, the performance of the table decreases dramatically. By counting the number of *probes* or association compares needed to find a value (a successful search), or to determine that the value is not among the elements of the dictionary (an unsuccessful search), we can observe the relative performance of the various hashing techniques (see Figures 13.11 and 13.12). Notice that the number of probes necessary to find an appropriate key is a function of the load factor, and not directly of the number of keys found in the table.

As we mentioned earlier, when a hash table exceeds the threshold load factor, the entire table is forced to expand, and each of the keys is rehashed. Looking at the graph in Figure 13.12, we select our threshold load factor to be 60 percent, the point at which the performance of linear-probing begins to degrade. When we expand the hash table, we make sure to at least double its size. For the same reasons that doubling is good when a vector is extended, doubling the size of the hash table improves the performance of the hash table without significant overhead.

13.3 Ordered Dictionaries and Tables

A significant disadvantage of the `Dictionary` interface is the fact that the values stored within the structure are not kept in any particular order. Often we wish to efficiently maintain an ordering among key–value pairs. The obvious solution is to construct a new `OrderedDictionary` that provides precisely the same interface as the `Dictionary`, but where methods may be allowed to assume parameters that are `Comparable`:

In fact, better hash functions probably avoid order!

```
public interface OrderedDictionary extends Dictionary
{
}
```

Ordered-
Dictionary

When we do this, the methods of the `Dictionary` are inherited. As a result, the types of the key-based methods manipulate `Objects` and not `Comparables`. Because we desire to maintain order among comparable keys, we have a general precondition associated with the use of the data structure—that keys provided and returned are treated as `Comparable` objects.

Even with comparable keys, it is not easy to construct a `Hashtable` whose `keys` iterator returns the keys in order. The hash codes provided for `Comparable` objects are not required (and unlikely) to be ordered in a way consistent with the `compareTo` function. We therefore consider other `OrderedStructures` to maintain the order among `ComparableAssociations`.

We will call our implementation of the `OrderedDictionary` a `Table`. As a basis for the implementation, we depend on the `SplayTree` class. `OrderedLists` and `OrderedVectors` could also provide suitable implementations for small applications. The `Table` maintains a single protected data item—the `SplayTree`.

The constructor is responsible for allocating the `SplayTree`, leaving it initialized in its empty state:

Table

```
protected OrderedStructure data;

public Table()
// post: constructs a new table
{
    data = new SplayTree();
}
```

When a key–value pair is to be put into the `Table`, a `ComparableAssociation` is constructed with the key–value pair, and it is used to look up any previous association using the same key. If the association is present, it is removed. In either case, the new association is inserted into the tree. While it seems indirect to remove the pair from the table to update it, it maintains the integrity of the `ComparableAssociation` and therefore the `SplayTree`. In addition, even though two **keys** may be logically equal, it is possible that they may be distinguishable. We insert the actual key–value pair demanded by the user, rather than perform a partial modification. Theoretically, removing and inserting a value into the `SplayTree` costs the same as finding and manipulating the value in place. Here we see the method for **put** (**get** is similar):

```
public Object put(Object key, Object value)
// pre: key is non-null object
// post: key-value pair is added to table
{
    ComparableAssociation ca =
        new ComparableAssociation((Comparable)key,value);
    // fetch old key-value pair
    ComparableAssociation old =
        (ComparableAssociation)data.remove(ca);
    // insert new key-value pair
    data.add(ca);
    // return old value
    if (old == null) return null;
    else return old.value();
}
```

While most of the other methods follow directly from considering `Hashtables` and `SplayTrees`, the `contains` method—the method that returns true exactly when a particular value is indexed by a key in the table—potentially requires a full traversal of the `SplayTree`. To accomplish this, we use an `Iterator` returned by the `SplayTree`'s `elements` methods. We then consider each association in turn, returning as soon as an appropriate value is found:

```
public boolean contains(Object value)
// pre: value is non-null object
// post: returns true iff value in table
```

```
{
    Iterator i = elements();
    for (;i.hasMoreElements();i.nextElement())
    {
        if (i.value() != null &&
            i.value().equals(value)) return true;
    }
    return false;
}
```

Next, our `Table` must provide an `Iterator` to be returned from the `keys` and `elements` methods. The approach is similar to the `Hashtable`—we construct a private `Association`-returning `Iterator` and then return its `KeyIterator` or `ValueIterator`. Because every value returned from the `SplayTree`'s iterator is useful,[3] we need not implement a special-purpose iterator for `Tables`; instead, we use the `SplayTree`'s iterator directly. Since `ComparableAssociations` extend `Associations`, the `KeyIterator` generates an `Iterator` that returns the comparable keys as `Objects` to be cast later:

```
public Iterator keys()
// post: returns an iterator for traversing keys of table
{
    return new KeyIterator(data.elements());
}

public Iterator elements()
// post: returns an iterator for traversing values in table
{
    return new ValueIterator(data.elements());
}
```

Previous hard work greatly simplifies this implementation! Since no hashing occurs, it is not necessary for any of the `keys` of a `Table` to implement the `hashCode` method. They must, though, implement the `compareTo` method since they are `Comparable`. Thus, each of the methods runs in amortized logarithmic time, instead of the near-constant time we get from hashing.

13.4   Example: Document Indexing

Indexing is an important task, especially for search engines that automatically index keywords from documents retrieved from the Web. Here we present the skeleton of a document indexing scheme that makes use of a `Dictionary` to keep track of the vocabulary.

---

[3] Compare this with, perhaps, a `Vector` iterator that might be used to traverse a `Vector`-based `Hashtable`.

Given a document we would like to generate a list of words, each followed by a list of lines on which the words appear. For example, when provided Gandhi's seven social sins:

```
  politics without principle
  pleasure without conscience
    wealth without work
 knowledge without character
  business without morality
   science without humanity
               and
   worship without sacrifice
```

The indexing program should generate the following output:

```
and: 7
business: 5
character: 4
conscience: 2
humanity: 6
knowledge: 4
morality: 5
pleasure: 2
politics: 1
principle: 1
sacrifice: 8
science: 6
wealth: 3
without: 1 2 3 4 5 6 8
work: 3
worship: 8
```

In this program we make use of Java's **StreamTokenizer** class. This class takes a stream of data and converts it into a stream of tokens, some of which are identified as words. The process for constructing this stream is a bit difficult, so we highlight it here.

Index

```java
public static void main(String args[])
{
    try {
        InputStreamReader isr = new InputStreamReader(System.in);
        Reader r = new BufferedReader(isr);
        StreamTokenizer s = new StreamTokenizer(r);
            ...
    } catch (java.io.IOException e) {
        Assert.fail("Got an I/O exception.");
    }
}
```

Each of the objects constructed here provides an additional layer of filtering on the base stream, **System.in**. The body of the main method is encompassed by the **try** statement in this code. The **try** statement catches errors generated by the **StreamTokenizer** and rewraps the exception as an assertion failure.

We begin by associating with each word of the input an initially empty list of line numbers. It seems reasonable, then, to use the vocabulary word as a key and the list of lines as the value. Our **Dictionary** provides an ideal mechanism to maintain the data.

The core of the program consists of reading word tokens from the stream and entering them into the **Dictionary**:

```
// allocate the symbol table (uses comparable keys)
Dictionary t = new Table();
int token;
// we'll not consider period as part of identifier
s.ordinaryChar('.');
// read in all the tokens from file
for (token = s.nextToken();
     token != StreamTokenizer.TT_EOF;
     token = s.nextToken())
{
    // only tokens we care about are whole words
    if (token == StreamTokenizer.TT_WORD)
    {
        // get wrapper for integer
        Integer line = new Integer(s.lineno());
        // each set of lines is maintained in a List
        List l;

        // look up symbol
        if (t.containsKey(s.sval))
        {   // symbol is there, get line # list
            l = (List)t.get(s.sval);
            l.addToTail(line);
        } else {
            // not found, create new list
            l = new DoublyLinkedList();
            l.addToTail(line);
            t.put(s.sval,l);
        }
    }
}
```

Here, we use a **Table** as our dictionary because it is important that the entries be sorted alphabetically. As the tokens are read from the input stream, they are looked up in the **Dictionary**. Since the **Dictionary** accepts comparable keys, it is important to use a (comparable) **String** to allow the words to index the structure. If the key is within the **Dictionary**, the value associated with the key (a list) is updated by appending the current line number (provided by the stream's **lineno** method) to the end of the list. If the word is not found, a new list is allocated with the current line appended, and the fresh word–list pair is inserted into the table.

The next section of the program is responsible for generating the output:

```
// printing table involves tandem key-value iterators
Iterator ti = t.keys();
Iterator ki = t.elements();
while (ti.hasMoreElements())
{
    // print symbol
    System.out.print(ti.value()+": ");
    // print out (and consume) each line number
    List l = (List)ki.value();
    while (!l.isEmpty())
    {
        System.out.print(l.removeFromHead()+" ");
    }
    System.out.println();
    // increment iterators
    ti.nextElement();
    ki.nextElement();
}
```

Here, two iterators—one for keys and one for values—are constructed for the **Dictionary** and are incremented in parallel. As each word is encountered, it is printed out along with the list of line numbers, generated by traversing the list with an iterator.

Because we used a **Table** as the underlying structure, the words are kept and printed in sorted order. If we had elected to use a **Hashtable** instead, the output would appear as follows:

Index2

```
humanity: 6
and: 7
worship: 8
sacrifice: 8
conscience: 2
wealth: 3
science: 6
knowledge: 4
without: 1 2 3 4 5 6 8
character: 4
work: 3
politics: 1
pleasure: 2
business: 5
principle: 1
morality: 5
```

The order of the words, here, reflects the order of the elements of the **Hashtable**. This order is neither alphabetical nor the order in which the words are encountered. It is the result of the particular hash function used to locate the data.

13.5   Conclusions

In this chapter we have investigated two structures that allow us to access values using a key or index from an arbitrary domain. When the keys can be uniformly distributed across a wide range of values, hashing is an excellent technique for providing constant time access to values within the structure. The cost is extra time necessary to hash the value, as well as the extra space needed to keep the load factor small enough to provide the expected performance.

When the keys are comparable, and order is to be preserved, we must depend on logarithmic behavior from ordered structures we have seen before. In our implementation of `Tables`, the `SplayTree` was used, although any other `OrderedStructure` could be used instead.

Because of the nonintuitive nature of hashing and hash tables, one of the more difficult tasks for the programmer is to generate useful effective hash code values. Hash functions should be designed specifically for each new class. They should be fast and deterministic and have wide ranges of values. While all `Objects` inherit a `hashCode` function, it is important to update the `hashCode` method whenever the `equals` method is changed; failure to do so leads to subtle problems with these useful structures.

Problems

13.1   Is it possible for a hash table to have two entries with equal keys?

13.2   Is it possible for a hash table to have two entries with equal values?

13.3   Suppose you have a hash table with seven entries (indexed 0 through 6). This table uses open addressing with the hash function that maps each letter to its alphabet code ($a = A = 0$, etc.) modulo 7. Rehashing is accomplished using linear-probing with a jump of 1. Describe the state of the table after each of the letters D, a, d, H, a, and h are added to the table.

13.4   Suppose you have a hash table with eight entries (indexed 0 through 7). The hash mechanism is the same as for Problem 13.3 (alphabet code mod 7), but with a linear-probe jump of 2. Describe what happens when one attempts to add each of the letters A, h, H, a, and H, in that order. How might you improve the hashing mechanism?

13.5   Design a `hashCode` method for a class that represents a telephone number.

13.6   Design a `hashCode` method for a class that represents a real number.

13.7   Suppose two identifiers—`Strings` composed of letters—were considered equal even if their cases were different. For example, `AGEdwards` would be equal to `AgedWards`. How would you construct a hash function for strings that was "case insensitive"?

13.8   When using linear-probing with rehashing jump size of greater than 1, why is it necessary to have the hash table size and jump size be relatively prime?

13.9 When 23 randomly selected people are brought together, chances are greater than 50 percent that two have the same birthday. What does this tell us about uniformly distributed hash codes for keys in a hash table?

13.10 Write a `hashCode` method for an `Association`.

13.11 Write a `hashCode` method for a `Vector`. It should only depend on hash codes of the `Vector`'s elements.

13.12 Write a `hashCode` method for a `BinaryTree`. Use recursion.

13.13 Write a `hashCode` method for a `Hashtable`. (For some reason, you'll be hashing hash tables into other hash tables!) Must the hashing mechanism look at the value of *every* element?

13.14⋆ The Java hash function for `String`s computes a hash code based on a fixed maximum number of characters of the string. Given that `String`s have no meaningful upper bound in length, describe how an effective, constant-time hashing algorithm can be constructed. (Hint: If you were to pick, say, eight characters to represent a string of length l, which would you choose?)

13.15⋆ Since URL's differ mostly toward their end (at high indices), write code that efficiently computes a hash code based on characters $l - x_i$ where $x_i = 2^i$ and $i = 0, 1, 2, \ldots$ How fast does this algorithm run? Is it better able to distinguish different URL's?

13.16 A hash table with *ordered linear-probing* maintains an order among keys considered during the rehashing process. When the keys are encountered, say, in increasing order, the performance of a failed lookup approaches that of a successful search. Describe how a key might be inserted into the ordered sequence of values that compete for the same initial table entry.

13.17⋆ Isn't the hash table resulting from the previous problem just an ordered vector? (Hint: No.) Why?

13.18⋆ If we were to improve the iterators for `Dictionary`s, we might add an iterator that returned key–value pairs. Is this an improvement in the interface?

13.19 Design a hash function for representing the state of a checkerboard.

13.20 Design a hash function for representing the state of a tic-tac-toe board. (It would—for strategy reasons—be useful to have mirror images of a board be considered equal.)

13.21 One means of potentially reducing the complexity of computing the hash code for `String`s is to compute it once—when the `String` is constructed. Future calls to `hashCode` would return the precomputed value. Since the value of a `String` never changes, this has potential promise. How would you evaluate the success of such a method?

13.22 Explain how a `Dictionary` might be useful in designing a spelling checker. (Would it be useful to have the words `bible` and `babble` stored near each other?)

Chapter 14

Graphs

"...314159..."
—π (digits 176452–176457)

RELATIONS ARE OFTEN AS USEFUL AS DATA. The process of building and accessing a data structure can be thought of as a means of effectively focusing the computation. Linear structures record the history of their accesses, ordered structures perform incremental sorting, and binary trees encode decisions about the partitioning of collections of data.

The most general mechanism for encoding relations between data is the *graph*. Simple structures, like arrays, provide implicit connections, such as adjacency, between stored values. Graphs are more demanding to construct but, as a result, they can encode more detailed information. Indeed, the versatility of graphs allows them to represent many of the most difficult theoretical problems of computer science.

This chapter investigates two traditional implementations of graphs, as well as several standard algorithms for analyzing their structure. We first agree on some basic terminology.

14.1 Terminology

A *graph*, G, consists of a collection of *vertices*, $v \in V_G$, and relations or *edges*, $(u, v) \in E_G$, between them (see Figure 14.1). An edge is *incident to* (or *mentions*) each of its two component vertices. A graph is *undirected* if each of its edges is considered a set of two unordered vertices, and *directed* if the mentioned vertices are ordered (e.g., referred to as the *source* and *destination*). A graph, S, is a *subgraph* of G if and only if $V_S \subseteq V_G$ and $E_S \subseteq E_G$. Simple examples of graphs include the *list* and the *tree*.

In an undirected graph, the number of edges (u, v) incident to a vertex u is its *degree*. In a directed graph, the outgoing edges determine its *out-degree* (or just *degree*) and incoming edges its *in-degree*. A *source* is a vertex with no incoming edges, while a *sink* is a vertex with no outgoing edges.

Two edges (u, v) and (v, w) are said to be *adjacent*. A *path* is a sequence of n distinct, adjacent edges, $(v_0, v_1), (v_1, v_2), \ldots, (v_{n-1}, v_n)$. In a *simple path* the vertices are distinct, except for, perhaps, the *endpoints* v_0 and v_n. When $v_0 = v_n$ the simple path is a *cycle*.

Two vertices u and v are *connected* (written $u \leadsto v$) if and only if a simple path of the graph mentions u and v as its endpoints. A subgraph, S, is a

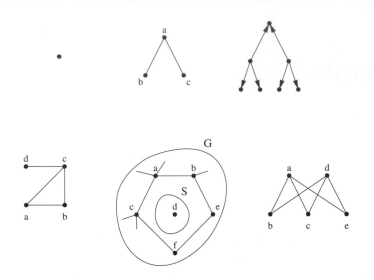

Figure 14.1 Some graphs. Each node a is adjacent to node b, but never to d. Graph G has two components, one of which is S. The directed tree-shaped graph is a directed, acyclic graph. Only the top left graph is complete.

Components are always connected. *connected component* (or, often, just a *component*) if and only if S is a largest subgraph of G such that for every pair of vertices $u, v \in V_S$ either $u \rightsquigarrow v$ or $v \rightsquigarrow u$. A connected component of a directed graph G is *strongly connected* if $u \rightsquigarrow v$ and $v \rightsquigarrow u$ for all pairs of vertices $u, v \in V_S$.

A graph containing no cycles is *acyclic*. A directed, acyclic graph (or *DAG*) plays an important role in solving many problems. A *complete graph G* contains an edge (u, v) for all vertices $u, v \in V_G$.

14.2   The Graph Interface

Vertices of a graph are usually labeled with application-specific information. As a result, our implementations of a graph structure depend on the user specifying unique labels for vertices. In addition, edges may be labeled, but not necessarily uniquely. It is common, for example, to specify weights or lengths for edges. As with all of our container classes, the graph allows addition and removal of vertices and edges. Here is the entire interface:

Graph

```
public interface Graph extends Collection
{
    public void add(Object label);
    // pre: label is a non-null label for vertex
    // post: a vertex with label is added to graph;
    //       if vertex with label is already in graph, no action
```

```
public void addEdge(Object vtx1, Object vtx2, Object label);
// pre: vtx1 and vtx2 are labels of existing vertices
// post: an edge (possibly directed) is inserted between
//       vtx1 and vtx2

public Object remove(Object label);
// pre: label is non-null vertex label
// post: vertex with "equals" label is removed, if found

public Object removeEdge(Object vLabel1, Object vLabel2);
// pre: vLabel1 and vLabel2 are labels of existing vertices
// post: edge is removed; its label is returned

public Object get(Object label);
// post: returns actual label of indicated vertex

public Edge getEdge(Object label1, Object label2);
// post: returns edge between vertices

public boolean contains(Object label);
// post: returns true iff vertex with "equals" label exists

public boolean containsEdge(Object vLabel1, Object vLabel2);
// post: returns true iff edge with "equals" label exists

public boolean visit(Object label);
// post: sets visited flag on vertex; returns previous value

public boolean visitEdge(Edge e);
// pre: sets visited flag on edge; returns previous value

public boolean isVisited(Object label);
// post: returns visited flag on labeled vertex

public boolean isVisitedEdge(Edge e);
// post: returns visited flag on edge between vertices

public void reset();
// post: resets visited flags to false

public int size();
// post: returns the number of vertices in graph

public int degree(Object label);
// pre: label labels an existing vertex
// post: returns the number of vertices adjacent to vertex

public int edgeCount();
// post: returns the number of edges in graph
```

```
        public Iterator elements();
        // post: returns iterator across all vertices of graph

        public Iterator neighbors(Object label);
        // pre: label is label of vertex in graph
        // post: returns iterator over vertices adj. to vertex;
        //       each edge beginning at label visited exactly once

        public Iterator edges();
        // post: returns iterator across edges of graph;
        //       iterator returns edges; each edge visited once

        public void clear();
        // post: removes all vertices from graph

        public boolean isEmpty();
        // post: returns true if graph contains no vertices

        public boolean isDirected();
        // post: returns true if edges of graph are directed
    }
```

Because edges can be fully identified by their constituent vertices, edge operations sometimes require pairs of vertex labels. Since it is useful to implement both directed and undirected graphs, we can determine the type of a specific graph using the `isDirected` method. In undirected graphs, the addition of an edge effectively adds a directed edge in both directions. Many algorithms keep track of their progress by visiting vertices and edges. This is so common that it seems useful to provide direct support for adding (`visit`), checking (`isVisited`), and removing (`reset`) marks on vertices and edges.

Two iterators—generated by **elements** and **edges**—traverse the vertices and edges of a graph, respectively. A special iterator—generated by **neighbors**—traverses the vertices adjacent to a given vertex. From this information, outbound edges can be determined.

Before we discuss particular implementations of graphs, we consider the abstraction of vertices and edges. From the user's point of view a vertex is a label. Abstractly, an edge is an association of two vertices and an edge label. In addition, we must keep track of objects that have been visited. These features of vertices and edges are independent of the implementation of graphs, thus we commit to an interface for these objects early. Let's consider the **Vertex** class:

Vertex

```
    class Vertex
    {
        public Vertex(Object label)
        // post: constructs unvisited vertex with label

        public Object label()
        // post: returns user label associated w/vertex
```

```
    public boolean visit()
    // post: returns, then marks vertex as being visited

    public boolean isVisited()
    // post: returns true iff vertex has been visited

    public void reset()
    // post: marks vertex unvisited

    public boolean equals(Object o)
    // post: returns true iff vertex labels are equal
}
```

This class is similar to an **Association**: the label portion of the **Vertex** cannot be modified, but the visited flag can be freely set and reset. Two **Vertex** objects are considered equal if their labels are equal. It is a bare-bones interface. It should also be noted that the **Vertex** is a nonpublic class. Since a **Vertex** is not visible through the **Graph** interface, there is no reason for the user to have access to the **Vertex** class.

Because the **Edge** class is visible "through" the **Graph** interface (you might ask why—see Problem 14.8), the **Edge** class is declared **public**:

Edge

```
public class Edge
{
    public Edge(Object vtx1, Object vtx2, Object label,
                boolean directed)
    // post: edge associates vtx1 and vtx2; labeled with label;
    //       directed if "directed" set true

    public Object here()
    // post: returns first node in edge

    public Object there()
    // post: returns second node in edge

    public void setLabel(Object label)
    // post: sets label of this edge to label

    public Object label()
    // post: returns label associated with this edge

    public boolean visit()
    // post: visits edge, returns whether previously visited

    public boolean isVisited()
    // post: returns true iff edge is visited

    public boolean isDirected()
    // post: returns true iff edge is directed
```

```
    public void reset()
    // post: resets edge's visited flag to initial state

    public boolean equals(Object o)
    // post: returns true iff edges connect same vertices
}
```

As with the `Vertex` class, the `Edge` can be constructed, visited, and reset. Unlike its `Vertex` counterparts, an `Edge`'s label may be changed. The methods `here` and `there` provide access to labels of the vertices mentioned by the edge. These method names are sufficiently ambiguous to be easily used with undirected edges, and convey a slight impression of direction for directed edges. Naming of these methods is important because they are used by those who wish to get vertex information while traversing a (potentially directed) graph.

14.3   Implementations

As "traditional" as this science gets, anyway!

Now that we have a good feeling for the graph interface, we consider traditional implementations. Nearly every implementation of a graph has characteristics of one of these two approaches. Our approach to specifying these implementations, however, will be dramatically impacted by the availability of object-oriented features. We first discuss the concept of a partially specified *abstract class* in Java.

14.3.1   Abstract Classes

Normally, when a class is declared, code for each of the methods must be provided. Then, when an instance of the class is constructed, each of the methods can be applied to the resulting object. Sometimes, however, it is useful to partially implement a class and later finish the implementation by *extending* the class in a particular direction. The partial base class is *abstract*; it cannot be constructed because some of the methods are not completely defined. The extension to the class *inherits* the methods that have been defined, and specifies any incomplete code to make the class *concrete*.

We will use abstract classes in our design of various graph implementations. Each implementation will be declared abstract, with the **abstract** keyword:

GraphMatrix

```
abstract public class GraphMatrix implements Graph
```

This is a warning to the Java compiler that we expect that parts of the implementation will be omitted. Our approach will be to provide all the code that can be written without considering whether the graph is undirected or directed. When we must write code that is dependent on the "directedness" of the graph, we delay it by writing just an abstract header for the particular method. For example, we will need to add edges to our graph, but the implementation depends on whether or not the graph is directed. Looking ahead, here is what the declaration for addEdge looks like in the abstract class GraphMatrix:

```
abstract public void addEdge(Object v1, Object v2, Object label);
// pre: v1 and v2 are labels of existing vertices, v1 & v2
// post: an edge (possibly directed) is inserted between v1 and v2;
//       if edge is new, it is labeled with label (can be null)
```

That's it! It is simply a *promise* that code will eventually be written.

Once the abstract class is described as fully as possible, we may then extend it, committing the graph to being undirected or directed. The directed version of the Graph implementation, called GraphMatrixDirected, specifies the addEdge method as follows:

```
public class GraphMatrixDirected extends GraphMatrix
{
    ...
    public void addEdge(Object vLabel1, Object vLabel2, Object label)
    // pre: vLabel1 and vLabel2 label existing vertices, v1 & v2
    // post: an edge is inserted between v1 and v2
    //       if edge is new, it is labeled with label (can be null)
    {
        GraphMatrixVertex vtx1,vtx2;
        ...
    }
    ...
}
```

GraphMatrix-
Directed

Because we declare the class GraphMatrixDirected to be an extension of the GraphMatrix class, all of the code written for the GraphMatrix class is inherited; it is as though it had been written for the GraphMatrixDirected class. By providing the missing pieces of code (tailored for directed graphs) the extension class becomes concrete. We can actually construct instances of the GraphMatrixDirected class.

A related concept, *subtyping*, allows us to use any extension of a class wherever the extended class could be used. We call the class that was extended the *basetype* or *superclass*, and the extension the *subtype* or *subclass*. Use of subtyping allows us to write code like

```
GraphMatrix g = new GraphMatrixDirected();

g.add("Alice");
g.add("Bob");
g.addEdge("Alice","Bob","helps"); // "Alice helps Bob!"
```

Because GraphMatrixDirected is an extension of GraphMatrix, it *is* a Graph-Matrix. Even though we cannot construct a GraphMatrix, we can correctly manipulate concrete subtypes using the methods described in the abstract class.

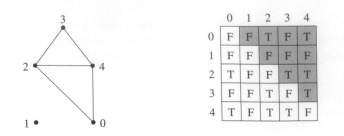

Figure 14.2 An undirected graph (left) and its adjacency matrix representation (right). Each nontrivial edge is represented twice across the diagonal—once in the gray and once in the white—making the matrix symmetric.

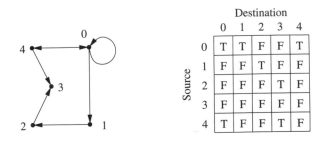

Figure 14.3 A directed graph (left) and its adjacency matrix representation (right). Each edge appears exactly once in the matrix.

In particular, a call to the method `addEdge` calls the method of `GraphMatrixDirected`.

We now return to our normally scheduled implementations!

14.3.2 Adjacency Matrices

An $n \times n$ matrix of booleans is sufficient to represent an arbitrary graph of relations among n vertices. We simply store `true` in the boolean at matrix location $[u][v]$ to represent the fact there is an edge between u and v (see Figure 14.2), and `false` otherwise. Since entries $[u][v]$ and $[v][u]$ are independent, the representation is sufficient to describe directed graphs as well. Our convention is that the first index (the row) specifies the source and the second index (the column) indicates the destination. To represent undirected graphs, we simply duplicate the entry $[u][v]$ at entry $[v][u]$. This is called an *adjacency matrix* representation of a graph. The abstract graphs on the left side of Figures 14.2 and 14.3 are represented by the matrices on the right.

Beware: Edges on the diagonal appear exactly once.

One difficult feature of our implementation is the arbitrary labeling of vertices and edges. To facilitate this, we maintain a `Dictionary` that translates a vertex label to a `Vertex` object. To help each vertex keep track of its associated index we extend the `Vertex` class to include methods that manipulate an `index` field. Each index is a small integer that identifies the dedicated row and column that maintain adjacency information about each vertex. To help allocate the indices, we keep a free list (see Section 6.2) of available indices.

One feature of our implementation has the potential to catch the unwary programmer by surprise. Because we keep a `Dictionary` of vertex labels, it is important that the vertex label class implement the `hashCode` function in such a way as to guarantee that if two labels are equal (using `equals`), they have the same `hashCode`.

We can now consider the protected data and constructors for the `GraphMatrix` class:

```
protected int size;          // allocation size for graph
protected Edge data[][];     // matrix - array of arrays
protected Dictionary dict;   // translates labels->vertices
protected List freeList;     // available indices in matrix
protected boolean directed;  // graph is directed
```

GraphMatrix

```
protected GraphMatrix(int size, boolean dir)
// pre: size > 0
// post: constructs an empty graph that may be expanded to
//       at most size vertices.  Graph is directed if dir true
//       and undirected otherwise
{
    this.size = size; // set maximum size
    directed = dir;   // fix direction of edges
    // the following constructs a size x size matrix
    data = new Edge[size][size];
    // label to index translation table
    dict = new Hashtable(size);
    // put all indices in the free list
    freeList = new SinglyLinkedList();
    for (int row = size-1; row >= 0; row--)
        freeList.add(new Integer(row));
}
```

To construct the graph, the user specifies an upper bound on the number of vertices. We allocate `size` arrays of length `size`—a two-dimensional array. By default, the array elements are `null`, so initially there are no edges. We then put each of the indices into the list of available vertex indices.

This constructor is declared protected. It takes a second parameter, `directed`, that identifies whether or not the graph constructed is to act like a directed graph. When we extend the graph to implement either directed or undirected graphs, we write a public constructor to call the abstract protected class's constructor with an appropriate boolean value:

GraphMatrix-
Directed

```
public GraphMatrixDirected(int size)
// pre: size > 0
// post: constructs an empty graph that may be expanded to
//       at most size vertices.  Graph is directed if dir true
//       and undirected otherwise
{
    super(size,true);
}
```

As we discussed before, this technique allows the implementor to selectively inherit the code that is common between directed and undirected graphs. Since we hide the implementation, we are free to reimplement either type of graph without telling our users, perhaps allowing us to optimize our code.

Returning to the `GraphMatrix` class, the `add` method adds a labeled vertex. If the vertex already exists, the operation does nothing. If it is new to the graph, an index is allocated from the free list, a new `Vertex` object is constructed, and the label–vertex association is recorded in the `Dictionary`. The newly added vertex mentions no edges, initially.

GraphMatrix

```
public void add(Object label)
// pre: label is a non-null label for vertex
// post: a vertex with label is added to graph;
//       if vertex with label is already in graph, no action
{
    // if there already, do nothing
    if (dict.containsKey(label)) return;

    Assert.pre(!freeList.isEmpty(), "Matrix not full");
    // allocate a free row and column
    int row = ((Integer) freeList.removeFromHead()).intValue();
    // add vertex to dictionary
    dict.put(label, new GraphMatrixVertex(label, row));
}
```

Removing a vertex reverses the `add` process. We must, however, be sure to set each element of the vertex's matrix row and column to `null`, removing any mentioned edges (we may wish to add a new, isolated vertex with this index in the future). When we remove the vertex from the `Dictionary`, we "recycle" its index by adding it to the list of free indices. As with all of our `remove` methods, we return the previous value of the label. (Even though the labels match using `equals`, they may not be precisely the same; once returned the user can extract any unknown information from the previous label before the value is collected as garbage.)

```
public Object remove(Object label)
// pre: label is non-null vertex label
// post: vertex with "equals" label is removed, if found
```

```
{
    // find and extract vertex
    GraphMatrixVertex vert;
    vert = (GraphMatrixVertex)dict.remove(label);
    if (vert == null) return null;
    // remove vertex from matrix
    int index = vert.index();
    // clear row and column entries
    for (int row=0; row<size; row++) {
        data[row][index] = null;
        data[index][row] = null;
    }
    // add node index to free list
    freeList.add(new Integer(index));
    return vert.label();
}
```

Within the graph we store references to **Edge** objects. Each **Edge** records all of the information necessary to position it within the graph, including whether it is directed or not. This allows the **equals** method to work on undirected edges, even if the vertices were provided in the opposite order (see Problem 14.12). To add an edge to the graph, we require two vertex labels and an edge label. The vertex labels uniquely identify the vertices within the graph and the edge label is used to form the value inserted within the matrix at the appropriate row and column. To add the edge, we construct a new **Edge** with the appropriate information. This object is written to appropriate matrix entries: undirected graphs update one or two locations; directed graphs update just one. Here is the **addEdge** method for undirected graphs:

```
public void addEdge(Object vLabel1, Object vLabel2, Object label)
// pre: vLabel1 and vLabel2 are labels of existing vertices, v1 & v2
// post: an edge (possibly directed) is inserted between v1 and v2;
//       if edge is new, it is labeled with label (can be null)
{
    GraphMatrixVertex vtx1,vtx2;
    // get vertices
    vtx1 = (GraphMatrixVertex) dict.get(vLabel1);
    vtx2 = (GraphMatrixVertex) dict.get(vLabel2);
    // update matrix with new edge
    Edge e = new Edge(vtx1.label(), vtx2.label(), label, false);
    data[vtx1.index()][vtx2.index()] = e;
    data[vtx2.index()][vtx1.index()] = e;
}
```

GraphMatrix-
Undirected

Here is a similar method for directed graphs:

```
public void addEdge(Object vLabel1, Object vLabel2, Object label)
// pre: vLabel1 and vLabel2 label existing vertices, v1 & v2
// post: an edge is inserted between v1 and v2
//       if edge is new, it is labeled with label (can be null)
```

GraphMatrix-
Directed

```
    {
        GraphMatrixVertex vtx1,vtx2;
        // get vertices
        vtx1 = (GraphMatrixVertex) dict.get(vLabel1);
        vtx2 = (GraphMatrixVertex) dict.get(vLabel2);
        // update matrix with new edge
        Edge e = new Edge(vtx1.label(), vtx2.label(), label, true);
        data[vtx1.index()][vtx2.index()] = e;
    }
```

The differences are quite minor, but the two different subtypes allow us to write specialized code without performing explicit runtime tests.[1]

The `removeEdge` method removes and returns the label associated with the `Edge` found between two vertices. Here is the undirected version (the directed version is similar):

GraphMatrix-
Undirected

```
public Object removeEdge(Object vLabel1, Object vLabel2)
// pre: vLabel1 and vLabel2 are labels of existing vertices
// post: edge is removed, its label is returned
{
    // get indices
    int row = ((GraphMatrixVertex)dict.get(vLabel1)).index();
    int col = ((GraphMatrixVertex)dict.get(vLabel2)).index();
    // cache old value
    Edge e = data[row][col];
    // update matrix
    data[row][col] = null;
    data[col][row] = null;
    if (e == null) return null;
    else return e.label();
}
```

The `get`, `getEdge`, `contains`, and `containsEdge` methods return information about the graph in an obvious way. Modifying the objects returned by these methods can be dangerous: they have the potential of invalidating the state of the underlying graph implementation.

Each of the `visit`-type methods passes on requests to the underlying object. For example, the `visit` method simply refers the request to the associated `Vertex`:

GraphMatrix

```
public boolean visit(Object label)
// post: sets visited flag on vertex; returns previous value
{
    Vertex vert = (Vertex) dict.get(label);
    return vert.visit();
}
```

---

[1] This is somewhat misleading, as the obvious runtime tests are replaced by less obvious decreases in performance due to subtyping. Still, the logical complexity of the code can be dramatically reduced using these techniques.

The process of resetting the visitation marks on a graph traverses each of the vertices and edges, resetting them along the way.

We now consider the implementation of each of the three iterators. The first, generated by `elements`, traverses the vertices. The values returned by the `Iterator` are vertex labels. This `Iterator` is easily constructed by returning the value of the `Dictionary`'s `keys` function!

But I reiterate myself.

```
public Iterator elements()
// post: returns iterator across all vertices of graph
{
    return dict.keys();
}
```

The `neighbors` iterator, which traverses the edges adjacent to a single vertex, considers only the outgoing edges. We simply look up the index associated with the vertex label and scan across the row, building up a list of vertex labels that are adjacent using each of the edges. By putting these values in a list, we can return a `ListIterator` that will give us iterative access to each of the adjacent vertex labels. With this information we may retrieve the respective edges with `getEdge` if necessary.

```
public Iterator neighbors(Object label)
// pre: label is label of vertex in graph
// post: returns iterator vertices adj. to labeled vertex
{
    GraphMatrixVertex vert;
    vert = (GraphMatrixVertex) dict.get(label);
    List list = new SinglyLinkedList();
    for (int row=size-1; row>=0; row--)
    {
        Edge e = data[vert.index()][row];
        if (e != null) {
            if (e.here().equals(vert.label()))
                list.add(e.there());
            else list.add(e.here());
        }
    }
    return list.elements();
}
```

All that remains is to construct an iterator over the edges of the graph. Again, we construct a list of the edges and return the result of the `elements` method invoked on the list. For directed edges, we include every edge; for undirected edges we include only the edges found in, say, the lower half of the array (including the diagonal). Here is the version for the undirected graph:

GraphMatrix-
Undirected

```
public Iterator edges()
// post: returns iterator across all edges of graph (returns Edges)
```

```
    {
        List list = new SinglyLinkedList();
        for (int row=size-1; row>=0; row--)
            for (int col=size-1; col >= row; col--) {
                Edge e = data[row][col];
                if (e != null) list.add(e);
            }
        return list.elements();
    }
```

The great advantage of the adjacency matrix representation is its simplicity. The access to a particular edge in a graph of size n can be accomplished in constant time. Other operations, like **remove**, appear to be more complex, taking $O(n)$ time. The disadvantage is that the implementation may vastly overestimate the storage required for edges. While we have room for storing $O(n^2)$ directed edges, some graphs may only need to make use of $O(n)$ edges. Graphs with superlinear numbers of edges are called *dense;* all other graphs are *sparse.* When graphs are sparse, most of the elements of the adjacency matrix are not used, leading to a significant waste of space. Our next implementation is particularly suited for representing sparse graphs.

14.3.3   Adjacency Lists

Recalling the many positive features of a linked list over a fixed size array, we now consider the use of an *adjacency list*. As with the adjacency matrix representation, we maintain a **Dictionary** for identifying the relationship between a vertex label and the associated **Vertex** object. Within the vertex, however, we store a collection (usually a linked list) of edges that mention this vertex. Figures 14.4 and 14.5 demonstrate the adjacency list representations of undirected and directed graphs. The great advantage of using a collection is that it stores only edges that appear as part of the graph.

As with the adjacency matrix implementation, we construct a privately used extension to the **Vertex** class. In this extension we reference a collection of edges that are incident to this vertex. In directed graphs, we collect edges that mention the associated vertex as the source. In undirected graphs any edge incident to the vertex is collected. Because the edges are stored within the vertices, most of the actual implementation of graphs appears within the implementation of the extended vertex class. We see most of the implementation below:

GraphList

```
class GraphListVertex extends Vertex
{
    protected Collection adjacencies; // adjacent edges

    public GraphListVertex(Object key)
    // post: constructs a new vertex, not incident to any edge
    {
        super(key); // init Vertex fields
        // new adjacency list
```

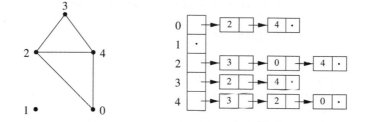

Figure 14.4 An undirected graph (left) and its adjacency list representation (right). Each edge is represented twice in the structure. (Compare with Figure 14.2.)

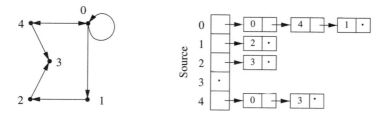

Figure 14.5 A directed graph (left) and its adjacency list representation (right). Each edge appears once in the source list. (Compare with Figure 14.3.)

```
        adjacencies = new SinglyLinkedList();
}

public void addEdge(Edge e)
// pre: e is an edge that mentions this vertex
// post: adds edge to this vertex's adjacency list
{
    if (!containsEdge(e)) adjacencies.add(e);
}

public boolean containsEdge(Edge e)
// post: returns true if e appears on adjacency list
{
    return adjacencies.contains(e);
}

public Edge removeEdge(Edge e)
// post: removes and returns adjacent edge "equal" to e
{
    return (Edge)adjacencies.remove(e);
}

public Edge getEdge(Edge e)
// post: returns the edge that "equals" e, or null
{
    Iterator edges = adjacencies.elements();
    while (edges.hasMoreElements())
    {
        Edge adjE = (Edge)edges.nextElement();
        if (e.equals(adjE)) return adjE;
    }
    return null;
}

public int degree()
// post: returns the degree of this node
{
    return adjacencies.size();
}

public Iterator adjacentVertices()
// post: returns iterator over adj. vertices
{
    return new GraphListAIterator(adjacentEdges(), label());
}

public Iterator adjacentEdges()
// post: returns iterator over adj. edges
{
    return adjacencies.elements();
```

```
    }
  }
```

The constructor initializes its `Vertex` fields, and then constructs an empty adjacency list. Elements of this list will be `Edge` objects. Most of the other methods have obvious behavior.

The only difficult method is `getEdge`. This method returns an edge from the adjacency list that logically equals (i.e., determined to be equal through a call to `Edge`'s `equals` method) the edge provided. In an undirected graph the order of the vertex labels may not correspond to the order found in edges in the edge list. As a result, `getEdge` returns a *canonical edge* that represents the edge specified as the parameter. This ensures that there are not multiple instances of edges that keep track of shared information.

We are now ready to implement most of the methods required by the `Graph` interface. First, we consider the protected `GraphList` constructor:

```
protected Dictionary dict;   // label to vertex dictionary
protected boolean directed;  // is graph directed?

protected GraphList(boolean dir)
// post: constructs an empty graph;
//       graph is directed iff dir is true
{
    dict = new Hashtable();
    directed = dir;
}
```

Our approach to extending the abstract `GraphList` type to support directed and undirected graphs is similar to that described in the adjacency matrix implementation. With the list-based implementation, though, we need not provide an upper bound on the number of vertices that will appear in the graph. This is because the underlying structures automatically extend themselves, if necessary.

The process of adding and removing a vertex involves simple manipulations of the `Dictionary`. Here, for example, is the code for adding a new vertex to the graph:

```
public void add(Object label)
// pre: label is a non-null label for vertex
// post: a vertex with label is added to graph;
//       if vertex with label is already in graph, no action
{
    if (dict.containsKey(label)) return; // vertex exists
    GraphListVertex v = new GraphListVertex(label);
    dict.put(label,v);
}
```

To add an edge to the graph we insert a reference to the `Edge` object in the appropriate adjacency lists. For a directed graph, we insert the edge in the list associated with the source vertex. For an undirected graph, a reference to the edge must be inserted into both lists. It is important, of course, that a *reference* to a single edge be inserted in both lists so that changes to the edge are maintained consistently. Here, we show the undirected version:

GraphList-
Undirected

```
public void addEdge(Object vLabel1, Object vLabel2, Object label)
// pre: vLabel1 and vLabel2 are labels of existing vertices, v1 & v2
// post: an edge (undirected) is inserted between v1 and v2;
//       if edge is new, it is labeled with label (can be null)
{
    GraphListVertex v1 = (GraphListVertex) dict.get(vLabel1);
    GraphListVertex v2 = (GraphListVertex) dict.get(vLabel2);
    Edge e = new Edge(v1.label(), v2.label(), label, false);
    v1.addEdge(e);
    v2.addEdge(e);
}
```

Removing an edge simply reverses this process:

```
public Object removeEdge(Object vLabel1, Object vLabel2)
// pre: vLabel1 and vLabel2 are labels of existing vertices
// post: edge is removed; its label is returned
{
    GraphListVertex v1 = (GraphListVertex) dict.get(vLabel1);
    GraphListVertex v2 = (GraphListVertex) dict.get(vLabel2);
    Edge e = new Edge(v1.label(), v2.label(), null, false);
    v2.removeEdge(e);
    e = v1.removeEdge(e);
    if (e == null) return null;
    else return e.label();
}
```

Notice that to remove an edge a "pattern" edge must be constructed to identify (through `equals`) the target of the remove.

Now that we can remove edges, we can remove a vertex. Since the removal of a vertex should remove incident edges, it is important that each of the adjacency lists be checked. Our approach is to iterate across each of the vertices and remove any edge that mentions that vertex. This requires some care. Here is the directed version:

GraphList-
Directed

```
public Object remove(Object label)
// pre: label is non-null vertex label
// post: vertex with "equals" label is removed, if found
{
    GraphListVertex v = (GraphListVertex)dict.get(label);

    Iterator vi = elements();
    while (vi.hasMoreElements())
    {
        Object v2 = vi.nextElement();
        if (!label.equals(v2)) removeEdge(v2,label);
```

```
        }
        dict.remove(label);
        return v.label();
    }
```

The complexity of this method counterbalances the simplicity of adding a vertex to the graph.

Many of the remaining edge and vertex methods have been greatly simplified by our having extended the **Vertex** class. Here, for example, is the **degree** method:

```
    public int degree(Object label)
    // pre: label is a label of a vertex
    // post: returns the degree of vertex
    {
        Assert.condition(dict.containsKey(label), "Vertex exists.");
        return ((GraphListVertex) dict.get(label)).degree();
    }
```

This code calls the **GraphListVertex degree** method. That, in turn, calls the **size** method of the underlying collection, a **SinglyLinkedList**. Most of the remaining methods are simply implemented.

At this point, it is useful to discuss the implementation of iterators for the adjacency list representation. Like the adjacency matrix implementation, the **elements** method simply returns the result of the **keys** iterator on the underlying **Dictionary**. Each of the values returned by the iterator is a vertex label, which is exactly what we desire.

The **neighbors** iterator should return an iterator over the neighbors of the provided vertex. Since each vertex maintains a **Collection** of edges, the **elements** method of the collection returns **Edge** values. Our approach is similar to the approach we used in constructing the iterators for **Dictionarys**: we construct a private, special purpose iterator that drives the **Collection** iterator as a slave. The process of extracting the "other" vertex from each edge encountered is made complex by the fact that "this" vertex can appear as either the source or destination vertex when the graph is undirected.

The **Edge**'s iterator has similar complexities. The easiest approach is to construct a list of edges by traversing each of the edge lists found in each of the vertices. The result is an iterator over the resulting list. Here is the code for the constructor of our private **GraphListEIterator** class:

```
    protected Iterator edges;

    public GraphListEIterator(Dictionary dict)
    // post: constructs a new iterator across edges of
    //       vertices within dictionary
    {
        List l = new DoublyLinkedList();
        Iterator dictIterator = dict.elements();
```

```
while (dictIterator.hasMoreElements())
{
    GraphListVertex vtx =
        (GraphListVertex)dictIterator.nextElement();
    Iterator vtxIterator = vtx.adjacentEdges();
    while (vtxIterator.hasMoreElements())
    {
        Edge e = (Edge)vtxIterator.nextElement();
        if (vtx.label().equals(e.here())) l.addToTail(e);
    }
}
edges = l.elements();
}
```

Each of the edges is traversed in the construction of the iterator, so there is considerable overhead just during initialization. Once constructed, however, the traversal is quick. An alternative implementation would distribute the cost over each step of the traversal. Construction of the iterator would be less expensive, but each step of the traversal would be slightly slower. In the end, both methods consume similar amounts of time. If, however, partial traversals of the edge lists are expected, the alternative implementation has its merits.

With two implementations of graphs in mind, we now focus on a number of examples of their use.

14.4   Examples: Common Graph Algorithms

Because the graph structure is so flexible there are many good examples of graph applications. In this section, we investigate a number of beautiful algorithms involving graphs. These algorithms provide a cursory overview of the problems that may be cast as graph problems, as well as techniques that are commonly used to solve them.

14.4.1   Reachability

Once data are stored within a graph, it is often desirable to identify vertices that are reachable from a common source (see Figure 14.6). One approach is to treat the graph as you would a maze and, using search techniques, find the reachable vertices. For example, we may use *depth-first search*: each time we visit an unvisited vertex we seek to further deepen the traversal.

The following code demonstrates how we might use recursion to search for unvisited vertices:

Reachability

```
static void reachableFrom(Graph g, Object vertexLabel)
// pre: g is a non-null graph, vertexLabel labels a vertex of g
// post: unvisited vertices reachable from vertex are visited
{
    g.visit(vertexLabel);   // visit this vertex
```

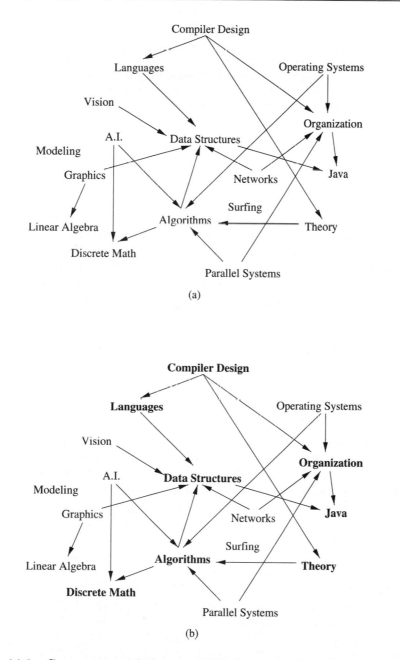

Figure 14.6 Courses you might be expected to have taken if you're in a compiler design class. The top figure (a) is a typical prerequisite graph (classes point to prerequisites). Note the central nature of data structures. Bold courses in the lower figure (b) can be reached as requisite courses for Compiler Design.

```
// recursively visit unvisited neighbor vertices
Iterator ni = g.neighbors(vertexLabel);
for (ni.reset(); ni.hasMoreElements(); ni.nextElement())
{
    Object neighbor = ni.value(); // adjacent node label
    if (!g.isVisited(neighbor))
    {
        reachableFrom(g,neighbor); // depth-first search
    }
    }
}
```

We clear each **Vertex**'s visited flag with a call to **reset**, and then call **reachableFrom** with the graph and the source vertex for the reachability test. Before the call to **reachableFrom**, the vertex labeled with the **vertexLabel** has not been visited. After the call, every vertex reachable from the vertex has been visited. Some vertices may be left unvisited and are not reachable from the source. So, to determine whether you may reach one vertex from another, the following code can be used:

```
g.reset();
reachableFrom(g,sourceLabel);
canGetThere = g.isVisited(destinationLabel));
```

In Section 7.3 we discussed the use of a **Linear** structure to maintain the state of a search of a maze. The use of a **Stack** led to a depth-first search. Here, however, no **Stack** appears! The reason is that the act of calling the procedure recursively maintains an implied stack of local variables.

How long does it take to execute the procedure? Suppose that, ultimately, we visit the reachable vertices V_r. Let E_r be the edges of the graph found among the vertices of V_r. Clearly, each vertex of V_r is visited, so there is one call to **reachableFrom** from each vertex $v \in V_r$. For each call, we ask each destination vertex if it has been visited or not. There is one such test for every edge within E_r. Thus, the total time is $O(|V_r| + |E_r|)$. Since $|E_r| \geq |V_r - 1|$ (every new vertex is visited by traversing a new edge), the algorithm is dominated by the number of edges actually investigated. Of course, if the graph is dense, this is bounded above by the square of the number of vertices.

In an undirected graph the reachable vertices form a component of the graph. To count the components of a graph (the undirected version of the graph of Figure 14.6 has three components), we iterate across the vertices of the graph, calling the **reachableFrom** procedure on any vertex that has not yet been visited. Since each unvisited vertex is not reachable from those that have been encountered before, the number of searches determines the number of components.

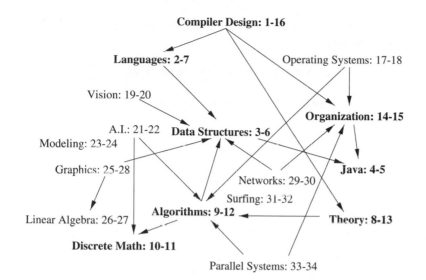

Figure 14.7 The progress of a topological sort of the course graph. The time interval following a node label indicates the time interval spent processing that node or its descendants. Dark nodes reachable from Compiler Design are all processed during the interval [1-16]—the interval associated with Compiler Design.

14.4.2 Topological Sorting

Occasionally it is useful to list the vertices of a graph in such a way as to make the edges point in one direction, for example, toward the front of the list. Such graphs have to be directed and acyclic (see Problem 14.13). A listing of vertices with this property is called a *topological sort*.

One technique for developing a topological sort involves keeping track of a counter or virtual timer. The timer is incremented every time it is read. We now visit each of the nodes using a depth-first search, labeling each node with two *timestamps*. These timestamps determine the span of time that the algorithm spends processing the descendants of a node. When a node is first encountered during the search, we record the *start time*. When the recursive depth-first search returns from processing a node, the timer is again read and the *finish time* is recorded. Figure 14.7 depicts the intervals associated with each vertex of the graph of Figure 14.6. (As arbitrary convention, we assume that a vertex iterator would encounter nodes in the diagram in "reading" order.)

One need only observe that the finish time of a node is greater than the finish time of any node it can reach. (This depth-first search may have to be started at several nodes if there are several independent components, or if the graph is not strongly connected.) The algorithm, then, simply lists the vertices in the order in which they are finished. For our course graph we generate one

of many course schedules that allow students to take courses without violating
course requirements:

Vertices Ordered by Finish Time					
5.	Java	15.	Organization	27.	Linear Algebra
6.	Data Structures	16.	Compiler Design	28.	Graphics
7.	Languages	18.	Operating Systems	30.	Networks
11.	Discrete Math	20.	Vision	32.	Surfing
12.	Algorithms	22.	A.I.	34.	Parallel Systems
13.	Theory	24.	Modeling		

Actually, the timestamps are useful only for purposes of illustration. In fact,
we can simply append vertices to the end of a queue at the time that they would
normally be finished. Here is sample code:

TopoSort

```
public static List topoSort(Graph g)
// pre: g is non-null
// post: returns list of all vertices of g, topologically ordered
{
    // construct result list
    List l = new DoublyLinkedList();
    Iterator vi = g.elements();
    for (vi.reset(); vi.hasMoreElements(); vi.nextElement())
    {
        // perform depth-first search on unvisited vertices
        if (!g.isVisited(vi.value()))
        {
            DFS(g,vi.value(),l);
        }
    }
    // result is queue of vertex labels
    return l;
}

static protected void DFS(Graph g, Object n, List l)
// post: performs depth-first search enqueuing
//       unvisited descendants of node n into l
{
    g.visit(n); // mark node visited
    Iterator ei = g.neighbors(n); // get neighbors
    for (ei.reset(); ei.hasMoreElements(); ei.nextElement())
    {
        // potentially deepen search if neighbor not visited
        if (!g.isVisited(ei.value())) {
            DFS(g,ei.value(),l);
        }
    }
    l.addToTail(n); // add this value once decendants added
}
```

These functions are declared as static procedures of a program that might make use of a topological sort. Alternatively, they could be written as methods of a graph, reducing the complexity of method calls.

14.4.3 Transitive Closure

Previously we discussed a reachability algorithm that determines if it is possible to reach any particular vertex from a particular source. It is also useful to compute the *transitive closure* of a graph: for *each pair* of vertices, $u, v \in V$, *Is v reachable from u?* These questions can be answered by $O(|V|)$ calls to the depth-first search algorithm, above (leading to an algorithm that is $O(|V|(|V|+|E|))$), or we can look for a more direct algorithm that has similar behavior.

One algorithm, *Warshall's algorithm*, computes reachability for each pair of vertices by modifying the graph. When the algorithm is applied to a graph, edges are added until there is an edge for every pair of connected vertices (u, v). The concept behind Warshall's algorithm is relatively simple. Two connected vertices u and v are either directly connected, or the path from u to v passes through an intermediate node w. The algorithm simply considers each node and connects all pairs of nodes u and v that can be shown to use w as an intermediate node. Here is a Java implementation:

Warshall

```
static void warshall(Graph g)
// pre: g is non-null
// post: g contains edge (a,b) if there is a path from a to b
{
    Iterator uiter = g.elements();
    Iterator viter = g.elements();
    Iterator witer = g.elements();

    for (witer.reset();
         witer.hasMoreElements();
         witer.nextElement())
    {
        Object w = witer.value();
        for (uiter.reset();
             uiter.hasMoreElements();
             uiter.nextElement())
        {
            Object u = uiter.value();
            for (viter.reset();
                 viter.hasMoreElements();
                 viter.nextElement())
            {
                Object v = viter.value();
                // check for edge from u to v via w
                if (g.containsEdge(u, w) &&
                    g.containsEdge(w, v))
                {
```

```
                                    g.addEdge(u, v, null);
                                }
                            }
                        }
                    }
                }
```

This algorithm is clearly $O(|V|^3)$: each iterator visits $|V|$ vertices and (for adjacency matrices) the check for existence of an edge can be performed in constant time.

To see how the algorithm works, we number the vertices in the order they are encountered by the vertex iterator. After k iterations of the outer loop, all "reachability edges" of the subgraph containing just the first k vertices are completely determined. The next iteration extends this result to a subgraph of $k + 1$ vertices. An inductive approach to proving this algorithm correct (which we avoid) certainly has merit.

14.4.4 All Pairs Minimum Distance

A slight modification of Warshall's algorithm gives us a method for computing the minimum distance between all pairs of points. The method is due to Floyd. Again, we use three loops to compute the new edges representing reachability, but these edges are now labeled or *weighted* with integer distances that indicate the current minimum distance between each pair of nodes. As we consider intermediate nodes, we merge minimum distance approximations by computing and updating the distance if the sum of path lengths through an intermediate node w is less than our previous approximation. Object orientation makes this code somewhat cumbersome:

Floyd

```
static void floyd(Graph g)
// post: g contains edge (a,b) if there is a path from a to b
{
    Iterator uiter = g.elements();
    Iterator viter = g.elements();
    Iterator witer = g.elements();

    for (witer.reset();
         witer.hasMoreElements();
         witer.nextElement())
    {
        Object w = witer.value();
        for (uiter.reset();
             uiter.hasMoreElements();
             uiter.nextElement())
        {
            Object u = uiter.value();
            for (viter.reset();
                 viter.hasMoreElements();
```

```
                        viter.nextElement())
        {
        Object v = viter.value();
        if (g.containsEdge(u,w) && g.containsEdge(w,v))
        {
            Edge leg1 = g.getEdge(u,w);
            Edge leg2 = g.getEdge(w,v);
            int leg1Dist =
                ((Integer)leg1.label()).intValue();
            int leg2Dist =
                ((Integer)leg2.label()).intValue();
            int newDist = leg1Dist+leg2Dist;

            if (g.containsEdge(u,v))
            {
                Edge across = g.getEdge(u,v);
                int acrossDist =
                    ((Integer)across.label()).intValue();
                if (newDist < acrossDist)
                    across.setLabel(new Integer(newDist));
            } else {
                g.addEdge(u,v,new Integer(newDist));
            }
        }
    }
    }
    }
}
```

Clearly, edge labels could contain more information than just the path length. For example, the path itself could be constructed, stored, and produced on request, if necessary. Again, the complexity of the algorithm is $O(|V|^3)$. This is satisfactory for dense graphs, especially if they're stored in adjacency matrices, but for sparse graphs the checking of all possible edges seems excessive. Indeed, other approaches can improve these bounds. We leave some of these for your next course in algorithms!

14.4.5 Greedy Algorithms

We now consider two examples of *greedy* algorithms—algorithms that compute optimal solutions to problems by acting in the optimal or "most greedy" manner at each stage in the algorithm. Because both algorithms seek to find the best choice for the next step in the solution process, both make use of a priority queue.

Minimum Spanning Tree

The solution to many network problems involves identifying a *minimum spanning tree* of a graph. A minimum spanning tree of an edge-weighted graph is a

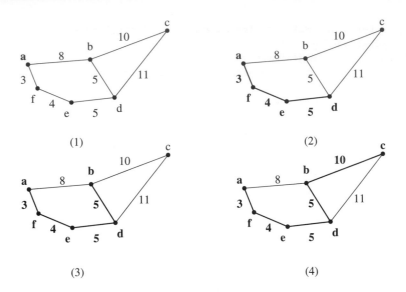

Figure 14.8 The progress of a minimum spanning tree computation. Bold vertices and edges are part of the tree. Vertex a is adjacent to the shortest edge. At each stage, a shortest external edge adjacent to the tree is incorporated.

tree that connects every vertex of a component whose edges have minimum total edge weight. Such a tree might represent the most inexpensive way to connect several cities with telephone trunk lines. For this reason, we will interpret the weights as edge lengths. For the purposes of our discussion, we will assume that the graph under consideration is composed of a single component. (If the graph contains multiple components, we can compute a minimum spanning forest with multiple applications of the minimum spanning tree algorithm.)

The process of constructing a minimum spanning tree involves starting with a shortest edge and then iteratively incorporating a shortest edge that connects a new node to the tree. The process stops when $|V| - 1$ edges have been added to the tree.

MCST

```
static public void mcst(Graph g)
// pre: g is a graph
// post: edges of minimum spanning tree of a component are visited
{
    // keep edges ranked by length
    PriorityQueue q = new SkewHeap();
    Object v = null;      // current vertex
    Edge e;               // current edge

    g.reset();            // clear visited flags
```

```
// select a smallest edge in graph for initial tree
ComparableEdge shortest = null;
Iterator ei = g.edges();

v = null;
while (ei.hasMoreElements())
{
    ComparableEdge possible =
        new ComparableEdge((Edge)ei.nextElement());
    if (shortest == null ||
        possible.compareTo(shortest) < 0)
        shortest = possible;
}
if (shortest == null) return; // no sortest edge
else v = shortest.here();

// at this point v is a vertex mentioned by shortest edge
e = null;
while (v != null)
{
    // v is a (possibly new) vertex
    if (!g.isVisited(v))
    {
        // visit incoming edge and vertex v
        if (e!=null) g.visitEdge(g.getEdge(e.here(),e.there()));
        g.visit(v);

        // now add all the outgoing edges from v
        Iterator ai = g.neighbors(v);
        while (ai.hasMoreElements()) {
            // turn it into outgoing edge
            e = g.getEdge(v,ai.nextElement());
            // add the edge to the queue
            q.add(new ComparableEdge(e));
        }
    }
    if (!q.isEmpty())
    {
        // grab next shortest edge
        e = (Edge)q.remove();

        // does this edge take us somewhere new?
        v = e.there();
        if (g.isVisited(v)) v = e.here();
    } else {
        // couldn't get to new vertex (we're done)
        v = null;
    }
}
}
```

First, we use a priority queue to rank edges based on length. As we remove the edges from the queue, the smallest edges are considered first (see Figure 14.8). When an edge is considered that includes an unvisited vertex, we visit it, logically adding it to the minimum spanning tree. We then add any edges that are outward-bound from the newly visited node. At any time, the priority queue contains only edges that mention at least one node of the tree. If, of course, an edge is considered that mentions two previously visited nodes, the edge is unnecessary, as the nodes are already connected by a path in the tree (albeit a potentially long one). When the priority queue "runs dry," the tree is fully computed.

The result of the algorithm will be visited marks on all nodes and edges that participate in the tree. The first loop looks for a shortest edge.[2] We use the source vertex to "prime" the greedy algorithm.

The main loop of the algorithm runs as long as a vertex is potentially added to the tree. If the vertex has already been visited, the next shortest edge is greedily considered. If the vertex has not been visited, then the edge that mentions it is visited and added to the tree (the initial vertex has no incoming edge). Its outbound edges are then added to the list of those to be considered. Eventually, all vertices and edges are processed once, leading to a running time of $O(|V| + |E|)$.

Notice that, indirectly, the initial vertex guarantees that a shortest edge is added to the tree first.

Single-Source Shortest Paths

The minimum spanning tree algorithm is related to a fast, single-source shortest path algorithm attributed to Dijkstra. In this algorithm, we desire the minimum length paths from a single source to all other nodes. We expect the algorithm, of course, to run considerably faster than the all-pairs version. This algorithm also runs in time proportional to $O(|V| + |E|)$ due to the fact that it uses much the same control as the minimum spanning tree. Here is the code:

Dijkstra

```
public static Dictionary dijkstra(Graph g, Object start)
// pre: g is a graph; start is source vertex
// post: returns a dictionary of vertex-based results
//       value is association (total-distance,prior-edge)
{
    // keep a priority queue of distances from source
    PriorityQueue q = new SkewHeap();
    Dictionary result = new Table(); // results, sorted by vertex
    Object v = start;        // last vertex added
    // result is a (total-distance,previous-edge) pair
    ComparableAssociation possible =
        new ComparableAssociation(new Integer(0),null);
```

---

[2] We use `ComparableEdges` here, an extension to an edge that assumes that the labels implement `Comparable`.

```
    // as long as we add a new vertex...
    while (v != null)
    {
        if (!result.containsKey(v))
        {
            // visit node v -- record incoming edge
            result.put(v,possible);
            // vDist is shortest distance to v
            int vDist = ((Integer)possible.key()).intValue();

            // compute and consider distance to each neighbor
            Iterator ai = g.neighbors(v);
            while (ai.hasMoreElements())
            {
                // get edge to neighbor
                Edge e = g.getEdge(v,ai.nextElement());
                // construct (distance,edge) pair for possible result
                possible = new ComparableAssociation(
                    new Integer(vDist+((Integer)e.label()).intValue()),
                    e);
                q.add(possible);      // add to priority queue
            }
        }
        // now, get closest (possibly unvisited) vertex
        if (!q.isEmpty())
        {
            possible = (ComparableAssociation)q.remove();
            // get destination vertex (take care w/undirected graphs)
            v = ((Edge)possible.value()).there();
            if (result.containsKey(v))
                v = ((Edge)possible.value()).here();
        } else {
            // no new vertex (algorithm stops)
            v = null;
        }
    }
    return result;
}
```

Unlike the previous algorithm, we return a `Table` of results. Each entry
in the `Table` has a vertex label as a key. The value is an association between
the total distance from the source to the vertex, and (in the nontrivial case) a
reference to the last edge that supports the minimum length path.

We initially record trivial results for the source vertex (setting its distance
to zero) and place every outgoing edge in the priority queue (see Figure 14.9).
Unlike the minimum spanning tree algorithm, we rank the edges based on *total*
distance from the source. These edges describe how to extend, in a nearest-first,
greedy manner, the paths that pass from the source through visited nodes. If, of
course, an edge is dequeued that takes us to a vertex with previously recorded

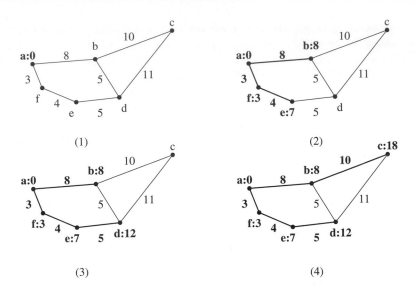

Figure 14.9 The progress of a single-source shortest path computation from source
a. As nodes are incorporated a minimum distance is associated with the vertex.
Compare with Figure 14.8.

results, it may be ignored: some other path from the source to the vertex is
shorter. If the vertex has not been visited, it is placed in the `Table` with the
distance from the source (as associated with the removed edge). New outbound
edges are then enqueued.

The tricky part is to rank the edges by the distance of the destination vertex
from the source. We can think of the algorithm as considering edges that fall
within a neighborhood of increasing radius from the source vertex. When the
boundary of the neighborhood includes a new vertex, its minimum distance from
the source has been determined.

Since every vertex is considered once and each edge possibly twice, the worst-
case performance is $O(|V|+|E|)$, an improvement over the $O(|V|^3)$ performance
for sparse graphs.

14.5 Conclusions

In this chapter we have investigated two traditional implementations of graphs.
The adjacency matrix stores information about each edge in a square matrix.
The adjacency list implementation keeps track of edges that leave each vertex.
The matrix implementation is ideal for dense graphs, where the number of
actual edges is high, while the list implementation is best for representing sparse
graphs.

Our approach to implementing graph structures is to use partial implementations, called abstract classes, and extend them until they are concrete, or complete. Other methods are commonly used, but this has the merit that common code can be shared among similar classes. Indeed, this inheritance is one of the features commonly found in object-oriented languages.

Our last section is, in effect, a stepping stone to an investigation of algorithms. There are many approaches to answering graph-related questions, and because of the dramatic differences in complexities in different implementations, the solutions are often affected by the underlying graph structure.

Finally, we note that many of the seemingly simple graph-related problems cannot be efficiently solved with *any* reasonable representation of graphs. Those problems are, themselves, a suitable topic for many future courses of study.

Problems

14.1   Draw the adjacency matrix and list representations of the following (undirected and complete) graph:

14.2   Draw the adjacency matrix and list representations of the following (directed) graph:

14.3   Draw the adjacency matrix and list representations of a complete tree with seven nodes and undirected edges.

14.4   What are the transitive closures of each of the following graphs?

(a)   (b)

14.5   Suppose that we use an $n \times n$ boolean matrix to represent the edges of a directed graph. Assume, as well, that the diagonal elements are all **true**. How should we interpret the nth power of this adjacency matrix?

14.6   What topological characteristics distinguish a general graph from a general tree?

14.7   Consider the following (simplified) map of the world.

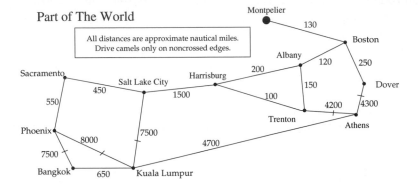

a. Compute the shortest air distance to each of the cities from scenic Montpelier, Vermont. Redraw the map with distances to cities and include only the air routes that support the most direct travel to Vermont.

b. Suppose you're interested in setting up a network among the capitals. Redraw the map to depict the minimum spanning network.

c. Suppose you're interested in setting up a Camel Express system. Redraw the map to depict the minimum spanning road systems that don't cross bodies of water (indicated by crossed edges).

14.8   Explain why it is necessary that the `Edge` class "show through" the `Graph` interface. (Hint: Consider implementations of the `Iterator` constructed by the `edges` method.)

14.9   Compare and contrast the performance of the adjacency list and adjacency matrix implementations of graphs.

14.10   For both implementations of graphs, write a method, `isSink`, that returns `true` iff the vertex indicated is a sink.

14.11   For both implementations of graphs, write a method, `isSource`, that returns `true` iff the vertex indicated is a source.

14.12   In an undirected graph, it is possible for a single edge to be represented by `Edge` objects whose vertices appear in opposite orders. Describe how a general `equals` method for `Edge`s might be written.

14.13   Explain why graphs with topologically sortable vertices must be (1) directed and (2) acyclic.

14.14 Suppose we had a graph that described the dependencies between Java modules, and that there were no cycles. How would you compute the order of compilations that had to occur?

Topological sorting solves this, given no cycles.

14.15 It is a fairly common practice to traverse the vertices and edges of a graph. Consider a new implementation of graphs that keeps a `Dictionary` of vertices as well as an unordered `List` of edges. This makes traversal of edges simple. What is the complexity of each of the other `Graph` operations?

14.16 Extend the all-pairs minimum distance algorithm to keep track of the shortest *path* between the nodes.

14.17 Explain why it is sometimes more efficient to compute the distance from a single source to all other nodes, even though a particular query may be answered with a partial solution.

14.18★ Under what conditions can a graph component have nonunique minimum spanning trees?

14.19★ Prove that a minimum spanning tree of a graph component must include a shortest edge.

14.20★ It is possible, in Dijkstra's algorithm, that an edge removed from the prioirty queue is not useful: it takes us to a previously visited node. Some of these extraneous edges can be avoided by not placing an edge in the priority queue if the destination has already been visited. Is it still possible to encounter an edge to a previously visited node?

14.21 Dijkstra's algorithm assumes certain basic operations that may be performed on the edge labels. Describe those operations and define a new `interface` that could be supported by classes like `Integer`, `Double`, and `String`. (It may be necessary to extend these classes to support the `interface`, but the support should be fairly trivial.) Then, indicate the changes necessary to make a single, general Dijkstra's algorithm work with each of these types of edge label.

Appendix A

A Sip of Java

"I love the java jive and it loves me."
—Milton Drake and Ben Oakland

THE JAVA PROGRAMMING LANGUAGE WAS DESIGNED at Sun Microsystems as a simple, object-oriented, portable programming language for supporting Internet-based products. With large numbers of students, educators, and developers writing applications once written in languages such as C, C++, Fortran, and Pascal, the language is developing rapidly. As it gains wider acceptance, it will be increasingly important for programmers of these other languages to become familiar with the important features and paradigms introduced by Java. This section serves as a quick introduction to the features of Java. Other, more in-depth treatments are available over the Internet or through your bookstore or local library.

A.1 A First Program

The main focus of a Java programmer is to write *classes*. These classes are templates for structures called *objects*. In most environments, the code supporting each class is placed in a dedicated file by the same name (class `Sort` is found in `Sort.java`). Writing a Java program involves writing a class definition. Here is a good first program to consider:

```java
import structure.*;

public class MyFirstProgram
{
    public static void main(String[] arguments)
    {
        // print a message to the standard output stream
        System.out.println("Look Mom: know Java!");
    }
}
```

At the top of the program, the `import` statement searches the programming environment for a *package* or library of classes called `structure`:

```java
import structure.*;
```

and makes all of them (.*) available for use within the program. The `structure` package is the subject of this book; the applications of this text will include this `import` statement. Other packages available with Java include `java.lang`—the package of items automatically imported (this includes, for example, the definition of `System` and `String`); `java.io`—the package that provides access to special-purpose I/O facilities; and `java.util`—a package that contains utility classes, including random number generators, date objects, and simple data structures. Documentation for these packages is freely available online from `javasoft.com` and in a wide variety of trade books.

The class is marked `public`:

```
public class MyFirstProgram
```

which means that it is available for access by anyone who wants to use the class—in particular anyone who wants to run the class as a program.

Classes that contain a procedure or *method* called `main` may be run as applications:

```
public static void main(String[] arguments)
```

When the application is run, the `main` method is executed, and its sole parameter is an array of `String`s that are passed to it from the programming environment.

Any text on a line following a double-slash (//) is considered a comment:

```
// print a message to the standard output stream
```

and is ignored by the compiler.

The computer prints a single string to the standard output:

```
System.out.println("Look Mom: know Java!");
```

The `print` method is part of the `out` stream from the `System` object. This dotted notation is used to provide names of data and methods within an object. For example, another name for the `main` procedure is `MyFirstProgram.main`.

Java is case sensitive; it is important to make sure identifiers are all in the same case. By convention, packages and methods begin with lowercase letters, while classes begin with uppercase.

Occasionally, two packages contain classes with the same name. If both classes are imported simultaneously, they are only accessible if prefixed by their respective package names. While the package system is a convenient means of compartmentalizing name-spaces, programmers are encouraged to consider potential naming conflicts with common packages before designing their own classes. Still over time, with a moving target like the Java runtime environment, naming conflicts are sometimes difficult to avoid.

A.2   Declarations

The *scope* of an identifier—the name of a variable, method, or class—is the range of code that may legally access the identifier. Variables in Java may be declared in a number of different places:

- Variables must be declared within a class or method. Variables declared within a method are local to the method, and many not be accessed outside the method. Variables declared within the class are "instance variables" whose access is determined by access keywords.

- Variables and values declared within a class are visible to any method declared as part of the class. Depending on the protection of the variable, it may be seen in subclasses, or within the class's package, or globally.

- Variables and values declared within a method can be seen within code following the declaration that is delimited by the tightest enclosing braces. Ideally variables are declared at the top of a method, but they may be declared at the top of the block where they are used.

Methods may only be declared within a class. Unlike Pascal, they may *not* be nested. An understanding of the access control keywords for Java is important to understanding their scope. The next appendix discusses this topic in considerable detail.

A.2.1   Primitive Types

Two types of data are available through Java–*primitive* types and *reference* types. Primitive types include integers, floating point numbers, booleans, and characters:

Name	Type	Range	Default Value
boolean	boolean	true or false	false
char	character data	any character	'\0' (null)
int	integer	$-2^{31} \ldots 2^{31}-1$	0
long	long integer	$-2^{63} \ldots 2^{63}-1$	0
float	real	$-3.4028E38 \ldots 3.4028E38$	0.0
double	double precision real	$-1.7977E308 \ldots 1.7977E308$	0.0

Java variables are automatically initialized to their default values, but programmers are best advised to initialize variables before they are used.

Java supports a large variety of operators for primitive data types. Here are the most common, in decreasing order of precedence:

Operator	Meaning
++	unary increment
--	unary decrement
!	logical not
* / %	multiplication, division, remainder
+ -	addition, subtraction
< <= => >	numeric comparison
== !=	primitive and reference equality test
&&	logical and
||	logical or
=	assignment

Notice that assignment (=) is an operator and can be used to generate complex (and unreadable) expressions:

```
int a, b, c = 0;
a = 1 + b = 1 + c; // a = (1 + (b = (1 + c)))
```

leaves c at 0 and sets b to 1 and a to 2. Pascal programmers should note that the assignment (=) and equality (==) operators are easily confused (although the compiler is often capable of detecting such mistakes). The assignment and equality tests work on references as well, but not the objects to which they refer.

Programmers should be aware that the division operator (/) returns only the integer portion of the quotient when both operands are integers. The remainder operator (%) recovers the remainder after division. As usual, one should perform integer division and remainder on negative numbers with care.

Characters in Java are encoded using a very general mechanism called *unicode*, which is a superset of ASCII characters. Characters are surrounded by apostrophes, and have the following shorthands familiar to C and C++ programmers:

Escaped character	Meaning	Escaped character	Meaning
'\b'	backspace	'\f'	form feed
'\r'	carriage return	'\n'	newline
'\t'	tab	'\''	apostrophe
'\"'	quotation mark	'\\'	backslash

Primitive types may be explicitly *converted* to other types through *casting*. When information would not be lost, Java may perform the type conversion automatically. The following removes the fractional component of a **double** value:

```
double d = -3.141;
int i = (int)d;
```

Unlike C-style languages, Java does not automatically convert **non-boolean** expressions to **true** or **false** values.

A.2.2 Reference Types

Java does not have explicit pointers. Instead, more tightly controlled *references* are provided. Reference types include arrays and objects. Arrays in Java must be explicitly allocated and, as a result, may have runtime-determined bounds. The following code demonstrates several means of initializing arrays; all are identical.

```
int primes1[] = {2,3,5,7,11};
int primes2[] = new int[5];
int primes3[] = primes2;
primes[0] = 2;
primes[1] = 3;
primes[2] = 5;
primes[3] = 7;
primes[4] = 11;
```

The arrays `primes2` and `primes3` refer to the same dynamically allocated memory; `primes1` refers to another chunk of memory with similar values. An array or object may be referred to by more than one reference variable at the same time. Thus, the result of comparing `primes1==primes2` is `false` (the references refer to different memory), but `primes2==primes3` is `true`. The length of an array may be determined by inspecting its length property: `primes2.length` is 5.

Every reference either refers to no object (it is called a `null` reference) or an instance of an object of the appropriate type. Arrays may be `null`, in which case they refer to no memory.

References to objects perform a level of indirection. Thus

```
String s;
s = new String("Measure for measure must be answered.");
System.out.println(s.length());
```

calls the `length` method referred to by the `String s`. If `s` were `null`, the indirection would be impossible, leading to a "null pointer exception." The following code, then, generates a null pointer exception:

But remember: Java has no pointers!

```
String s; // a null reference since no string allocated
System.out.println(s.length()); // illegal!
```

Java works hard to ensure that references do not point to invalid objects. In traditional languages, significant errors can be incorporated into programs by incorrectly allocating or freeing dynamic memory. Java's approach is to force the user to explicitly allocate each nonprimitive object and rely on a *garbage collector* to free allocated memory, but only after it is known to be unreferenced. This approach has some cost associated with it (the garbage collector has no hints as to where to find likely garbage), but a reference is guaranteed to never point to invalid memory.

A.3 Important Classes

Several classes are used in nearly every Java program. As with all classes, they are also fully documented online.

A.3.1 The ReadStream Class

Strangely, Java makes little effort to support input of primitive types from streams. As a result, the **structure** package provides a simple class for performing Pascal-like reading of primitive values from the keyboard. A **ReadStream** can be attached (much like a filter) to an input stream and can then be made to read primitive values. It is, perhaps, best to learn observing an example:

ReadStream

```
ReadStream r = new ReadStream();
int i;

for (r.skipWhite(); !r.eof(); r.skipWhite())
{
    i = r.readInt();
    if (isPrime(i)) System.out.println(i);
}
r.close();
```

Here, a new **ReadStream** is created. By default, it is attached to the standard input stream, **System.in**. The method **skipWhite** scans and disposes of characters on the input, as long as they are white space (including tabs and end-of-line marks). The **eof** method returns **true** if no more data are available on the **readStream**. Finally, **readInt** reads in an integer from the stream. The value is stored in **i**. **ReadStreams** are capable of reading in all of the primitive types, including **doubles** and **booleans**:

Method	Reads
r.readChar()	next char from stream r
r.readBoolean()	next boolean from stream r
r.readInt()	next int from stream r
r.readLong()	next long from stream r
r.readFloat()	next float from stream r
r.readDouble()	next double from stream r
r.readString()	next word, returned as String, from stream r
r.readLine()	next line, returned as String, from stream r
r.readln()	next line, returning no value, from stream r
r.skipWhite()	until next nonwhitespace from stream r
r.eof()	returns true iff no more data in stream r
r.eoln()	returns true iff no more data on line from stream r

A.3.2 PrintStreams

Simple output can be accomplished by writing the `PrintStream System.out`. While the interface for the standard output is not as flexible as it is in many languages, it is suitable for rudimentary communication. The methods include:

Method	Writes
`System.out.print(<primitive>)`	primitive to standard output
`System.out.println(<primitive>)`	primitive, followed by newline
`System.out.print(o)`	representation of `Object o`
`System.out.println(o)`	`Object o` followed by newline

An important feature of this interface is that any subclass of `Object`—really, any class—has a `toString` method. This method is invoked by the `print` and `println` methods to generate a readable form of the `Object`.

A.3.3 Strings

Strings, in Java, are implemented as nonmutable objects. These objects are special in a number of ways. First, strings may be initialized to string constants, which are delimited by double quotation marks ("). Secondly, the addition operator (+) is overloaded to mean string concatenation. When strings are concatenated with other primitive types, the primitive type is converted to a string before concatenation. Thus, the following program constructs and prints one string of the first n integers:

```
String s = "";
int i;
for (i = 1; i <= 10; i++)
{
    s = s + " " + i;
}
System.out.println(s);
```

Each `String` value is allocated dynamically from the heap, and may not be modified. Thus, the above program actually constructs 11 different `String`s, and we are printing only the last.

Other `String` methods include:

Method	Computes
`s.length()`	s's length
`s.charAt(i)`	the ith character (starts at 0)
`s.compareTo(t)`	integer relating s and t
`s.equals(t)`	`true` if string s has same value as t
`s.indexOf(c)`	index of c in s
`s.indexOf(t)`	index of beginning of match of t in s
`s.substring(start,end)`	substring of s between `start` and `end`

A.4   Control Constructs

Java provides many of the forms of control found in other languages, including conditional and multiple-choice statements, and various forms of looping constructs. Also included are a number of convenience operations that allow unusual forms of control.

A.4.1   Conditional Statements

Java provides several conditional statements. The `if` statement allows code to be conditionally executed, based on a `boolean` expression. Its general form is

```
if (<condition>) <statement>
```

If the boolean `<condition>` is `true`, the `<statement>` is executed. If the `<condition>` is `false`, `<statement>` is ignored. Unlike Pascal-style languages, there is no `then` keyword; instead, the parentheses about the `<condition>` are required. An alternative form is the `if-then-else` statement:

```
if (<condition>)
    <then-statement>
else
    <else-statement>
```

In this form the `<then-statement>` is executed if the `<condition>` is `true`; otherwise the `<else-statement>` is executed. Since the semicolon is part of many statements, it is often the case that the `then` part of the `if` terminates with a semicolon just before the keyword `else`. When `if` statements are nested, the `else` matches the closest `if` statement that doesn't yet contain an `else`. Thus, the following statement checks for various values of integer `i`:

```
if (i == 0)
    System.out.println("zero");
else if (i == 1)
    System.out.println("one");
else if (i == 2)
    System.out.println("two");
```

Such instances of cascading `if` statements are so common it is useful to express them as multiple-choice `switch` statements:

```
switch (<expression>)
{
    case <constant1>: <statement1>; break;
    case <constant2>: <statement2>; break;
        ...
    default: <default-statement>; break;
}
```

When the `<expression>` takes on any of the values `<constant1>`, `<constant2>`, and so forth, the respective `<statement>` is executed. The `break` statement is not strictly part of the `switch`, but if it is missing the control falls through the various cases until a `break` is encountered. It is a good habit to introduce `break` statements regularly in the switch. The `default` case is executed if none of the `cases` match. It is a good idea to include a `default` statement in `switch` statements and perform an appropriate action. It is interesting to note that the `structure` package does not make use of the `switch` statement. The cascading `if` statements, from above, might be recoded as:

```
switch (i)
{   // note: order doesn't matter if breaks are used:
    case 1: System.out.println("one"); break;
    case 0: System.out.println("zero"); break;
    case 2: System.out.println("two"); break;
    default: // do nothing!
}
```

A.4.2 Loops

Loops are an important part of most programs. Casting your code using the appropriate loop is important to making your programs as understandable as possible. Java, like C-based languages, provides three types of looping constructs. In order of popularity, they are the `for` loop, the `while` loop, and the `do-while` loop. Unlike Fortran and Pascal, each of the loops can be used—with some modification—as a substitute for any of the others. As a result, most programmers use rules-of-thumb. Some prefer to always cast loops as `for` loops, while others attempt to avoid the `for` loop altogether. The best advice is to use the style of loop that seems most natural—but be prepared to defend your choice.

The "most general" of the three looping constructs is the `for` loop. It has the form

```
for (<initialization>; <continue-test>; <iteration>)
    <statement>
```

When the loop is encountered the `<initialization>` is executed. At that point, the loop is started and the `<continue-test>` (a `boolean`) is evaluated. If `true`, the body of the loop (`<statement>`) is executed. If `false`, the loop is finished, and the execution continues at the statement that follows. After each execution of the loop body, the `<iteration>` statement is executed before reevaluation of the `<continue-test>`.

Here are some idiomatic `for` loops. First, to loop `n` times, the statement

```
for (i = 0; i < n; i++) ...
```

is used. Programmers unfamiliar with C-style languages might prefer

```
for (i = 1; i <= n; i++) ...
```

but this often detracts from the readability of the code. Besides, many operations on `Strings` and arrays require a range of values from 0 to `n-1`. Stick with the idiom, whenever possible.

The statement

```
for (i = r.readInt(); i != 0; i = r.readInt());
```

reads in integers from a stream until one is zero. Notice that the empty statement (a lone semicolon) provides the body of the loop.

To loop forever, one need only use:

```
for (;;) ...
```

Here, the empty `<continue-test>` is interpreted as `true`. The equivalent

```
for (;true;) ...
```

is less idiomatic and not frequently used, but just as effective.

Often—as in the last example—it is useful to be able to terminate or control the loop from within its body. If, for example, we wish to consume the characters in a file before the first space we write:

```
for ( ; !r.eof(); )
{
    char c = r.readChar();
    if (c == ' ') break;
}
```

This loop terminates when the end-of-file mark is read on the `ReadStream`, or when a space character is encountered; `break` statements terminate the tightest enclosing loop or `switch` statement.

Sometimes it is useful to jump to the next iteration of the loop from within the body. Here's an example of the use of `continue`:

```
for (i = 0; i < n; i++)
{
    if (i == 2) System.out.println("two is prime");
    if ((i % 0) == 0) continue;
    // only odd numbers remain
    ... test for prime ...
}
```

The above loop does not look for primes among even numbers (other than 2). When an even number is encountered, it jumps to the `i++` statement to begin the next iteration of the loop.

The two remaining loops are straightforward in comparison. The `while` loop has the form

```
while (<continue-condition>) <statement>
```

It is equivalent to the `while` loop in many languages. It could be cast as an equivalent `for` loop:

```
for (; <continue-condition>; ) <statement>
```

Another loop, the `do-while` loop, is a `while` loop with its test at the bottom:

```
do {
    <statement>
} while (<continue-condition>)
```

The `<statement>` is executed at least once, and the loop continues as long as the `<continue-condition>` is `true`. (Compare with the `repeat-until` loop of Pascal, whose condition is an *exit* condition.)

In the `structure` package, there are approximately 100 `for` loops, 70 `while` loops, and exactly one `do-while` loop. At this moment, I'm considering rewriting the code that uses the `do-while`!

A.5   Methods

Methods are declared within classes. Unless declared otherwise, methods may only act on instances of an object. If there are no instances of an object, these methods may not be called. If, on the other hand, a method is declared `static`, it exists (and may be called) no matter the number of instances. This explains the need to bootstrap the Java application with a `static` method, `main`.

Methods are declared much as they are in C. Here, for example, is a (very inefficient) method that checks to see if `n` is prime:

```
static boolean isPrime(int n)
{
    int factor;
    for (factor = 2; factor < n; factor++)
    {
        if ((n % factor) == 0) return false;
    }
    return true;
}
```

Somewhere later we find:

```
if (isPrime(2)) System.out.println("Two is prime.");
```

`n` is passed by value—changing the value of `n` will not change the value of the actual parameter passed to it. Unlike Pascal and C++ there are no means of passing the parameter by reference or as a variable parameter. And, unlike C, we have no means of generating a pointer to simulate passing by reference. *All primitive values are passed by value.* Being references, all variables referring to objects pass the object by reference. The reference, of course, cannot be changed. All of this makes it difficult, for example, to exchange the value of two parameters as you can easily do in most other languages.

A.6   Inheritance and Subtyping

Many object-oriented languages provide support for two useful concepts: inheritance and subtyping. Java is no exception.

A.6.1   Inheritance

Suppose, for example, we develop a class to perform the functions of a stopwatch. It might be declared as follows:

```
public class stopWatch
{
    protected double currentTime;
    protected boolean running;
    public stopWatch() {...} // code omitted for brevity
    public void start() {...} // start the watch
    public void stop() {...} // stop the watch
    public double read() {...} // read the time
}
```

This watch provides three methods once the `stopWatch` is constructed. The state of the watch is maintained in the protected `running` and `currentTime` variables. A watch with more features could be declared as

```
public class lapWatch extends stopWatch
{
    protected double memory[50];
    protected int lapNumber;
    public lapWatch() {...}
    public void startLap() {...}
    public double recallLap(int number) {...}
}
```

This class inherits the definitions in the `stopWatch` definition. It is as though all the definitions found in the `stopWatch` class were textually included in the definition of the `lapWatch`. In this way we think of the definitions added by the `lapWatch` class as extending the definition of the `stopWatch`.

Every class declared in Java is an extension of some other class. Even the `stopWatch` definition is a type extension: it extends the definition of `Object` (short for `java.lang.Object`). The `Object` class provides several interesting methods, including `toString`—which generates a `String` representation of the watch—and `hashCode`—which generates an integer that ideally represents the state of the watch (see Section 13.2.1). Since the `lapWatch` extends the `stopWatch` it indirectly extends `Object`, inheriting methods like `toString`.

Type extension is useful in reducing the amount of code that must be rewritten for each class. Whenever a new class must be written, a similar type of object may be extended to inherit the hard work of previous programmers. In Java, however, the extension of types actually serves to promote a stronger relationship between types of objects—that one type of object may be substituted for another wherever it appears. This is called *subtyping*.

A.6.2   Subtyping

It is often the case that programmers do not realize the full potential of the code they write. Thus, in Pascal-like languages, it is difficult to design data structures that are capable of holding "generic" information. For example, it is not obvious how to write a general-purpose definition of "a list of things" because the definition of "thing" must be completely determined when the code is written. Another result is that a "list of integers" and a "list of reals" must be distinct definitions since the lists contain different types.

Java increases the utility of types by relaxing the type-checking system so that wherever a class `stopWatch` is referred to, any type extension of a `stopWatch` (including our `lapWatch`) works just as well. We say that `stopWatch` is a *supertype* or *baseclass* and `lapWatch` is a *subtype* or *subclass*. The rule is that

Wherever a supertype can be used, a subtype works just as well.

The following code makes use of subtyping:

```
stopWatch minny = new lapWatch();
minny.start();
    ...
minny.stop();
System.out.println("Elapsed time is "+minny.read());
```

Even though `minny` refers to a `lapWatch`, we are informing the compiler that we want to use only the `stopWatch` features of `minny`. Since `minny`'s actual type (`lapWatch`) is an extension of the `stopWatch`, certainly the `stopWatch` methods are all available (though they may have `lapWatch`-like behavior if the `lapWatch` *overrides* their behavior).

In C++ the compiler and programmer are responsible for ensuring that operations work on compatible types. In Java the object to which `minny` refers keeps track of its actual type. On occasion it is useful to verify that the type information known to the compiler is consistent with that known to the object. This is accomplished by a form of casting. We can improve the program's knowledge of `minny`'s type in the following manner:

```
( (lapWatch)minny ).startLap()
```

By placing the `lapWatch` type in parentheses, the runtime system verifies that `labWatch` is a supertype of `minny`'s actual type (it is). The object is not modified in any way. After casting the value of the expression is of type `lapWatch` and the `startLap` method can be correctly invoked.

In Java, the way that subtypes are determined is by inheritance. Any type that extends another is automatically a subtype. Language designers are not completely convinced that subtyping and inheritance go hand-in-hand, but in Java they do.

A.6.3   Interfaces and Abstract Classes

The Java *interface* allows the programmer to specify a template for verifying the methods provided by a class definition. An interface is specified much like a class, but methods may not have associated bodies. We might, for example, have an interface for things that may be started and stopped:

```
public interface timer
{
    public void start();  // this can be started
    public void stop();   // and stopped
}
```

As new classes are developed, their `public` methods may support one or more interfaces. Since the `stopWatch` supports both the `start` and `stop` methods, the following definition of `stopWatch` requests that the compiler verify that the `stopWatch` supports the `timer` interface. The result is a `stopWatch` that is also a `timer`:

```
public class stopWatch implements timer
{
    protected double currentTime;
    protected boolean running;
    public stopWatch() {...}
    public void start() {...} // start the watch
    public void stop() {...} // stop the watch
    public double read() {...} // read the time
}
```

Since interfaces have no actual code associated with them, it is impossible to explicitly create objects of the interface type. It is possible, however, to use subtyping to generate references to objects that implement `timer` features:

```
timer minny = new lapWatch();
```

`minny`, in this case, is a `timer` that (via the `stopWatch` class) is really a reference to a `lapWatch`. The previous discussion of casting would apply to this example as well.

Sometimes it is useful to develop partial or *abstract* classes. These classes are partially implemented and demand extension before the class becomes *concrete*. If, for example, we had several choices for actually constructing a `stopWatch`, we might use the following definition:

```
abstract public class stopWatch
{
    protected double currentTime;
    protected boolean running;
    public stopWatch() {...}
    abstract public void start(); // start the watch
    abstract public void stop(); // stop the watch
    public double read() {...} // read the time
}
```

Here, we indicate to the compiler that the `start` and `stop` methods are part of the `stopWatch` definition, be we're not willing to commit to an actual implementation at this time (perhaps there are choices, or we just don't know how). Notice, by the way, that we have committed to the protected data, and the definition of the `read` method, so this is *not* like an `interface`. Still, because there is no code associated with the `start` and `stop` methods, no instances of the class can actually be constructed. We must depend on references to subtypes—instances of extensions to this class—if we want to use a `stopWatch` in our code. We warn the compiler that we are working with an incompletely specified class by attaching the `abstract` keyword to the definition of the class, and any method headers that are left unspecified.

Notice, by the way, any concrete extension of the latest `stopWatch` class must specify code for the `start` and `stop` methods. Thus, the last definition of `lapWatch` must either specify those methods completely or be declared abstract itself.

Java suffers somewhat from a desire to avoid mistakes of this past. As a result it is impossible to have a single class extend multiple superclasses at the same time. This *multiple inheritance* introduces some sticky problems into language design. Still, it *is* possible for a single class to implement multiple interfaces at the same time. The careful and conservative programmer is often rewarded with easily understood code.

Appendix B

Use of the Keyword Protected

*"Before I built a wall I'd ask to know
What I was walling in or walling out,
And to whom I was like to give offense."*
—Robert Frost

AT EVERY TURN, this text has advocated the use of the access control keyword **protected**. Because of the complexity of access control in the Java language, it is important that the case for the use of **protected** be adequately argued. With some reservation, we do that here.

To make the best use of data abstraction, we have argued that each data structure be considered from two vantage points: the *interface* and the *implementation*. Again, the interface describes a public "contract" between the implementor and the user. The private implementation informs the machine how the demands of the contract may be met.

For both parties—the user and implementor to agree on a structure's behavior, its interface must be visible wherever it is used. The "user," of course, may be the structure itself, another structure within the same package, or some entity external to the package. We suggest the use of the word **public** to describe classes, methods, and fields that are to be visible to the user. (It is almost never necessary to make data fields public since they are only accessed through public methods.)

The implementation, on the other hand, should be hidden from the user as much as possible. Only the implementor should be able to see the internal workings of the structure. When implementations are protected in this way, then it is possible for the implementor to make changes to the implementation without effect on the user's applications—as long as contracts are met. Indeed, languages with *dynamic loading* of classes, like Java, make it possible for implementors of data structures to update applications that have already been compiled. For maintenance and reliability reasons, this is a feature.

Unfortunately, the *means* of protecting the implementation is not very clear in Java. To understand the problem we review access control briefly, and suggest further investigation by the reader.

Of the widely used languages, Java is the first to provide two levels of encapsulation: *class* and *package*. Clearly, the class provides a means of grouping together related fields and methods. It is important for an implementor to be able to see all the fields and methods within a class, but only selected elements should be visible to the user.

The package provides an (increasingly common) method for grouping related classes together. It also serves to partition the name space (we can refer to two types of `Vectors`: `structure.Vector` and `java.util.Vector`). Since access protections are sensitive to whether or not access to a field or method occurs from within the same package, the language designers clearly had a feeling that there should be a difference in visibility between interpackage and intrapackage access.

There are two types of access for classes: `public` and default. Default classes are "private" and not visible outside the containing package. For methods (and data) there are four types of access. In increasing constraint, they are `public`, `protected`, "default," and `private`:

- `public`—methods declared `public` are always visible. This is an ideal keyword for use in describing interfaces.

- `protected`—class methods declared as `protected` are visible to any class declared in the same package, as well as any extension to the class whether or not it is in the same package.

- "default" or "friendly"—class methods declared without any keyword are visible to any class declared in the same package, as well as any extension to the class *within the same package*.

- `private`—class methods are not visible outside of the class.

For our purposes it seems best to commit to one level of protection for the implementation: `protected`. What follows is an informal defense of that decision.

First, the use of `public` provides no control over the access of methods and fields. It would be possible, then, for users to access the implementation directly, undermining the control provided by the interface. For even the simplest data structures, access to the implementation undermines any effort to keep the structure in a consistent state. The following principle has been demonstrated regularly in major software systems:

Principle 27 *Make it* `public` *and they will use it.*

Even if you don't want them to.

The use of the `private` access control is far too restrictive. Suppose we are interested in constructing two types of lists—a `SimpleList` and an extension, a `ComplexList`. The `SimpleList` has a field, `head`, that references the first element of the list. Clearly, this field should be declared `protected`; manipulating the head of the list without going through a method is likely to put the list into an inconsistent state. Now, suppose that the `ComplexList` manipulates the list in a way that requires manipulating the head of the list in a manner not previously provided. Declaring `head` to be `private` makes it impossible for the `ComplexList` to access the field directly. We might be tempted to provide the access through a method of `SimpleList`, but *we are then forced to restate the argument as it applies to methods.* If, then, we are to have an effective extension of types, the `private` keyword cannot be the preferred method of access control.

If one uses the "default" access control, it is possible for any class inside, but not outside, the package to access the associated field. While it seems unconstrained to allow all classes within the same package to access the field (after all, we may be interested in protecting fields from a package co-resident), the protection against extension outside the package is *too* constraining. If the concern is access to implementation information outside the package, the class should be declared `final` to indicate that extension is not allowed.[1] If extension is allowed, *all extensions should have equal access.*

What remains, then, is the use of the `protected` access control. Fields and methods of a class are available to classes within the same package, *as well as extensions to the class that reside outside the package.* Use of this keyword protects fields and methods from unrelated agents outside the package. Since all extensions are provided equal access, extensions to the package are welcomed and are likely to occur.

A special warning is necessary for the "everyday programmer." Since the motivation for use of packages is subtle and their use introduces considerable bureaucratic overhead in current programming environments, the tendency is to develop one's software in the *default* or *user package.* This is particularly dangerous since, within that package, there is no distinction between access controls that are not `private`. It follows, then, that absolute hiding of the implementation is particularly dangerous since, within that package, there is no distinction between `public`, `protected`, and `default` access. It follows, then, that absolute hiding of the implementation is only possible with the `private` keyword.

For most purposes, the `protected` keyword is suitable. The reader should be aware, however, that its use here is not an adoption of an ideal, but an acceptance of what's available. In short, while Java is not perfect, it is a work in progress and we may reasonably expect improvements in its access control.

Principle 28 *Fight imperfection.*

---

[1] It should be pointed out that Sun's widespread use of `final` in their own classes serves to destroy one of the features most sought in this type of language—type extension and code reuse. As it stands now, it is impossible to implement many reasonable class extensions without rewriting the baseclass, and even then the subtype relation is lost.

Appendix C
Principles

"As I knew, or thought I knew, what was right and wrong,
I did not see why I might not always
do the one and avoid the other.
But I soon found I had undertaken
a task of more difficulty than I had imagined."
—Benjamin Franklin

1. THE PRINCIPLED PROGRAMMER understands a principle well enough to form an opinion about it. (Page 1)

2. Free the future: reuse code. (Page 18)

3. Design and abide by interfaces as though you were the user. (Page 20)

4. Declare data fields protected. (Page 20)

5. Test assertions in your code. (Page 26)

6. Maintaining a consistent interface makes a structure useful. (Page 39)

7. Recursive structures must make "progress" toward a "base case." (Page 60)

8. When manipulating references, draw pictures. (Page 105)

9. Every public method of an object should leave the object in a consistent state. (Page 108)

10. Symmetry is good. (Page 111)

11. Test the boundaries of your structures and methods. (Page 114)

12. Question asymmetry. (Page 117)

13. Understand the complexity of the structures you use. (Page 142)

14. Never modify a data structure while an associated Enumeration is live. (Page 156)

15. Assume that values returned by iterators are read-only. (Page 162)

16. Declare parameters of overriding methods with the most general types possible. (Page 170)

17. Avoid multiple casts of the same object by assigning the value to a temporary variable. (Page 172)

18. Consider your code from different points of view. (Page 181)

19. Don't let opposing references show through the interface (Page 196)

20. Use wrappers to provide a consistent interface to recursive structures. (Page 201)

21. Write methods to be as general as possible. (Page 211)

22. Avoid unnaturally extending a natural interface. (Page 227)

23. Seek structures with reduced friction. (Page 228)

24. Declare object-independent functions `static`. (Page 230)

25. Provide a method for hashing the objects you implement. (Page 279)

26. Equivalent objects should return equal hash codes. (Page 279)

27. Make it `public` and they will use it. (Page 346)

At least 28 is perfect!
28. Fight imperfection. (Page 347)

Appendix D
Structure Package Hierarchy

"'My name is Ozymandius, King of Kings,
Look on my Works, ye Mighty, and despair!'
Nothing beside remains. Round the decay
Of the colossal Wreck, boundless and bare
The lone and level sands stretch far away."
—Percy Bysshe Shelley

The **structure** package contains a large number of interfaces and implementations of common data structures. The relationship between these is indicated below. Private structures are, of course, not available for direct use by users. Indentation indicates extension or implementation: **GraphList** is an implementation of the **Graph**, **Collection**, and **Store** interfaces.

Appendix E
Selected Answers

"From north, south, east, and west
every man who had a shade of red in his hair
had tramped into the city
to answer the advertisement."
—Sir Arthur Conan Doyle

Chapter 0

0.1   Right here, in the back of the book.

0.2   1—Relax. 2—Get more sleep. 3—Experiment. 4—Read books.
5—Consider programming a form of art.

0.4   All but `BitSet`. Documentation is provided online, though.

0.6   Only `BitSet`, `Dictionary`, and `Hashtable`.

Chapter 1

1.1   `int`, `double`, `char`, `boolean`.

1.2   Constructors for variables `a`, `f`, and `h` are all legal.

1.14   A solution is available online.

Chapter 2

2.1   The pre- and postconditions provide a slight increase in formality that allows the user of the data structure to identify exactly what will happen when a method is run.

2.4   Because hidden code is called by other methods. These methods act, essentially, like users of your hidden code.

2.5   Precondition: none. Postcondition: returns the length of the string.

2.6   Precondition: $0 <= index < length()$. Postcondition: returns the (index+1)th character of string.

2.7   Precondition: the string provided as parameter is non-null. Postcondition: returns a new string consisting of chars of this string followed by characters of parameter string.

Chapter 3

3.1   The size is the actual number of elements in use; the capacity is the number of cells allocated in the underlying array.

3.2   The value 10 was selected because it seemed to the author that many arrays would never be extended past 10 elements. One million is not a good value because it allocates large amounts of memory for even trivial applications.

3.7   The proof is relatively straightforward. First, we realize that when the array is extended the first time, to size 1, no values are copied. In general, when the array is extended to size i, $i-1$ elements must be preserved by copying. By the time the array has been incrementally expanded to size n,

$$0 + 1 + 2 + \cdots + (n-1) = \frac{n(n-1)}{2}$$

elements must be copied. This value is approximately n^2. See the proof of Observation 4.1 for details in demonstrating the closed form of this sum.

3.8   Using the default settings of Sun's Java 1.1.2 compiler under Solaris, an array of approximately 1 million strings can be allocated. Can you write a program to determine the upper bound?

3.9   This method is available within the class.

3.10   These methods are available online.

Chapter 4

4.9   The function grows as a linear function, $O(n)$. The linear term, n, outstrips the logarithmic term $\log n$. Select $c = 2$ and $n_0 = 1$. (Proof omitted.)

4.11   The rate is $O(1)$. Select $c = 1.5$ and $n_0 = 1$. (Proof omitted.)

4.12   Since $\sin n$ has magnitude no greater than unity, $\frac{\sin n}{n}$ has magnitude no greater than $\frac{1}{n}$. Therefore, the rate of growth is $O(\frac{1}{n})$

4.13 $O(\tan n)$. If no "traditional" bound can be found, we can make use of the fact that every function f is $O(f)$.

4.14   An array (or **Vector**) of 366 entries will help you solve small problems. For $n > 366$ the problem can be solved in constant time because it is known a duplicate exists. Growth is $O(1)$.

4.21   Let us prove this by induction. First, note that if $n = 0$, then

$$5^n - 4n - 1 = 1 + 0 - 1 = 0$$

Since 16 divides 0 evenly, the observation holds for $n = 0$. Now, assume that the observation holds for all values less than n, and specifically in the case of $n-1$. We have, then, that

$$5^{n-1} - 4(n-1) - 1$$

is divisible by 16. Multiplying by 5 we get

$$5^n - 20(n-1) - 5$$

which is also divisible by 16. That is not quite the desired expression. At this point we add $16(n-1)$, a multiple of 16:

$$5^n - 20(n-1) + 16(n-1) - 5 =$$

$$5^n - 4(n-1) - 5 =$$

$$5^n - 4n + 4 - 5 =$$

$$5^n - 4n - 1$$

Clearly, this expression is divisible by 16, so the observation holds for n. By induction on n, we see the result holds for all $n \geq 0$.

4.23   It is clear to see that n^d can be rewritten as $n^{c+(d-c)} = n^c \cdot n^{d-c}$. Since $d \geq c$, then $d - c \geq 0$ and, for $n \geq 1$, $n^{d-c} \geq 1$. We have, therefore, that $n^d \geq n^c$ for all $n \geq 1$. This is sufficient to demonstrate that n^c is $O(n^d)$ for any $d \geq c$.

4.25   The sum is simply twice the sum of the first n integers greater than 0. Therefore, the total is $2 \cdot \frac{n(n+1)}{2} = n(n+1)$.

4.26   Clearly, the sum of the first n odd integers is

$$2 \left(\sum_{i=0}^{n} i \right) - n = n(n+1) - n = n^2$$

4.27   We prove this by induction. First, consider the base case, when $n = 0$. We have $\sum_{i=0}^{n=0} c^i = c^0 = 1$. At the same time

$$\frac{c^{n+1} + (c-2)}{c-1} - 1 = \frac{c^1 + c - 2}{c-1} - 1 = \frac{2c - 2}{c-1} - 1 = 2 - 1 = 1$$

so the observation holds for $n = 0$. Now, assume that it is true for all values less than n. We extend the result to n as follows: The sum

$$\sum_{i=0}^{n} c^i = c^0 + c^1 + \ldots + c^{n-1} + c^n$$

Using our assumption, this can be rewritten as

$$\left(\frac{c^n + (c-2)}{c-1} - 1 \right) + c^n =$$

$$\frac{(c-1)c^n + c^n + (c-2)}{c-1} - 1 =$$

$$\frac{c^{n+1} + (c-2)}{c-1} - 1$$

which is the desired result. By induction on n, the observation holds for all values $n \geq 0$.

4.33   The best strategy is to decrease the size of the **Vector** by a factor of two when the number of elements within the **Vector** falls below $\frac{1}{3}$.

Chapter 5

5.1   The two values `a` and `b` can be exchanged with the following code:

```
a=b-a;
b=b-a;
a=a+b;
```

5.8   Quicksort uses more space keeping track of the progress of recursion.

5.11   As presented, insertion and mergesort are stable. Selection and quicksort are not stable. Selection sort can easily be made stable. For quicksort to be made stable, the partition function needs to be reconsidered.

5.12   While the pivot is in the correct location, it does not partition the data, and thus does not sort. It is possible, for example, for a larger value to appear to the left of the pivot in the final arrangement.

5.16   Data can (and should) be shuffled in $O(n)$ time.

5.17   The worst-case running time cannot be determined since given any particular upper bound, there is a nonzero probability that a run of shuffle sort will exceed that bound. The revised assumption allows a worst-case running time to be determined.

Chapter 6

6.9   I will design a method for inserting an element into a list, making it the nth element of the list. Clearly, the list must be long enough to support such an operation. This begs a question, about what it means for something to be the nth. Do we begin counting at 1 or 0? Well, since vectors start at 0, we have some precedent for doing just that. So another way to think about the value of n is that it indicates how many elements will appear before the inserted element, once the operation is complete. We present the code here:

```
public void insert(int n, Object value)
// pre: list has at least n values; value not null
// post: list includes element with value "value," occurring at
//       location n+1
{
    Assert.pre(n >= size(),"index is less than or equal to size.");
    Assert.pre(value != null,"value is non-null");
    SinglyLinkedList finger = head; // element we're traversing
    SinglyLinkedList previous = null; // element above traversed
    int skipped = 0; // count of number of elements traversed
    while (skipped < n)
    {
        previous = finger;
        finger = finger.next;
        skipped = skipped + 1;
    }
    // create a new element that points to remainder of list
    SinglyLinkedListElement e = new
        SinglyLinkedListElement(value,finger);
```

```
        if (previous == null) // we must be inserting at head
        {
            head = e;  // head points to new element
        } else
        {
            previous.next = e;  // element above finger points to e
        }
    }
```

6.10 Clearly, for long lists, you would like to keep track of the count in a dedicated integer. Computing the length of a million-element list is time consuming since the process of counting is proportional to the length of the list. For the million short lists, we would be able to save a considerable amount of space (several megabytes) if we avoided keeping track of the counts. Also, we will need this value less frequently.

There are 1,048,576 bytes in a megabyte.

6.11 Because we have backed up the reference, it is farther away from the references that need to be manipulated. In general, the construction of the head and tail references will take longer and operations will execute more slowly. Clearly, though, the method `removeFromTail` has the potential for great improvement; it becomes an $O(1)$ operation, instead of $O(n)$.

6.13 A constant factor of space reduction.

Chapter 7

7.7 The sequence 3, 1, 2 is not possible.

7.9 The only sequence that is possible is 1, 2, and 3. All others are impossible.

Chapter 8

8.1 Because the `Iterator` is an extension of the `Enumeration` class, it must inherit the methods of the `Enumeration`. There is, essentially, no way to change or retract the methods provided through inheritance. If there were, then the interface for an `Iterator` would be different from the interface for an `Enumeration`, and the `Iterator` would not be a subtype of `Enumeration`.

Chapter 9

9.3 The older value is found in a location with a lower index.

9.7 The source code for the `String` class is available for noncommercial use from Sun. Check it out!

9.8 This problem demonstrates the error-prone nature of the `compareTo`-style method for ordering objects. The easiest method is to return three integers -1, 0, and 1, based on two different comparisons of the two values.

9.10 The `lessThan` method is more versatile. It can simulate the action of the `compareTo` method, as well as support partial orders. For example, the `lessThan` method can be provided as a "proper subset" operator for a `Set` class, but a meaningful `compareTo` cannot.

Chapter 10

10.4 Each node of a tree can have degree greater than one. Lists are limited to degrees of 1 or less.

10.9 A `setParent` method has ambiguous semantics: should this node be inserted as a left or right child of the new parent? Allowing the user to explicitly `setParent` makes it easier for data structure to become inconsistent.

10.21 This method is similar to an `isComplete` method, except that subtrees can differ in height by 1 or -1.

Chapter 11

11.12 | 0 | 1 | 4 | 3 | 2 | 7 | 5 | 6 |
|---|---|---|---|---|---|---|---|

11.14 Reverse the meaning of `compareTo` in the data class. This might be accomplished in an extension of the original class.

11.21 The vector could be as large as $2^n - 1$ elements.

11.22 If comparisons of the underlying type can be accomplished in constant time, the entire operation is linear in the number of elements of the `PriorityVector`.

11.23 Certainly this can be accomplished in $O(n \log n)$ time.

Chapter 12

12.1 The nodes of a binary search tree are ordered.

12.8 The performance of binary search is $O(\log n)$. A binary search tree may be unbalanced, however, and may have linear worst-case performance.

12.9 One need only observe that values are added as a leaf in a unique location. A levelorder traversal of the binary search tree desired gives an appropriate order for insertion.

12.11 This is, effectively, the construction of a `Linear` structure, a degenerate right-most search tree. Behavior is $O(n^2)$. (The best-case running time for arbitrary order is $O(n \log n)$.)

12.13 Have it first use the successor, then predecessor, then successor, and so on.

12.16 Construct two iterators and compare the values produced.

Chapter 13

13.14 For short strings (say, less than eight characters), use a traditional hashing function. For longer strings, pick characters located at $i\frac{l}{8}$, where $i = 0 \ldots 7$.

13.15 The value of i can get to be as large as $\log_2 l$, so the algorithm is potentially logarithmic in the length of the string.

13.17 No. It's only ordered from the perspective of rehashing. The smallest value, for example, may appear in any location to which it hashes—anywhere in the table.

13.18 It is not ideal, because it forces the user to know about and use `Associations`; this gives away part of the implementation.

Chapter 14

14.18 A graph can have a nonunique minimum spanning tree any time that only one of many similarly weighted edges mentioning a common vertex participates in a minimum spanning tree.

14.19 Suppose it did not. This assumption leads to a contradiction.

14.20 Yes. Many edges to the same vertex may be added to the priority queue before the vertex is visited. Totally eliminating the extra edges would obviate the need for the priority queue—an unlikely event.

Index